MEDITATION

OSHO

MEDITATION

THE FIRST AND LAST FREEDOM

A PRACTICAL GUIDE TO MEDITATION

ST. MARTIN'S GRIFFIN
NEW YORK

Compilation by Swami Deva Wadud
Assisted by Ma Anand Svarup
Editing by Ma Yoga Ranjana

Library of Congress Cataloging-in-Publication Data

Osho.
    Meditation: the first and last freedom : a practical guide to meditation /
Osho ; compiled by Swami Deva Wadud.—1st U.S. ed.
        p.   cm.
    Includes bibliographical references (p. 271) and index.
    ISBN 0-312-16927-2
    1. Meditation. I. Deva Wadud, Swami. II. Title.
    BP605.R34M432 1996   96-9227
    299'.93—DC20   CIP

First Published by the Rebel Publishing House GmbH in Germany
First St. Martin's Griffin Edition: December 1997

10 9 8 7 6 5 4 3 2

*Music tapes are available for these meditations from any of the addresses given in the back of the book

Introduction

The enlightened master Osho is creating a worldwide rebellion for the sake of man's freedom and meditation. You may think this is an odd choice. How are they related? Yet the subtle connection between the two is a crucial point in the understanding of man's future potential. The door to opening our capacity for love, intimacy, creativity and expansion *is* meditation. And according to Osho there is no other door, no other path.

Since his enlightenment in 1953 Osho has been giving talks to disciples and seekers, deciphering many of the world's great religious, mystical, and esoteric traditions. His talks are contained in more than 400 volumes, where he has brought to life countless ancient and contemporary mystics, making the wisdom of their teachings understandable and relevant to our lives today.

This book is a compilation drawn from Osho's profound work on meditation. It contains a wide variety of methods which can help us to discover what he calls "Meditation: The First and Last Freedom." The Master has said, "Meditation is not something new; you have come with it into the world. Mind is something new, meditation is your nature. It is your nature, it is your very being. How can it be difficult?" [1]

We make it difficult by struggling against something which we think is *preventing* us from being free, or, by searching for something which we presume will *give* us freedom. It is actually found simply by relaxing into who we are, living life moment to moment.

All over the world people are struggling to be free *from* something. The struggle may be against a nagging wife, or a controlling husband, a domineering parent, or a boss at work who is quashing creativity. My struggle was either a fight against a repressive political system or an effort to free myself of my childhood conditionings through countless therapies. This struggle did not make me free; it was simply a reaction against something which I thought was not allowing me to be free.

The freedom of meditation is not a search to find freedom *for* something, either. How many of us have dreams of being in some situation or utopia which would allow us just to relax and be ourselves, free from the competition and tension of everyday life? My experiences have demonstrated to me that the freedom we are searching for does not depend upon something *outside* ourselves.

So what is the freedom we are longing for? I have heard Osho describe it as "just freedom": living in the here and now, moment to moment, living neither in the memory and oppression of the past nor the dreams of the future.

He has said:

"Eating – simply eat, be with it. Walking – simply walk, be there. Don't go ahead, don't jump here and there. Mind always goes ahead or lags behind. Remain with the moment." [2]

Many of us have certainly experienced what the Master is saying about the mind. Mind is always jumping ahead or lagging behind, but it is never in the moment: it is a constant chattering. When this chattering takes place, it robs us of being in the moment and living life totally. How can we live totally when our mind is chattering to itself even while we are engaged in daily activities?

To illustrate this for yourself you can try a small experiment. Put this book down for a few moments and close your eyes. See how long you can just sit and enjoy the feel of your body, and any sounds that may be around you.

The chances are it will not be very long, perhaps only a minute, before your mind starts chattering. If you sit for a while and notice what the chatterings are, you will be amazed: you will find that you are carrying on many different incoherent inner conversations with yourself which, if you overheard someone else saying them out loud, you would think

crazy. This constant chattering literally robs us of life, preventing us from enjoying what each moment of life holds for us.

So what to do about this out-of-control chattering which separates us from, and robs us of, the precious moments of life? I have heard the Master tell us over and over again to meditate. I have heard him say that we can't stop the chattering mind directly, but that through meditation the chattering can slow down and eventually disappear.

With meditation the mind becomes a useful instrument, instead of enslaving us with its constant chatter. However, we often are confused by the profusion of countless meditation techniques which are generally obscure and not relevant for today's living. Osho has taken these techniques, weeded out the true from the false, and penetrated to their very core, giving us a key which can open the door to a universe beyond our imagination. This master key is *witnessing:* a simple but profound state of watching and accepting ourselves as we are.

Osho tells us that:

"Witnessing simply means a detached observation, unprejudiced; that's the whole secret of meditation." [3]

It's actually so simple that I went

on missing it for years. We all certainly think we know what watching is; we observe things around us all day long. We watch television, we watch other people go by and notice what they are wearing, what they look like, but we don't generally watch ourselves. When we do, it is usually through self-conscious criticism. We will notice something about ourselves which we don't like and then start worrying about what others will think. Usually these inner chatterings of the mind make us feel miserable. This is not witnessing.

Osho reminds us:

"Nothing needs to be done; just be a witness, an observer, a watcher, looking at the traffic of the mind – thoughts passing by, desires, memories, dreams, fantasies. Simply stand aloof, cool, watching it, seeing it, with no judgment, with no condemnation, neither saying 'This is good,' nor saying 'This is bad.' " [4]

Through the meditations that are in this book, you will discover what witnessing is. While sitting in the Master's presence, witnessing just starts happening spontaneously. Moments occur when you are just sitting, listening, feeling, watching whatever is happening with an inner silence. This silence is like the vast empty sky, yet vibrating with life.

Osho's home is the sky and his very being is silence. His words caress the very depth of the heart, his song is the song of the empty sky.

"Your inner being is
nothing but the inner sky.
Clouds come and go,
planets are born and disappear,
stars arise and die,
and the inner sky remains the same,
untouched, untarnished, unscarred.
We call that inner sky *sakshin,*
the witness,
and that is the whole goal
of meditation.

"Go in, enjoy the inner sky.
Remember, whatsoever you can see,
you are not it.
You can see thoughts,
then you are not thoughts;
you can see your feelings,
then you are not your feelings;
you can see your dreams,
desires, memories, imaginations,
projections,
then you are not them.
Go on eliminating all
that you can see.
Then one day a tremendous
moment arises, the most significant
moment of one's life,
when there is nothing left
to be rejected.

"All the seen has disappeared and
only the seer is there.

The seer is the empty sky.
"To know it is to be fearless,
and to know it is to be full of love.
To know it is to be God,
is to be immortal." [5]

Through this book you are invited to experience your own inner sky. My gratitude and love for my Master cannot be put into words; only tears can convey my feeling. Through hearing his call to freedom I am beginning to awaken to the beauty and grace that each moment of life can bring. Thank you, Beloved Master.

Swami Deva Wadud
Poona, January 1992

In using this book as a guide in meditation you do not have to read it from cover to cover before trying any of the meditations. Use the book intuitively. Glance through it and choose some section or meditation that appeals to you. For example, you may prefer to jump

How to use this book

right into one of the meditations in part III and get your feet wet before reading the guidelines. Go by what feels good to you.

After choosing a meditation try it for at least three days and if it feels good, continue doing it and go deeper. The important thing is to experiment playfully and simply ask yourself: Does this meditation help my joy and sensitivity to keep growing?

Meditating to music

Music and meditation can go well together. About this, Osho once said:

"To me music and meditation are two aspects of the same phenomenon. And without music, meditation lacks something; without music, meditation is a little dull, unalive. Without meditation, music is simply noise – harmonious, but noise. Without meditation, music is an entertainment; music and meditation should go together. That adds a new dimension to both. Both are enriched by it." [6]

Hence music tapes have been prepared to guide Dynamic Meditation and many of the active methods, including Kundalini, The Mystic Rose and No-Mind Meditations, Mandala, Nataraj, Devavani, Prayer, and Gourishankar, as well as Nadabrahma. The music tapes for the meditations are available from the distributors listed at the back of this book.

Material printed in italics

Many of the meditations in part III are based on the teachings of various enlightened masters, including Buddha, Patanjali and Shiva from India, Atisha and Tilopa from Tibet, and the Chinese master Lu Tsu. Where Osho quotes their verses or sutras, the selection has been introduced with the name of the earlier master in italics.

Finally, there are a few selections in this book, for example the summary instructions for several of the meditations, which are based on Osho's teachings but are not actually given in his own words. To show the difference, these pieces have been printed in italics.

PART ONE

About Meditation

What is Meditation?

Witnessing, the spirit of meditation

Meditation is adventure, the greatest adventure the human mind can undertake. Meditation is just to be, not doing anything – no action, no thought, no emotion. You just are and it is a sheer delight. From where does this delight come when you are not doing anything? It comes from nowhere, or it comes from everywhere. It is uncaused, because existence is made of the stuff called joy.[1]

When you are not doing anything at all – bodily, mentally, on no level – when all activity has ceased and you simply are, just being, that's what meditation is. You cannot do it, you cannot practice it: you have only to understand it.

Whenever you can find time for just being, drop all doing. Thinking is also doing, concentration is also doing, contemplation is also doing. Even if for a single moment you are not doing anything and you are just at your center, utterly relaxed – that is meditation. And once you have got the knack of it, you can remain in that state as long as you want; finally you can remain in that state for twenty-four hours a day.

Once you have become aware of the way your being can remain undisturbed, then slowly you can start doing things, keeping alert that your being is not stirred. That is the second part of meditation – first, learning how just to be, and then learning little actions: cleaning the floor, taking a shower, but keeping yourself centered. Then you can do complicated things.

For example, I am speaking to you, but my meditation is not disturbed. I can go on speaking, but at my very center there is not even a ripple; it is just silent, utterly silent.

So meditation is not against action. It is not that you have to escape from life. It simply teaches you a new way of life: you become the center of the cyclone.

Your life goes on, it goes on really

more intensely – with more joy, with more clarity, more vision, more creativity – yet you are aloof, just a watcher on the hills, simply seeing all that is happening around you.

You are not the doer, you are the watcher.

That's the whole secret of meditation, that you become the watcher.

Doing continues on its own level, there is no problem: chopping wood, drawing water from the well. You can do small and big things; only one thing is not allowed and that is, your centering should not be lost.

That awareness, that watchfulness, should remain absolutely unclouded, undisturbed. 2

In Judaism there is a rebellious school of mystery called Hassidism. Its founder, Baal Shem, was a rare being. In the middle of the night he was coming from the river – that was his routine, because at the river in the night it was absolutely calm and quiet. And he used to simply sit there, doing nothing – just watching his own self, watching the watcher. This night when he was coming back, he passed a rich man's house and the watchman was standing by the door.

And the watchman was puzzled because *every* night at exactly this time, this man would come back. He came out and he said, "Forgive me for interrupting but I cannot contain my curiosity anymore. You are haunting me day and night, every day. What is your business? Why do you go to the river? Many times I have followed you, and there is nothing – you simply sit there for hours, and in the middle of the night you come back."

Baal Shem said, "I know that you have followed me many times, because the night is so silent I can hear your footsteps. And I know every day you are hiding behind the gate. But it is not only that you are curious about me, I am also curious about you. What is your business?"

He said, "My business? I am a simple watchman."

Baal Shem said, "My God, you have given me the key word. This is my business too!"

The watchman said, "But I don't understand. If you are a watchman you should be watching some house, some palace. What are you watching there, sitting in the sand?"

Baal Shem said, "There is a little difference: you are watching for somebody outside who may enter the palace; I simply watch *this watcher*. Who is this watcher? This is my whole life's effort; I watch myself."

The watchman said, "But this is a strange business. Who is going to pay you?"

He said, "It is such bliss, such a joy, such immense benediction, it pays itself profoundly. Just a single moment, and all the treasures are nothing in comparison to it."

The watchman said, "This is strange. I have been watching my whole life. I never came across such a beautiful experience. Tomorrow night I am coming with you. Just teach me. Because I know how to watch – it seems only a different direction is needed; you are watching in some different direction."

There is only one step, and that step is of direction, of dimension. Either we can be focused outside or we can close our eyes to the outside and let our whole consciousness be centered inwards – and you will know, because you are a knower, you *are* awareness. You have never lost it. You simply got your awareness entangled in a thousand and one things. Withdraw your awareness from everywhere and just let it rest within yourself, and you have arrived home. 3

The essential core, the spirit of meditation is to learn how to witness.

A crow crowing…you are listening.

These are two – object and subject. But can't you see a witness who is seeing both? – the crow, the listener, and still there is someone who is watching both. It is such a simple phenomenon.

You are seeing a tree: you are there, the tree is there, but can't you find one thing more? – that you are seeing the tree, that there is a witness in you which is seeing you seeing the tree. [4]

Watching is meditation. What you watch is irrelevant. You can watch the trees, you can watch the river, you can watch the clouds, you can watch children playing around. Watching *is* meditation. What you watch is not the point; the object is not the point.

The quality of observation, the quality of being aware and alert – that's what meditation is.

Remember one thing: meditation means awareness. Whatsoever you do with awareness is meditation. Action is not the question, but the quality that you bring to your action. Walking can be a meditation if you walk alert. Sitting can be a meditation if you sit alert. Listening to the birds can be a meditation if you listen with awareness. Just listening to the inner noise of your mind can be a meditation if you remain alert and watchful.

The whole point is, one should not move in sleep. Then whatsoever you do is meditation. [5]

The first step in awareness is to be very watchful of your body. Slowly slowly one becomes alert about each gesture, each movement. And as you become aware, a miracle starts happening: many things that you used to do before simply disappear; your body becomes more relaxed, your body becomes more attuned. A deep peace starts prevailing even in your body, a subtle music pulsates in your body.

Then start becoming aware of your thoughts; the same has to be done with thoughts. They are more subtle than the body and of course, more dangerous too. And when you become aware of your thoughts, you will be surprised what goes on inside you. If you write down whatsoever is going on at any moment, you are in for a great surprise. You will not believe that this is what is going on inside you.

And after ten minutes read it – you will see a mad mind inside! Because we are not aware, this whole madness goes on running like an undercurrent. It affects whatsoever you are doing, it affects whatsoever you are not doing; it affects everything. And the sum total of it is going to be your life! So this madman has to be

changed. And the miracle of awareness is that you need not do anything *except* just become aware.

The very phenomenon of watching it changes it. Slowly slowly the madman disappears, slowly slowly the thoughts start falling into a certain pattern; their chaos is no more, they become more of a cosmos. And then again, a deeper peace prevails. And when your body and your mind are at peace you will see that they are attuned to each other too, there is a bridge. Now they are not running in different directions, they are not riding different horses. For the first time there is accord, and that accord helps immensely to work on the third step – that is becoming aware of your feelings, emotions, moods.

That is the subtlest layer and the most difficult, but if you can be aware of the thoughts then it is just one step more. A little more intense awareness is needed and you start reflecting your moods, your emotions, your feelings. Once you are aware of all these three they all become joined into one phenomenon. And when all these three are one – functioning together perfectly, humming together, you can feel the music of all the three; they have become an orchestra – then the fourth happens, which you cannot do. It happens on its own accord. It is a gift from the whole, it is a reward for those who have done these three.

And the fourth is the ultimate awareness that makes one awakened. One becomes aware of one's awareness – that is the fourth. That makes a buddha, the awakened. And only in that awakening does one come to know what bliss is.

The body knows pleasure, the mind knows happiness, the heart knows joy, the fourth knows bliss. Bliss is the goal of sannyas, of being a seeker, and awareness is the path towards it. 6

The important thing is that you are watchful, that you have not forgotten to watch, that you are watching…watching…watching. And slowly slowly, as the watcher becomes more and more solid, stable, unwavering, a transformation happens. The things that you were watching disappear.

For the first time, the watcher itself becomes the watched, the observer itself becomes the observed.

You have come home. 7

The Flowering of Meditation

Meditation is not an Indian method; it is not simply a technique. You cannot learn it. It is a growth: a growth of your total living, out of your total living. Meditation is not something that can be added to you as you are. It cannot be added to you; it can only come to you through a basic transformation, a mutation. It is a flowering, a growth. Growth is always from the total; it is not an addition. Just like love, it cannot be added to you. It grows out of you, out of your totality. You must grow towards meditation. [8]

The great silence

Silence usually is understood to be something negative, something empty, an absence of sound, of noises. This misunderstanding is prevalent because very few people have ever experienced silence.

All that they have experienced in the name of silence is noiselessness. But silence is a totally different phenomenon. It is utterly positive. It is existential, it is not empty. It is overflowing with a music that you have never heard before, with a fragrance that is unfamiliar to you, with a light that can only be seen by the inner eyes.

It is not something fictitious; it is a reality, and a reality which is already present in everyone – just we never look in.

Your inner world has its own taste, has its own fragrance, has its own light. And it is utterly silent, immensely silent, eternally silent. There has never been any noise, and there will never be any noise. No word can reach there, but *you* can reach.

Your very center of being is the center of a cyclone. Whatever happens around it does not affect it. It is eternal silence: days come and go, years come and go, ages come and pass. Lives come and go, but the eternal silence of your being remains exactly the same – the same soundless music, the same fragrance of godliness, the same transcendence from all that

6

is mortal, from all that is momentary.

It is not *your* silence.

You *are* it.

It is not something in your possession; you are possessed by it, and that's the greatness of it. Even you are not there, because even your presence will be a disturbance.

The silence is so profound that there is nobody, not even you. And this silence brings truth, and love, and thousands of other blessings to you. [9]

Growing in sensitivity

Meditation will bring you sensitivity, a great sense of belonging to the world. It is our world – the stars are ours, and we are not foreigners here. We belong intrinsically to existence. We are part of it, we are the *heart* of it.

You become so sensitive that even the smallest blade of grass takes on an immense importance for you. Your sensitivity makes it clear to you that this small blade of grass is as important to existence as the biggest star; without this blade of grass, existence would be less than it is. This small blade of grass is unique, it is irreplaceable, it has its own individuality.

And this sensitivity will create new friendships for you – friendships with trees, with birds, with animals, with mountains, with rivers, with oceans, with stars. Life becomes richer as love grows, as friendliness grows. [10]

Love, the fragrance of meditation

If you meditate, sooner or later you will come upon love. If you meditate deeply, sooner or later you will start feeling a tremendous love arising in you that you have never known before – a new quality to your being, a new door opening. You have become a new flame and now you want to share.

If you love deeply, by and by you will become aware that your love is becoming more and more meditative. A subtle quality of silence is entering in you. Thoughts are disappearing, gaps appearing…silences! You are touching your own depth.

Love makes you meditative if it is on the right lines.

Meditation makes you loving if it is on the right lines. [11]

You want a love which is born out of meditation, not born out of the mind. That is the love I continually talk about.

Millions of couples around the world are living as if love is there. They are living in a world of 'as if'. Of course, how can they be joyous? They are drained of all energy. They are trying to get something out of a false love; it cannot deliver the goods. Hence the frustration, hence the continuous boredom, hence the continuous nagging, fighting between the lovers. They are both trying to do something which is impossible: they are trying to make their love affair something of the eternal, which it cannot be. It has arisen out of the mind and mind cannot give you any glimpse of the eternal.

First go into meditation, because love will come out of meditation – it is the fragrance of meditation. Meditation is the flower, the one-thousand-petaled lotus. Let it open. Let it help you to move in the dimension of the vertical, no-mind, no-time, and then suddenly you will see the fragrance *is* there. Then it is eternal, then it is unconditional. Then it is not even directed to anybody in particular, it *cannot* be directed to anybody in particular. It is not a relationship, it is more a quality that surrounds you. It has nothing to do with the other. You are loving, you are love; then it is eternal. It is your fragrance. It has been around a Buddha, around a Zarathustra, around a Jesus. It is a totally different kind of love, it is qualitatively different. [12]

Compassion

Buddha has defined compassion as "love plus meditation." When your love is not just a desire for the other, when your love is not only a need, when your love is a sharing, when your love is not that of a beggar but that of an emperor, when your love is not asking for something in return but is ready only to give – to give for the sheer joy of giving – then add meditation to it and the pure fragrance is released, the imprisoned splendor is released. That is compassion; compassion is the highest phenomenon. Sex is animal, love is human, compassion is divine. Sex is physical, love is psychological, compassion is spiritual. [13]

Abiding joy for no reason at all

For no reason at all you suddenly feel yourself joyous. In ordinary life, if there is some reason, you are joyful. You have met a beautiful woman and you are joyous, or you have got the money that you always wanted and you are joyous, or you have purchased the house with a beautiful garden and you are joyous, but these joys cannot last long. They are momentary, they cannot remain continuous and uninterrupted.

If your joy is caused by something it will disappear, it will be momentary. It will soon leave you in deep sadness; all joys leave you in deep sadness. But there is a different kind of joy that is a *confirmatory sign*: you are suddenly joyous for no reason at all. You cannot pinpoint why. If somebody asks, "Why are you so joyous?" you cannot answer.

I cannot answer why I am joyous. There is no reason. It's simply so. Now *this* joy cannot be disturbed. Now whatsoever happens, it will continue. It is there, day in, day out. You may be young, you may be old, you may be alive, you may be dying – it is always there. When you have found some joy that remains – circumstances change but it abides – then you are certainly coming closer to Buddhahood. [14]

Intelligence: the ability to respond

Intelligence simply means ability to respond, because life is a flux. You have to be aware and to see what is demanded of you, what is the challenge of the situation. The intelligent person behaves according to the situation and the stupid behaves according to the ready-made answers. Whether they come from Buddha, Christ or Krishna, it does not matter. He always carries scriptures around himself, he is afraid to depend on himself. The intelligent person depends on his own insight; he trusts his own being. He loves and respects himself. The unintelligent person respects others.

Intelligence can be rediscovered. The only method to rediscover it is meditation. Meditation only does one thing: it destroys all the barriers that the society has created to prevent you from being intelligent. It simply removes the blocks. Its function is negative: it removes the rocks that are preventing your waters from flowing, your springs from becoming alive.

Everybody is carrying the great potential, but society has put great rocks to prevent it. It has created China Walls around you; it has imprisoned you.

To come out of all prisons is intelligence – and never to get into another again. Intelligence can be discovered through meditation because all those prisons exist in your mind; they cannot reach your being, fortunately. They cannot pollute your being, they can only pollute your mind – they can only cover your mind. If you can get out of the mind you will get out of Christianity, Hinduism, Jainism, Buddhism, and all kinds of rubbish will be just finished. You can come to a full stop.

And when you are out of the mind, watching it, being aware of it, just being a witness, you are intelligent. Your intelligence is discovered. You have undone what the society has done to you. You have destroyed the mischief; you have destroyed the conspiracy of the priests and the politicians. You have come out of it, you are a free man. In fact you are for the first time a real man, an authentic man. Now the whole sky is yours.

Intelligence brings freedom, intelligence brings spontaneity. [15]

Aloneness: your self-nature

Aloneness is a flower, a lotus blooming in your heart. Aloneness is positive, aloneness is health. It is the joy of being yourself. It is the joy of having your own space.

Meditation means: bliss in being alone. One is *really* alive when one has become capable of it, when there is no dependence anymore on anybody, on any situation, on any condition. And because it is one's own, it can remain morning, evening, day, night, in youth or in old age, in health, in illness. In life, in death too, it can remain because it is not something that is happening to you from the outside. It is something welling up in you. It is your very nature, it is self-nature. [16]

An inside journey is a journey towards absolute aloneness; you cannot take anybody there with you. You cannot share your center with anybody, not even with your beloved. It is not in the nature of things; nothing can be done about it. The moment you go in, all connections with the outside world are broken; all bridges are broken. In fact, the whole world disappears.

That's why the mystics have called the world illusory, *maya*, not that it does not exist, but for the meditator, one who goes in, it is almost as if the world does not exist. The silence is so profound; no noise penetrates it. The aloneness is so deep that one needs guts. But out of that aloneness explodes bliss. Out of that aloneness – the experience of God. There is no other way; there has never been any and there is never going to be. [17]

Celebrate aloneness, celebrate your pure space, and a great song will arise in your heart. And it will be a song of awareness, it will be a song of meditation. It will be a song of a lone bird calling in the distance – not calling to somebody in particular, but just calling because the heart is full and wants to call, because the cloud is full and wants to rain, because the flower is full and the petals open and the fragrance is released…unaddressed. Let your aloneness become a dance. [18]

Your real self

Meditation is nothing but a device to make you aware of your real self – which is not created by you, which need not be created by you, which you already are. You are born with it. You *are* it! It needs to be discovered. If this is not possible, or if the society does not allow it to happen – and no society allows it to happen, because the real self is dangerous: dangerous for the established church, dangerous for the state, dangerous for the crowd, dangerous for the tradition, because once a man knows his real self, he becomes an individual.

He belongs no more to the mob psychology; he will not be

superstitious, and he cannot be exploited, and he cannot be led like cattle, he cannot be ordered and commanded. He will live according to his light; he will live from his own inwardness. His life will have tremendous beauty, integrity. But that is the fear of the society.

Integrated persons become individuals, and the society wants you to be non-individuals. Instead of individuality, the society teaches you to be a personality. The word 'personality' has to be understood. It comes from the root, *persona* – *persona* means a mask. The society gives you a false idea of who you are; it gives you just a toy, and you go on clinging to the toy your whole life. [19]

As I see it, almost everybody is in the wrong place. The person who would have been a tremendously happy doctor is a painter and the person who would have been a tremendously happy painter is a doctor. Nobody seems to be in his right place; that's why this whole society is in such a mess. The person is directed by others; he is not directed by his own intuition.

Meditation helps you to grow your own intuitive faculty. It becomes very clear what is going to fulfill you, what is going to help you flower. And whatsoever it is, it is going to be different for each individual – that is the meaning of the word 'individual': everybody is unique. And to seek and search for your uniqueness is a great thrill, a great adventure. [20]

PART TWO

The Science of Meditation

Methods and Meditation

With a master, with scientific techniques, you can save much time, opportunity and energy. And sometimes within seconds you can grow so much that even within lives you would not have been able to grow that much. If a right technique is used, growth explodes. And these techniques have been used in thousands of years of experiments. They were not devised by one man; they were devised by many, many seekers, and only the essence is given here.

You will reach the goal, because the life energy within you will move unless it comes to the point where no movement is possible; it will go on moving to the highest peak. And that is the reason why one goes on being born again and again. Left to yourself you will reach, but you will have to travel very, very long, and the journey will be very tedious and boring. [1]

Techniques are helpful

Techniques are helpful because they are scientific. You are saved from unnecessary wandering, unnecessary groping; if you don't know any techniques, you will take a long time.

All techniques can be helpful but they are not exactly meditation, they are just a groping in the dark. Suddenly one day, doing something, you will become a witness. Doing a meditation like Dynamic, or Kundalini or Whirling, suddenly one day the meditation will go on but you will not be identified. You will sit silently behind, you will watch it – that day meditation has happened; that day the technique is no more a hindrance, no more a help. You can enjoy it if you like, like an exercise; it gives a certain vitality, but there is no need now – the real meditation has happened. Meditation is witnessing. To meditate means to become a witness. Meditation is not a technique at all! This will be very confusing to you because I go on giving you techniques. In the ultimate sense meditation is not a technique; meditation is an understanding, awareness. But you need techniques because that final understanding is very far away from you; hidden deep in you but still very far away from you. Right this moment you can attain it. But you will not attain it, because your mind goes on. This very moment it is possible and yet impossible. Techniques will bridge the gap; they are just to bridge the gap.

So in the beginning techniques are meditations; in the end you will laugh – techniques are not meditation. Meditation is a totally different quality of being, it has nothing to do with anything. But it will happen only in the end; don't think it has happened in the beginning, otherwise the gap will not be bridged. [2]

Begin with effort

Meditation techniques are doings, because you are advised to do something – even to meditate is to do something; even to sit silently is to do something, even to *not* do anything is a sort of doing. So in a superficial way, all meditation techniques are doings. But in a deeper way they are not, because if you succeed in them, the doing disappears.

Only in the beginning it appears like an effort. If you succeed in it, the effort disappears and the whole thing becomes spontaneous and effortless. If you succeed in it, it is not a doing. Then no effort on your part is needed: it becomes just like breathing, it is there. But in the beginning there is bound to be effort, because the mind cannot do anything which is not an effort. If you tell it to be effortless, the whole thing seems absurd.

In Zen, where much emphasis is put on effortlessness, the masters say to the disciples, "Just sit. Don't do anything." And the disciple tries. Of course – what can you do other than trying?

In the beginning, effort will be there, doing will be there – but only in the beginning, as a necessary evil. You have to remember constantly that you have to go beyond it. A moment must come when you are not doing anything about meditation; just being there and it happens. Just sitting or standing and it happens. Not doing anything, just being aware, it happens.

All these techniques are just to help you to come to an effortless moment. The inner transformation, the inner realization, cannot happen through effort, because effort is a sort of tension. With effort you cannot be relaxed totally; the effort will become a barrier. With this back-

ground in mind, if you make effort, by and by you will become capable of leaving it also. [3]

These methods are simple

Each of these methods which we will be discussing has been told by someone who has achieved. Remember this. They will look too simple, and they are. To our minds, things which are so simple cannot be appealing. Because if techniques are so simple and the abode is so near, if you are already in it, and the home is so near, you will look ridiculous to yourself – then why are you missing it? Rather than feel the ridiculousness of your own ego, you will think that such simple methods cannot help.

That is a deception. Your mind will tell you that these simple methods cannot be of any help – that they are so simple, they cannot achieve anything. "To achieve Divine existence, to achieve the Absolute and the Ultimate, how can such simple methods be used? How can they be of any help?" Your ego will say that they cannot be of any help.

Remember one thing – ego is always interested in something which is difficult because when something is difficult, there is a challenge. If you can overcome the difficulty, your ego will feel fulfilled. The ego is never attracted toward anything which is simple – never! If you want to give your ego a challenge, then you have to have something difficult devised. If something is simple, there is no appeal, because even if you can conquer it, there will be no fulfillment of the ego. In the first place, there was nothing to be conquered: the thing was so simple. Ego asks for difficulties – some hurdles to be crossed, some peaks to be conquered. And the more difficult the peak, the more at ease your ego will feel.

Because these techniques are so simple, they will not have any appeal to your mind. Remember, that which appeals to the ego cannot help your spiritual growth.

These techniques are so simple that you can achieve all that is possible to human consciousness to achieve, at any moment that you decide to achieve it. 4

First understand the technique

I have heard a story about an old doctor. One day his assistant phoned him because he was in very great difficulty: his patient was choking to death; a billiard ball was stuck in his throat, and the assistant was at a loss for what to do. So he asked the old doctor, "What am I supposed to do now?" The old doctor said, "Tickle the patient with a feather."

After a few minutes the assistant phoned again, very happy and jubilant, and said, "Your treatment proved wonderful! The patient started laughing and he spat the ball out. But tell me – from where have you learned this remarkable technique?"

The old doctor said, "I just made it up. This has always been my motto: when you don't know what to do, do something."

But this will not do as far as meditation is concerned. If you don't know what to do, don't do anything. Mind is very intricate, complex, delicate. If you don't know what to do, it is better not to do anything, because whatsoever you do without knowing is going to create more complexities than it can solve. It may even prove fatal, it may even prove suicidal.

If you don't know anything about the mind…. And really, you don't know anything about it. Mind is just a word. You don't know the complexity of it. Mind is the most complex thing in existence; there is nothing comparable to it. And it is the most delicate; you can destroy it, you can do something which then can not be undone. These techniques are based on a very deep knowledge, on a very deep encounter with the human mind. Each technique is based on long experimentation.

So remember this: don't do anything on your own, and don't mix two techniques, because their functioning is different, their ways are different, their bases are different. They lead to the same end, but as means they are totally different. Sometimes they may even be diametrically opposite. So don't mix two techniques. Really, don't mix anything; use the technique as it is given.

Don't change it, don't improve it – because you cannot improve it, and any change you bring to it will be fatal.

And before you start doing a technique, be fully alert that you have understood it. If you feel confused and you don't really know what the technique is, it is better not to do it, because each technique is for bringing about a revolution in you.

First try to understand the technique absolutely rightly. When you have understood it, then try it. And don't use this old doctor's motto that when you don't know what to do, do something. No, don't do anything. Non-doing will be more beneficial. [5]

The right method will click

Really, when you try the right method it clicks immediately. So I will go on talking about methods here every day. You try them. Just play with them: go home and try. The right method, whenever you happen upon it, just clicks. Something explodes in you, and you know that "This is the right method for me." But effort is needed, and you may be surprised that suddenly one day one method has gripped you.

I have found that while you are playing, your mind is more open. While you are serious your mind is not so open; it is closed. So just play. Do not be too serious, just play. And these methods are simple. You can just play with them.

Take one method: play with it for at least three days. If it gives you a certain feeling of affinity, if it gives you a certain feeling of well-being, if it gives you a certain feeling that this is for you, *then* be serious about it. Then forget the others. Do not play with other methods; stick to it – at least for three months.

Miracles are possible. The only thing is that the technique must be for you. If the technique is not for you, then nothing happens. Then you may go on with it for lives together, but nothing will happen. If the method is for you, then even three minutes are enough. [6]

When to drop the method

All the great masters say this, that one day you have to drop the method. And the sooner you drop it, the better. The moment you attain, the moment awareness is released in you, immediately drop the method.

Buddha used to tell a story again and again. Five idiots passed through a village. Seeing them, people were surprised, because they were carrying a boat on their heads. The boat was really big; they were almost dying under the weight of it. And people asked, "What are you doing?"

They said, "We cannot leave this boat. This is the boat that helped us to come from the other shore to this shore. How can we leave it? It is because of it that we have been able to come here. Without it we would have died on the other shore. The night was coming close, and there were wild animals on the other shore; it was as sure as anything that by the morning we would have been dead. We will never leave this boat. We are indebted forever. We will carry it on our heads in sheer gratitude."

Methods are dangerous only if you are unaware; otherwise they can be used beautifully. Do you think a boat is dangerous? It is dangerous if you are thinking to carry it on your head for your whole life, out of sheer gratitude. Otherwise it is just a raft to be used and discarded, used and abandoned, used and never looked back at again; there is no need, no point!

If you drop the remedy, automatically you will start settling in your being. The mind clings; it never allows you to settle in your being. It keeps you interested in something that you are not: the boats.

When you don't cling to anything, there is nowhere to go; all boats have been abandoned, you cannot go anywhere; all paths have been dropped, you cannot go anywhere; all dreams and desires have disappeared, there is no way to move. Relaxation happens of its own accord.

Just think of the word *relax*. Be... settle...you have come home.

One moment all is fragrance, and the next moment you are searching

15

for it and you cannot find it, where it has gone.

Only glimpses will happen in the beginning. Slowly slowly, they become more and more solid, they abide more and more. Slowly, slowly, slowly, slowly, very slowly, they settle forever. Before that, you cannot be allowed to take it for granted; that will be a mistake.

When you are sitting in meditation, a session of meditation, this will happen. But it will go. So what are you supposed to do between sessions?

Between sessions, continue to use the method. Drop the method when you are deep in meditation. The moment comes, as awareness is getting purer and purer, when suddenly it is utterly pure: drop the method, abandon the method, forget all about the remedy, just settle and be.

But this will happen only for moments in the beginning. Sometimes it happens here listening to me. Just for a moment, like a breeze, you are transported into another world, the world of no-mind. Just for a moment, you know that you know, but only for a moment. And again the darkness gathers and the mind is back with all its dreams, with all its desires and all its stupidities.

For a moment the clouds had separated and you had seen the sun. Now the clouds are there again; it is all dark and the sun has disappeared. Now even to believe that the sun exists will be difficult. Now to believe that what you had experienced a moment before was true will be difficult. It may have been a fantasy. The mind may say it might have been just imagination.

It is so incredible, it looks so impossible that it could have happened to *you*. With all this stupidity in the mind, with all these clouds and darknesses, it happened to you: you saw the sun for a moment. It doesn't look probable, you must have imagined it; maybe you had fallen into a dream and seen it.

Between sessions start again, be in the boat, use the boat again. [7]

Imagination can work for you

First you must understand what imagination is. It is condemned very much nowadays. The moment you hear the word "imagine" you will say this is useless, we want something real, not imaginary. But imagination is a reality, it is a capacity, it is a potentiality within you. You can imagine. That shows that your being is capable of imagination. This capacity is a reality. Through this imagination you can destroy or you can create yourself, that depends on you. Imagination is very powerful. It is potential power.

What is imagination? It is getting into an attitude so deeply that the very attitude becomes reality. For example, you may have heard about a technique which is used in Tibet. They call it heat yoga. The night is cold, snow is falling, and the Tibetan lama is standing naked under the open sky. The temperature is below zero. You would simply start dying, you would freeze. But the lama is practicing a particular technique – he is imagining that his body is a burning fire and he is imagining that he is perspiring – the heat is so much that he is perspiring. And he actually starts perspiring although the temperature is below zero and even the blood should freeze. He starts perspiring. What is happening? This perspiration is real, his body is really hot – but this reality is created through imagination.

Once you get in tune with your imagination, the body starts functioning. You are already doing many things without knowing that it is your imagination working. Many times you create illnesses just through imagination; you imagine that now this disease is here, infectious, it is all over the place. You have become receptive; now there is every possibility that you will fall ill – and that illness is real. But it has been created through imagination. Imagination is a force, an energy, and the mind moves through it. And when the mind moves through it, the body follows. [8]

This is the difference between the tantra tradition and Western hypnosis: hypnotists think that by imagination you are creating something; tantra thinks that you are not creating it – by imagination you are simply becoming attuned to something that is already there.

Whatsoever you create by imagination cannot be permanent. If it is not a reality, then it is false, unreal, and you are creating a hallucination. [9]

Suggestions for Beginners

Enough space

When you are trying to meditate, put the phone off the hook, disengage yourself. Put a notice on the door that for one hour nobody should knock, that you are meditating. And when you move into the meditation room, take your shoes off, because you are walking on sacred ground. Not only take your shoes off, but everything that you are preoccupied with. Consciously, leave everything with the shoes. Go inside unoccupied.

One can take one hour out of twenty-four hours. Give twenty-three hours for your occupations, desires, thoughts, ambitions, projections. Take one hour out of all this, and in the end you will find that only that one hour has been the real hour of your life; those twenty-three hours have been a sheer wastage. Only that one hour has been saved and all else has gone down the drain. [10]

The right place

You should find a place which enhances meditation. For example, sitting under a tree will help. Rather than going and sitting in front of a movie house or going to the railway station and sitting on the platform, go to nature, to the mountains, to the trees, to the rivers where tao is still flowing, vibrating, pulsating, streaming all around. Trees are in constant meditation. Silent, unconscious, is that meditation. I'm not saying to become a tree; you have to become a buddha! But Buddha has one thing in common with the tree: he's as green as a tree, as full of juice as a tree, as celebrating as a tree – of course with a difference. He is conscious, the tree is unconscious. The tree is unconsciously in tao; a buddha is consciously in tao. And that is a great difference, the difference between the earth and the sky.

But if you sit by the side of a tree surrounded by beautiful birds singing, or a peacock dancing, or just a river flowing, and the sound of running water, or by the side of a waterfall, and the great music of it....

Find a place where nature has not

yet been disturbed, polluted. If you cannot find such a place, then just close your doors and sit in your own room. If it is possible have a special room for meditation in your house. Just a small corner will do, but especially for meditation. Why especially for meditation? – because every kind of act creates its own vibration. If you simply meditate in that place, that place becomes meditative. Every day you meditate it absorbs your vibration when you are in meditation. Next day when you come, those vibrations start falling back on you. They help, they reciprocate, they respond.

When a person has really become a meditator, he can meditate sitting before a picture house, he can meditate on the railway platform.

For fifteen years I was continuously traveling around the country, continuously traveling – day in, day out, day in, day out, year in, year out – always on a train, on a plane, in a car. That makes no difference. Once you have become really *rooted* in your being, nothing makes a difference. But this is not for the beginner.

When the tree has become rooted, let winds come and let rains come and let clouds thunder; it is all good. It gives integrity to the tree. But when the tree is small, tender, then even a small child is dangerous

enough, or just a cow passing by, that is enough to destroy it. [11]

Be comfortable

A posture should be such that you can forget your body. What is comfort? When you forget your body, you are comfortable. When you are reminded continuously of the body, you are uncomfortable. So whether you sit in a chair or you sit on the ground, that is not the point. Be comfortable, because if you are not comfortable in the body you cannot long for other blessings which belong to deeper layers: the first layer missed, all other layers closed. If you really want to be happy, blissful, then start from the very beginning to be blissful. Comfort of the body is a basic need for anybody who is trying to reach inner ecstasies. [12]

Begin with catharsis

I never tell people to begin with just sitting. Begin from where beginning is easy. Otherwise, you will begin to feel many things unnecessarily – things that are not there.

If you begin with sitting, you will feel much disturbance inside. The

more you try to just sit, the more disturbance will be felt. You will become aware only of your insane mind and nothing else. It will create depression; you will feel frustrated, you will not feel blissful. Rather, you will begin to feel that you are insane. And sometimes you may really go insane!

If you make a sincere effort to 'just sit', you may really go insane. Only because people do not really try sincerely does insanity not happen more often. With a sitting posture you begin to know so much madness inside you that if you are sincere and continue it, you may really go insane. It has happened before, so many times. So I never suggest anything that can create frustration, depression, sadness… anything that will allow you to be too aware of your insanity. You may not be ready to be aware of all the insanity that is inside you.

You must be allowed to get to know certain things gradually. Knowledge is not always good. It must unfold itself slowly, as your capacity to absorb it grows.

I begin with your insanity, not with a sitting posture. I allow your insanity. If you dance madly, the opposite happens within you. With a mad dance, you begin to be aware of a silent point within you; with sitting silently, you begin to be aware of madness. The opposite is always the point of awareness.

With you dancing madly, chaotically, with crying, with chaotic breathing, I allow your madness. Then you begin to be aware of a subtle point, a deep point inside you which is silent and still, in contrast to the madness on the periphery. You will feel very blissful; at your center there is an inner silence. But if you are just sitting, then the inner one is the mad one. You are silent on the outside, but inside you are mad.

If you begin with something active – something positive, alive, moving – it will be better. Then you will begin to feel an inner stillness growing. The more it grows, the more it will be possible for you to use a sitting posture or a lying posture – the more silent meditation will be possible. But by then things will be different, totally different.

A meditation technique that begins with movement, action, helps you in other ways also. It becomes a catharsis. When you are just sitting, you are frustrated: your mind wants to move and you are just sitting. Every muscle turns, every nerve turns. You are trying to force something upon yourself that is not natural for you. Then you have divided yourself into the one who is forcing and the one who is being forced. And really, the part that is being forced and sup-

pressed is the more authentic part. It is a more major part of your mind than the part that is suppressing, and the major part is bound to win.

That which you are suppressing is really to be thrown, not suppressed. It has become an accumulation within you because you have been constantly suppressing it. The whole upbringing, the civilization, the education, is suppressive. You have been suppressing much that could have been thrown very easily with a different education, with a more conscious education, with a more aware parenthood. With a better awareness of the inner mechanism of the mind, the culture could have allowed you to throw many things.

For example, when a child is angry we tell him, "Do not be angry." He begins to suppress anger. By and by, what was a momentary happening becomes permanent. Now he will not *act* angry, but he will remain angry. We have accumulated so much anger from what were just momentary things. No one can be angry continuously unless anger has been suppressed. Anger is a momentary thing that comes and goes; if it is expressed, then you are no longer angry. So with me, I would allow the child to be angry more authentically. Be angry, but be deep in it. Do not suppress it.

Of course, there will be problems.

If we say, "Be angry," then you are going to be angry *at* someone. But a child can be molded. He can be given a pillow and told, "Be angry with the pillow. Be violent with the pillow." From the very beginning, a child can be brought up in a way in which the anger is just deviated. Some object can be given to him: he can go on throwing the object until his anger goes. Within minutes, within seconds, he will have dissipated his anger and there will be no accumulation of it.

You have accumulated anger, sex, violence, greed – everything. Now this accumulation is a madness within you. It is there, inside you. if you begin with any suppressive meditation – for example, with just sitting – you are suppressing all of this, you are not allowing it to be released. So I begin with a catharsis. First, let the suppressions be thrown into the air. And when you can throw your anger into the air, you have become mature.

If I cannot be loving alone, if I can be loving only with someone I love, then I am not really mature yet. Then I am depending on someone even to be loving. Someone must be there; only then can I be loving. That loving can be only a very superficial thing. It is not my nature. If I am alone in the room I am not loving at all, so the loving quality has not gone deep; it has not become a part of my being.

You become more and more mature when you are less and less dependent. If you can be angry alone, you are more mature. You do not need any object to be angry. So I make a catharsis in the beginning a must. You must throw everything into the sky, into the open space, without being conscious of any object.

Be angry without the person with whom you would like to be angry. Weep without finding any cause. Laugh, just laugh, without anything to laugh at. Then you can just throw the whole accumulated thing. You can just throw it! And once you know the way, you are unburdened of the whole past.

Within moments you can be unburdened of the whole life – of lives even. If you are ready to throw everything, if you can allow your madness to come out, within moments there is a deep cleansing. Now you are cleansed: fresh, innocent. You are a child again. Now, in your innocence, sitting meditation can be done – just sitting or just lying or anything – because now there is no mad one inside to disturb the sitting.

Cleansing must be the first thing – a catharsis. Otherwise, with breathing exercises, with just sitting, with practicing *asanas*, yogic postures –

you are just suppressing something. And a very strange thing happens: when you have allowed everything to be thrown out, sitting will just happen, *asanas* will just happen. It will be spontaneous.

Begin with catharsis and then something good can flower within you. It will have a different quality, a different beauty – altogether different. It will be authentic.

When silence comes to you, when it descends on you, it is not a false thing. You have not been cultivating it. It comes to you; it happens to you. You begin to feel it growing inside you just like a mother begins to feel a child growing. [13]

When I used to lead meditation camps myself, there was one method where every afternoon all the participants in the camp used to sit together and everybody was allowed to do whatsoever he wanted – no restriction, just he was not to interfere in anybody else's work. Whatever he wants to say, he can say; if he wants to cry, he can cry; if he wants to laugh, he can laugh – and one thousand people! It was such a hilarious scene! People you could never have imagined – serious people – doing such stupid things! Somebody was making faces, putting out his tongue as far

as he can, and you know that this man is a police commissioner!

One man I cannot forget, because he used to sit in front of me every day. He was a very rich man from Ahmedabad, and because his whole business was the share market, he was just continually on the phone. Whenever this one hour meditation would begin, within two or three minutes he would take up the phone. He would start dialing the numbers: "Hello!" And he would say – it looked from his face as if he was getting the answer – "Purchase it."

This would continue for one hour, and he was again and again phoning to this place, to that place, and once in a while he would look at me and smile: "What nonsense I'm doing!" But I had to keep absolutely serious. I never smiled at him. So he would again start phoning: "Nobody is taking any notice, everybody is engaged in his own work."

One thousand people doing so many things … and these things were continuously going on in their minds. This was a great chance for them to bring them out. It was such a drama.

Jayantibhai used to be in charge of the camp in Mount Abu, and one of his closest friends took off all his clothes. That was a surprise! Jayantibhai was standing by my side, and he could not believe it. That man was a very serious man, very rich; what was he doing in front of one thousand people? And then he started pushing the car in which I had come to the place – it was Jayantibhai's car. We were in the mountains, and just ahead there was a thousand-foot drop, and he was naked pushing the car.

Jayantibhai asked me, "What has to be done? He is going to destroy the car, and I had never thought that this man was against my car. We are close friends."

So I told him, "You push it from the other side; otherwise he is going to...."

So he was stopping the car and his friend was jumping around and shouting, "Get out of my way! I have always hated this car" – because he did not have an imported car, and this was an imported car which Jayantibhai was keeping for me. I was coming to Mount Abu three or four times a year, so he was keeping that car just for me.

His friend must have been feeling jealous inside that he did not have an imported car. And then a few people seeing the situation rushed to help. When he saw that so many people were preventing him, just out of protest he climbed a tree in front of me. Naked he sat in the top of the tree, and he started shaking

the tree. There was every danger that he would fall with the tree on top of the thousand people. Jayantibhai asked me, "What has to be done now?"

I said, "He is your friend. Let him be, don't be worried. Just move the people to this side and that, and let him do whatsoever he is doing. Now he is not destroying the car. At the most he will have multiple fractures."

As people moved away, he also stopped. Silently he sat in the tree. After the meditation was over, he was still sitting in the tree, and Jayantibhai said, "Now get down. The meditation is over."

As if he woke up from a sleep, he looked all around and saw that he was naked! He jumped out of the tree, rushed to his clothes, and said, "What happened to me?" In the night he came to see me and he said, "This was a very dangerous meditation! I could have killed myself or somebody else. I could have destroyed the car, and I am a great friend of Jayantibhai, and I had never thought...but certainly there must have been this idea in me.

"I hated the idea that you come in his car always, and I hated the idea that he has got an imported car, but it was not at all conscious in me. And what I was doing in the tree? I must have been carrying so much

violence in me, I wanted to kill people."

That meditation was immensely helpful. It relaxed people in one hour so much that they told me, "It seems a heavy load has disappeared from the head. We were not aware what we were carrying in the mind." But to become aware of it, there was no other way except an unlimited expression.

It was only a small experiment, I told people to continue it: soon you will come to many more things, and one day you will come to a point where all is exhausted. Remember only not to interfere with anybody, not to be destructive. Say anything you want to say, shout abuse, whatever you want – and exhaust all that you have been collecting.

But this is a strange world. The government of Rajasthan passed a resolution in their assembly that I cannot have camps in Mount Abu, because they had heard all these things were happening there – people who are perfectly right become almost mad, start doing any kinds of things. Now the politicians in the assembly don't have any idea of the human mind, its inhibitions and how to exhaust them, how to burn them. I had to stop that meditation because otherwise they were not going to allow me to have camps in Mount Abu. [14]

Guidelines to Freedom

The three essentials

Meditation has a few essential things in it, whatever the method, but those few essentials are necessary in every method. The first is a relaxed state: no fight with the mind, no control of the mind, no concentration. Second, just watch with a relaxed awareness whatever is going on, without any interference – just watching the mind, silently, without any judgment, evaluation.

These are the three things: relaxation, watching, no judgment, and slowly, slowly a great silence descends over you. All movement within you ceases. You are, but there is no sense of 'I am' – just a pure space. There are one hundred and twelve methods of meditation. I have talked on all those methods. They differ in their constitution, but the fundamentals remain the same: relaxation, watchfulness, a non-judgmental attitude. [15]

Be playful

Millions of people miss meditation because meditation has taken on a wrong connotation. It looks very serious, looks gloomy, has something of the church in it; it looks as if it is only for people who are dead, or almost dead – those who are gloomy, serious, have long faces, who have lost festivity, fun, playfulness, celebration....

These are the qualities of meditation: a really meditative person is playful; life is fun for him, life is a *leela*, a play. He enjoys it tremendously. He is not serious. He is relaxed. [16]

Be patient

Don't be in a hurry. So often, hurrying causes delay. As you thirst, wait patiently – the deeper the waiting, the sooner it comes.

You have sown the seed, now sit in the shade and watch what happens. The seed will break, it will blossom, but you cannot speed the process. Doesn't everything need time? Work you must, but leave the results to God. Nothing in life is ever wasted, especially steps taken towards truth.

But at times impatience comes; impatience comes with thirst, but this is an obstacle. Keep the thirst and throw the impatience.

Do not confuse impatience with thirst. With thirst there is yearning but no struggle; with impatience there is struggle but no yearning. With longing there is waiting but no demanding; with impatience there is demanding but no waiting. With thirst there are silent tears; with impatience there is restless struggle.

Truth cannot be raided; it is attained through surrender, not through struggle. It is conquered through total surrender. [17]

Don't look for results

The ego is result-oriented, the mind always hankers for results. The mind is never interested in the act itself, its interest is in the result. "What am I going to gain out of it?" If the mind can manage to gain without going through any action, then it will choose the shortcut.

That's why educated people become very cunning, because they are able to find shortcuts. If you earn money through a legal way, it may take your whole life. But if you can earn money by smuggling, by gambling, or by something else – by becoming a political leader, a prime minister, a president – then you have all the shortcuts available to you. The educated person becomes cunning. He does not become wise, he simply becomes clever. He becomes so cunning that he wants to have everything without doing anything for it.

Meditation happens only to those who are not result-oriented. Meditation is a non-goal-oriented state. [18]

Appreciate unawareness

While aware enjoy awareness, and while unaware enjoy unawareness. Nothing is wrong, because unawareness is like a rest. Otherwise awareness would become a tension. If you are awake twenty-four hours, how many days do you think you can be alive? Without food a man can live for three months; without sleep, within three weeks he will go mad, and he will try to commit suicide. In the day you are alert; in the night you relax, and that relaxation helps you in the day to be more alert, fresh again. Energies have passed through a rest period so they are more alive in the morning again.

The same will happen in meditation: for a few moments you are perfectly aware, at the peak and for a few moments you are in the valley, resting. Awareness has disappeared, you have forgotten. But what is wrong in it?

It is simple. Through unawareness awareness will arise again, fresh, young, and this will go on. If you can enjoy both you become the third, and that is the point to be understood: if you can enjoy both, it means that you are neither – neither awareness nor unawareness – you are the one who enjoys both. Something of the beyond enters.

In fact, this is the real witness. Happiness you enjoy, what is wrong with it? When happiness has gone and you have become sad, what is wrong with sadness? Enjoy it. Once you become capable of enjoying sadness, then you are neither.

And this I tell you: if you enjoy sadness, it has its own beauties. Happiness is a little shallow; sadness is very deep, it has a depth to it. A man who has never been sad will be shallow, just on the surface. Sadness is like a dark night, very deep. Darkness has a silence to it, and sadness also. Happiness bubbles; there is a sound in it. It is like a river in the mountains; sound is created. But in the mountains, a river can never be very deep; it is always shallow. When the river comes to the plain it becomes deep, but the sound stops. It moves as if not moving. Sadness has a depth.

Why create trouble? While happy, be happy, enjoy it. Don't get identified with it. When I say be happy, I mean enjoy it. Let it be a climate which will move and change. The morning changes into noon, noon changes into evening, and then comes night. Let happiness be a climate around you. Enjoy it, and then when sadness comes, enjoy that too. I teach you enjoyment whatsoever is the case. Sit silently and enjoy sadness, and suddenly sadness is no longer sadness; it has become a silent peaceful moment, beautiful in itself. Nothing is wrong in it.

And then comes the ultimate alchemy, the point where suddenly you realize that you are neither – neither happiness nor sadness. You are the watcher: you watch peaks, you watch valleys; but you are neither.

Once this point is attained, you can go on celebrating everything. You celebrate life, you celebrate death. [19]

Machines help but don't create meditation

So many machines are being developed around the world, pretending that they can give you meditation; you just have to put on earphones and relax, and within ten minutes you will reach the state of meditation.

This is utter stupidity, but there is a reason why such an idea has come to the minds of technical people. Mind functions on a certain wavelength when it is awake. When it is dreaming it functions on another wavelength. When it is fast asleep it functions on a different wavelength. But none of these are meditation.

For thousands of years we have called meditation *turiya,* "the fourth." When you go beyond the deepest sleep and still you are aware, that awareness is meditation. It is not an experience; it is you, your very being.

But these hi-tech mechanisms can be of tremendous use in the right hands. They can help to create the kind of waves in your mind so that you start feeling relaxed, as if half asleep…thoughts are disappearing and a moment comes that everything becomes silent in you. That is the moment when the waves are those of deep sleep. You will not be

aware of this deep sleep, but after ten minutes, when you are unplugged from the machine, you will see the effects: you are calm, quiet, peaceful, no worry, no tension; life seems to be more playful and joyous. One feels as if one has had an inner bath. Your whole being is calm and cool.

With machines things are very certain, because they don't depend on any doing of yours. It is just like listening to music: you feel peaceful, harmonious. Those machines will lead you up to the third state – deep sleep, sleep without dreams.

But if you think this is meditation then you are wrong. I will say this is a good experience, and while you are in that moment of deep sleep, if you can also be aware from the very beginning, as the mind starts changing its waves… You have to be more alert, more awake, more watchful – what is happening? – and you will see that mind is by and by falling asleep. And if you can see the mind falling asleep…the one who is seeing the mind falling asleep is your being, and that is the purpose of all authentic meditation.

These machines cannot create that awareness. That awareness you will have to create, but these machines can certainly create within ten minutes a possibility that you may not be able to create in years of effort.

So I am not against these hi-tech instruments, I am all for them. It is just that I want the people who are spreading those machines around the world to know that they are doing good work, but it is incomplete. It will be complete only when the person in the deepest silence is also alert, like a small flame of awareness which goes on burning. Everything disappears, all around is darkness, and silence, and peace – but an unwavering flame of awareness. So if the machine is in the right hands and people can be taught that the real thing will come not through the machine, the machine can create the very essential ground in which that flame can grow. But that flame depends on you, not on the machine.

So I am in favor of those machines on the one hand and on the other hand I am very much against them, because many, many people will think, "This is meditation," and they will be deceived. These machines will do immense harm, but they will spread all over the world very soon. And they are simple – there is nothing much in it; it is only a question of creating certain waves. Musicians can learn from those machines, what waves they create in people, and they can start creating those waves through their instruments. There is no need for the machines, just the musicians can create those waves

for you, and you will start falling asleep! But if you can remain awake even in the deepest sleep, when you see that just one step more and you will become unconscious, you have learned a secret. That machine can be used beautifully.

And this is true about all the machines of the world: in the right hands they can be used tremendously for the benefit of mankind. In the wrong hands they can become hindrances. And unfortunately, there are so many wrong hands....

But it is not meditation, it is simply a change in the radio waves that are continuously moving around you in the air. It can be certainly helpful as an experience; otherwise for many people meditation remains only a word. They think that some time they will meditate. And there remains a doubt, whether anybody meditates or not?

But in the West the mind is mechanical, the approach is mechanical; everything they want to reduce to a machine – and they are capable of it. But there are things which are beyond the capacity of any machine. Awareness cannot be created by any machine; it is beyond the scope of any hi-tech. But what technology can give you can certainly be used. This can be used as a very beautiful jumping ground into meditation.

And once you have tasted aware-

ness, perhaps a few times the machine may be helpful so that it becomes more and more clear, so your awareness becomes more and more separate from the silence that machine is creating. And then you should start doing it without the machine. Once you have learned to do it without the machine, the machine has helped you immensely. [20]

You are not your experiences

One of the most fundamental things to remember – not only by you but by everyone – is that whatever you come across in your inner journey, you are not it.

You are the one who is witnessing it – it may be nothingness, it may be blissfulness, it may be silence. But one thing has to be remembered – however beautiful and however enchanting an experience you come by, you are not it.

You are the one who is experiencing it, and if you go on and on and on, the ultimate in the journey is the point when there is no experience left – neither silence, nor blissfulness, nor nothingness. There is nothing as an object for you but only your subjectivity.

The mirror is empty. It is not reflecting anything. It is you.

Even great travelers of the inner world have got stuck in beautiful experiences, and have become identified with those experiences thinking, "I have found myself." They have stopped before reaching the final stage where all experiences disappear.

Enlightenment is not an experience. It is the state where you are left absolutely alone, nothing to know. No object, however beautiful, is present. Only in that moment does your consciousness, unobstructed by any object, take a turn and move back to the source.

It becomes self-realization. It becomes enlightenment.

I must remind you about the word 'object'. Every object means hindrance. The very meaning of the word is hindrance, objection.

So the object can be outside you, in the material world; the object can be inside you in your psychological world, the objects can be in your heart, feelings, emotions, sentiments, moods. And the objects can be even in your spiritual world. And they are so ecstatic that one cannot imagine there can be more. And many mystics of the world have stopped at ecstasy. It is a beautiful spot, a scenic spot, but they have not arrived home yet.

When you come to a point when all experiences are absent, there is no object, then consciousness without obstruction moves in a circle – in existence everything moves in a circle, if not obstructed – it comes from the same source of your being, goes around. Finding no obstacle to it – no experience, no object – it moves backwards. And the subject itself becomes the object.

That is what J. Krishnamurti continued to say for his whole life: when the observer becomes the observed, know that you have arrived. Before that there are thousands of things in the way. The body gives its own experiences, which have become known as the experiences of the centers of kundalini; seven centers become seven lotus flowers. Each is bigger than the other and higher, and the fragrance is intoxicating. The mind gives you great spaces, unlimited, infinite. But remember the fundamental maxim that still the home has not come.

Enjoy the journey and enjoy all the scenes that come on the journey – the trees, the mountains, the flowers, the rivers, the sun and the moon and the stars – but don't stop anywhere, unless your very subjectivity becomes its own object. When the observer is the observed, when the knower is the known, when the seer is the seen, the home has arrived.

This home is the real temple we have been searching for, for lives together, but we always go astray. We become satisfied with beautiful experiences.

A courageous seeker has to leave all those beautiful experiences behind, and go on moving. When all experiences are exhausted and only he himself remains in his aloneness…no ecstasy is bigger than that, no blissfulness is more blissful, no truth is truer. You have entered what I call godliness, you have become a god.

An old man went to his doctor. "I have got toilet problems," he complained.

"Well, let us see. How is your urination?"

"Every morning at seven o'clock, like a baby."

"Good. How about your bowel movement?"

"Eight o'clock each morning, like clockwork."

"So, what is the problem?" the doctor asked.

"I don't wake up until nine."

You are asleep and it is time to wake up.

All these experiences are experiences of a sleeping mind. The awakened mind has no experiences at all. [21]

The observer is not the witness

The observer and the observed are two aspects of the witness. When they disappear into each other, when they melt into each other, when they are one, the witness for the first time arises in its totality.

But a question arises to many people. The reason is that they think the witness is the observer. In their mind, the observer and the witness are synonymous. It is fallacious; the observer is not the witness, but only a part of it. And whenever the part thinks itself as the whole, error arises.

The observer means the subjective, and the observed means the objective: the observer means that which is outside the observed, and the observer means that which is inside. The inside and the outside can't be separate; they are together, they can only be together. When this togetherness, or rather oneness, is experienced, the witness arises.

You cannot practice the witness. If you practice the witness, you will be practicing only the observer, and the observer is not the witness.

Then what has to be done? Melting has to be done, merging has to be done. Seeing a rose flower, forget completely that there is an object seen and a subject as a seer. Let the beauty of the moment, the benediction of the moment, overwhelm you both, so the rose and you are no more separate, but you become one rhythm, one song, one ecstasy.

Loving, experiencing music, looking at the sunset, let it happen again and again. The more it happens the better, because it is not an art but a knack. You have to get the hunch of it; once you have got it, you can trigger it anywhere, any moment.

When the witness arises, there is nobody who is witnessing and there is nothing to be witnessed. It is a pure mirror, mirroring nothing. Even to say it is a mirror is not right; it would be better to say it is a mirroring. It is more a dynamic process of melting and merging; it is not a static phenomenon, it is a flow. The rose reaching you, you reaching into the rose: it is a sharing of being.

Forget that idea that the witness is the observer; it is not. The observer can be practiced, the witness happens. The observer is a kind of concentration, and the observer keeps you separate. The observer will enhance, strengthen your ego. The more you become an observer, the more you will feel like an island – separate, aloof, distant.

Down the ages, the monks all over the world have been practicing the observer. They may have called it the witness, but it is not the witness. The witness is something totally different, qualitatively different. The observer can be practiced, cultivated; you can become a better observer through practicing it.

The scientist observes, the mystic witnesses. The whole process of science is that of observation: very keen, acute, sharp observation, so nothing is missed. But the scientist does not come to know God. Although his observation is very very expert, yet he remains unaware of God. He never comes across God; on the contrary, he denies that God is, because the more he observes – and his whole process is that of observation – the more he becomes separate from existence. The bridges are broken and walls arise; he becomes imprisoned in his own ego.

The mystic witnesses. But remember, witnessing is a happening, a byproduct – a byproduct of being total in any moment, in any situation, in any experience. Totality is the key: out of totality arises the benediction of witnessing.

Forget all about observing; that will give you more accurate information about the observed object, but you will remain absolutely oblivious of your own consciousness. [22]

28

Meditation is a knack

Meditation is such a mystery that it can be called a science, an art, a knack, without any contradiction.

From one point of view it is a science because there is a clear-cut technique that has to be done. There are no exceptions to it, it is almost like a scientific law.

But from a different point of view it can also be said to be an art. Science is an extension of the mind – it is mathematics, it is logic, it is rational. Meditation belongs to the heart, not to the mind – it is not logic, it is closer to love. It is not like other scientific activities, but more like music, poetry, painting, dancing; hence, it can be called an art.

But meditation is such a great mystery that calling it 'science' and 'art' does not exhaust it. It is a knack – either you get it or you don't get it. A knack is not a science, it cannot be taught. A knack is not an art. A knack is the most mysterious thing in human understanding. 23

In my childhood I was sent to a master, a master swimmer. He was the best swimmer in the town, and I have never come across a man who has been so tremendously in love with water. Water was god to him, he worshiped it, and the river was his home. Early – at three o'clock in the morning – you would find him on the river. In the evening you would find him on the river and at night you would find him sitting, meditating by the side of the river. His whole life consisted of being close to the river.

When I was brought to him – I wanted to learn swimming – he looked at me, he felt something. He said, "But there is no way to learn swimming; I can just throw you in the water and then swimming comes of its own accord. There is no way to learn it, it cannot be taught. It is a knack, not knowledge."

And that's what he did – he threw me in the water and he was standing on the bank. For two, three times I went down and I felt I was almost drowning. He was just standing there, he would not even try to help me! Of course when your life is at stake, you do whatsoever you can. So I started throwing my hands about – they were haphazard, hectic, but the knack came. When life is at stake, you do whatsoever you can do …and whenever you do whatsoever you can do totally, things happen!

I could swim! I was thrilled! "Next time," I said, "you need not throw me into it – I will jump myself. Now I know that there is a natural buoyancy of the body. It is not a question of swimming, it is only a question of getting in tune with the water element. Once you are in tune with the water element it protects you."

And since then I have been throwing many people into the river of life! And I just stand there…. Almost nobody ever fails *if* he takes the jump. One is bound to learn. 24

It may take a few days for you to get the knack. It is a knack! It is not an art! If meditation were an art, it would have been very simple to teach. Because it is a knack, you have to try; slowly you get it. One of the Japanese professors of psychology is trying to teach small children, six months old, to swim, and he has succeeded. Then he tried with children three months old – and he has succeeded. Now he is trying with the newly born, and I hope that he succeeds. There is every possibility – because it is a knack. It does not need any other kind of experience: age, education…it is simply a knack. And if a six-month or three-month old baby can swim, that means we are naturally endowed with the idea of "how" to swim…it is just that we have to discover it. Just a little bit of effort and you will be able to discover it. The same is true about meditation – more true than about swimming. You just have to make a little effort. 25

PART THREE

The Meditations

Two Powerful Methods for Awakening

These are not really meditations. You are just getting in tune. It is like...if you have seen Indian classical musicians playing...for half an hour, or sometimes even more, they simply go on fixing their instruments. They will move their knobs, they will make the strings tight or loose, and the drum player will go on checking his drum – whether it is perfect or not. For half an hour they go on doing this. This is not music, this is just preparation.

Kundalini is not really meditation. It is just preparation. You are preparing your instrument. When it is ready, then you stand in silence, then meditation starts. Then you are utterly there. You have woken yourself up by jumping, by dancing, by breathing, by shouting – these are all devices to make you a little more alert than you ordinarily are. Once you are alert, then the waiting. Waiting is meditation. Waiting with full awareness. And then it comes, it descends on you, it surrounds you, it plays around you, it dances around you, it cleanses you, it purifies you, it transforms you.

Meditation is an energy phenomenon. One very basic thing has to be understood about all types of energies, and this is the basic law to be understood: energy moves in a dual polarity. That is the only way it moves; there is no other way for its movement. It moves in a dual polarity.

For any energy to become dynamic, the anti-pole is needed. It is just like electricity moving with negative and positive polarities. If there is only negative polarity, electricity will not happen; or if

Dynamic Meditation: Catharsis and Celebration

there is only positive polarity, electricity will not happen. Both poles are needed. And when both poles meet, they create electricity; then the spark comes up.

And this is so for all types of phenomena. Life goes on: between man and woman, the polarity. The woman is the negative life-energy; man is the positive

pole. They are electrical – hence so much attraction. With man alone, life would disappear; with woman alone there could be no life, only death. Between man and woman there exists a balance. Between man and woman – these two poles, these two banks – flows the river of life.

Wherever you look you will find

the same energy moving in polarities, balancing itself.

This polarity is very meaningful for meditation because mind is logical, and life is dialectical. When I say mind is logical, it means mind moves in a line. When I say life is dialectical, it means life moves with the opposite, not in a line. It zigzags from negative to positive –

positive to negative, negative to positive. It zigzags; it *uses* the opposites.

Mind moves in a line, a simple straight line. It never moves to the opposite – it denies the opposite. It believes in one, and life believes in two.

So whatsoever mind creates, it always chooses the one. If mind chooses silence – if mind has become fed up with all the noise that is created in life and it decides to be silent – then the mind goes to the Himalayas. It wants to be silent, it doesn't want anything to do with any type of noise. Even the song of the birds will disturb it; the breeze blowing through the trees will be a disturbance. The mind wants silence; it has chosen the line. Now the opposite has to be denied completely.

But this man living in the Himalayas – seeking silence, avoiding the other, the opposite – will become dead; he will certainly become dull. And the more he chooses to be silent, the duller he will become – because life needs the opposite, the challenge of the opposite.

There is a different type of silence which exists between two opposites. The first is a dead silence, the silence of the cemetery. A dead man is silent, but you would not like to be a dead man. A dead man is absolutely silent. Nobody can disturb him, his concentration is perfect. You cannot do anything to distract his mind; his mind is absolutely fixed. Even if the whole world goes mad all around, he will remain in his concentration. But still, you would not like to be a dead man. Silence, concentration, or whatever it is called…you would not like to be dead – because if you are silent and dead the silence is meaningless.

Silence must happen while you are absolutely alive, vital, bubbling with life and energy. Then silence is meaningful. But then silence will have a different, altogether different quality to it. It will not be dull. It will be alive. It will be a subtle balance between two polarities.

A man who is seeking a live balance, a live silence, would like to move to both the market and the Himalayas. He would like to go to the market to enjoy noise, and he would also like to go to the Himalayas to enjoy silence. And he will create a balance between these two polar opposites, and he will remain in that balance. And that balance cannot be achieved through linear efforts.

That is what is meant by the Zen technique of effortless effort. It uses contradictory terms – effortless effort, or gateless gate, or pathless path.

Zen always uses the contradictory term immediately, just to give you the hint that the process is going to be dialectical, not linear. The opposite is not to be denied but absorbed. The opposite is not to be left aside – it has to be used. Left aside, it will always be a burden on you. Left aside, it will hang with you. Unused, you will miss much.

The energy can be converted and used. And then, using it, you will be more vital, more alive. The opposite has to be absorbed, then the process becomes dialectical.

Effortlessness means not doing anything, inactivity – *akarma*.

Effort means doing much, activity – *karma*. Both have to be there.

Do much, but don't be a doer – then you achieve both. Move in the world, but don't be a part of it. Live in the world, but don't let the world live in you.

Then the contradiction has been absorbed….

And that's what I'm doing. Dynamic meditation is a contradiction. Dynamic means effort, much effort, absolute effort. And meditation means silence, no effort, no activity. You can call it a dialectical meditation. [1]

Instructions for Dynamic Meditation

Music to support this meditation and to signal the beginning of each stage has been composed with Osho's guidance. For availability, see back page.

First stage: 10 minutes

*B*reathing *rapidly in and out through the nose, let breathing be intense and chaotic. The breath should move deeply into the lungs. Be as fast as you can in your breathing, making sure breathing stays deep. Do this as totally as you possibly can; without tightening up your body, make sure neck and shoulders stay relaxed. Continue on, until you literally become the breathing, allowing breath to be chaotic (that means not in a steady, predictable way). Once your energy is moving, it will begin to move your body. Allow these body movements to be there, use them to help you build up even more energy. Moving your arms and body in a natural way will help your energy to rise. Feel your energy building up; don't let go during the first stage and never slow down.*

Second stage: 10 minutes

Follow your body. Give your body freedom to express whatever is there …. EXPLODE! …. Let your body take over. Let go of everything that needs to be thrown out. Go totally mad…. Sing, scream, laugh, shout, cry, jump, shake, dance, kick, and throw yourself around. Hold nothing back, keep your whole body moving. A little acting often helps to get you started. Never allow your mind to interfere with what is happening. Remember to be total with your body.

Third stage: 10 minutes

Leaving your shoulders and neck relaxed, raise both arms as high as you can without locking the elbows. With raised arms, jump up and down shouting the mantra HOO!…HOO!…HOO! as deeply as possible, coming from the bottom of your belly. Each time you land on the flats of your feet (making sure heels touch the ground), let the sound hammer deep into the sex center. Give all you have, exhaust yourself completely.

Fourth stage: 15 minutes

*STOP! Freeze where you are in whatever position you find your-*self. Don't arrange the body in any way. A cough, a movement, anything will dissipate the energy flow and the effort will be lost. Be a witness to everything that is happening to you.*

Fifth stage: 15 minutes

Celebrate!…with music and dance express whatsoever is there. Carry your aliveness with you throughout the day. [2]

Giving birth to yourself

Helpful hints

*M*y system of Dynamic Meditation begins with breathing, because breathing has deep roots in the being. You may not have observed it, but if you can change your breathing, you can change many things. If you observe your breathing carefully, you will see that when you are angry you have a particular rhythm of breathing. When you are in love, a totally different rhythm comes to you. When you are relaxed you breathe differently; when you are tense you breathe differently. You cannot breathe the way you do when you are relaxed and be angry at the same time. It is impossible.

When you are sexually aroused, your breathing changes. If you do not allow the breathing to change, your sexual arousal will drop automatically. This means that breathing is deeply related to your mental state. If you change your breathing, you can change the state of your mind. Or, if you change the state of your mind, breathing will change.

So I start with breathing and I suggest ten minutes of chaotic breathing in the first stage of the technique. By chaotic breathing I mean deep, fast, vigorous breathing, without any rhythm – just taking the breath in and throwing it out, taking it in and throwing it out, as vigorously, as deeply, as intensely as possible. Take it in; then throw it out.

This chaotic breathing is to create a chaos within your repressed system. Whatever you are, you are with a certain type of breathing. A child breathes in a particular way. If you are sexually afraid, you breathe in a particular way. You cannot breathe deeply because every deep breath hits the sex center. If you are fearful, you cannot take deep breaths. Fear creates shallow breathing.

This chaotic breathing is to destroy all your past patterns. What you have made out of yourself, this chaotic breathing is to destroy. Chaotic breathing creates a chaos within you because unless a chaos is created, you cannot release your repressed emotions. And those emotions have now moved into the body.

You are not body *and* mind; you are body/mind, psycho/somatic. You are both together. So whatever is done with your body reaches to the mind and whatever is done with the mind reaches to the body. Body and mind are two ends of the same entity.

Ten minutes of chaotic breathing is wonderful! But it must be chaotic. It is not a type of *pranayama,* yogic breathing. It is simply creating chaos through breathing. And it creates chaos for many reasons.

Deep, fast breathing gives you more oxygen. The more oxygen in the body, the more alive you become, the more animal-like. Animals are alive and man is half-dead, half-alive. You have to be made into an animal again. Only then can something higher develop in you.

If you are only half-alive, nothing can be done with you. So this chaotic breathing will make you like an animal: alive, vibrating, vital – with more oxygen in your blood, more energy in your cells. Your body cells will become more alive. This oxygenation helps to create body electricity – or, you can call it bio-energy. When there is electricity in the body you can move deep within, beyond yourself. The electricity will work within you.

The body has its own electrical sources. If you hammer them with more breathing and more oxygen, they begin to flow. And if you become really alive, then you are no longer a body. The more alive you become, the more energy flows in your system and the less you will feel yourself physically. You will feel more like energy and less like matter.

And whenever it happens that you are more alive, in those moments you are not body-oriented. If sex has so much appeal, one of the reasons is this: that if you are really in the act, totally moving, totally alive, then you are no longer a body – just energy. To feel this energy, to be alive with this energy, is very necessary if you are to move beyond.

The second step in my technique of Dynamic Meditation is a catharsis. I tell you to be *consciously* insane. Whatever comes to your mind – *whatever* – allow it to express itself; cooperate with it. No resistance; just a flow of emotions.

If you want to scream, then scream. Cooperate with it. A deep scream, a total scream in which your whole being becomes involved, is very therapeutic, deeply therapeutic. Many things, many diseases, will be released just by the scream. If the scream is total, your whole being will be in it.

So for the next ten minutes (this second step is also for ten minutes) allow yourself expression through crying, dancing, screaming, weeping, jumping, laughing – 'freaking out' as they say. Within a few days, you will come to feel what it is.

In the beginning it may be forced, an effort, or it may even be just acting. We have become so false that nothing real or authentic can be done by us. We have not laughed, we have not cried, we have not screamed authentically. Everything is just a facade – a mask. So when you begin to do this technique – in the beginning – it may be forced. It may need effort; there may be just acting. But do not bother about it. Go on. Soon you will touch those sources where you have repressed many things. You will touch those sources, and once they are released, you will feel unburdened. A new life will come to you; a new birth will take place.

This unburdening is basic and without it there can be no meditation for man as he is. Again, I am not talking about the exceptions. They are irrelevant.

With this second step – when things are thrown out – you become vacant. And this is what is meant by emptiness: to be empty of all repressions. In this emptiness something can be done. Transformation can happen; meditation can happen.

Then in the third step I use the sound *hoo*. Many sounds have been used in the past. Each sound has something specific to do. For example, Hindus have been using the sound *aum*. This may be familiar to you. But I won't suggest *aum*. *Aum* strikes at the heart center, but man is no longer centered in the heart. *Aum* is striking at a door where no one is home.

Sufis have used *hoo,* and if you say *hoo* loudly, it goes deep to the sex center. So this sound is used just as a hammering within. When you have become empty and vacant, this sound can move within you.

The movement of the sound is possible only when you are empty. If you are filled with repressions, nothing will happen. And sometimes it is even dangerous to use any mantra or sound when you are filled with repressions. Each layer of repression will change the path of the sound and the ultimate result may be something of which you never dreamed, never expected, never wished. You need a vacant mind; only then can a mantra be used.

So I never suggest a mantra to anyone as he is. First there must be a catharsis. This mantra *hoo* should never be done without doing the first two steps. It should *never* be done without them. Only in the third step (for ten minutes) is this *hoo* to be used – used as loudly as possible, bringing your total energy to it. You are to hammer your energy with the sound. And when you are empty – when you have been emptied by the catharsis of the second step – this *hoo* goes deep down and hits the sex center.

The sex center can be hit in two ways. The first way is naturally. Whenever you are attracted to a member of the opposite sex, the sex center is hit from without. And that hit is also a subtle vibration. A man is attracted to a woman or a woman is attracted to a man. Why? What is there in a man and what is there in a woman to account for it? A positive or negative electricity hits them, a subtle vibration. It is a sound, really. For example, you may have observed that birds use sound for sex appeal. All their singing is sexual. They are repeatedly hitting each other with particular sounds. These sounds hit the sex centers of birds of the opposite sex.

Subtle vibrations of electricity are hitting you from without. When your sex center is hit from without, your energy begins to flow outward – toward the other. Then there will be reproduction, birth. Someone else will be born out of you.

Hoo is hitting the same center of energy, but from within. And when the sex center is hit from within, the energy starts to flow within. This inner flow of energy changes you completely. You become transformed: you give birth to yourself.

You are transformed only when your energy moves in a totally opposite direction. Right now it is flowing out, but then it begins to flow within. Now it is flowing down, but then it flows upward. This upward flow of energy is what is known as *kundalini.* You will feel it actually flowing in your spine, and the higher it moves, the higher you will move with it. When this energy reaches the *brahmarandhra* – the last center in you: the seventh center, located at the top of the head – you are the highest man possible.

In the third step, I use *hoo* as a vehicle to bring your energy upward. These first three steps are cathartic. They are not meditation, but just preparation for it. They are a 'getting ready' to take the jump, not the jump itself.

The fourth step is the jump. In the fourth step I tell you to *stop!* When I say "Stop!" stop completely.

Don't do anything at all because anything you do can become a diversion and you will miss the point. Anything – just a cough or a sneeze – and you may miss the whole thing because the mind has become diverted. Then the upward flow will stop immediately because your attention has moved.

Don't do anything. You are not going to die. Even if a sneeze is coming and you do not sneeze for ten minutes, you will not die. If you feel like coughing, if you feel an irritation in the throat and you do not do anything, you are not going to die. Just let your body remain dead so that the energy can move in one upward flow.

When the energy moves upward, you become more and more silent. Silence is the by-product of energy moving upward and tension is the by-product of energy moving downward. Now your whole body will become so silent – as if it has disappeared. You will not be able to feel it. You have become bodiless. And when you are silent, the whole existence is silent because the existence is nothing but a mirror. It reflects you. In thousands and thousands of mirrors, it reflects you. When you are silent, the whole existence has become silent. In your silence I will tell you to just be a witness – a constant alertness:

not doing anything, but just remaining a witness, just remaining with yourself; not doing *anything* – no movement, no desire, no becoming – but just remaining then and there, silently witnessing what is happening.

That remaining in the center, in yourself, is possible because of the first three steps. Unless these three are done, you cannot remain with yourself. You can go on talking about it, thinking about it, dreaming about it, but it will not happen because you are not ready.

These first three steps will make you ready to remain with the moment. They will make you aware. That is meditation. In that meditation something happens that is beyond words. And once it happens you will never be the same again; it is impossible. It is a growth; it is not simply an experience. It is a growth. [3]

Remember,
remain a witness

This is a meditation in which you have to be continuously alert, conscious, aware, whatsoever you do. Remain a witness. Don't get lost.

It is easy to get lost. While you are breathing you can forget. You can become one with the breathing so much that you can forget the witness. But then you miss the point. Breathe as fast, as deep as possible, bring your total energy to it, but still remain a witness.

Observe what is happening, as if you are just a spectator, as if the whole thing is happening to somebody else, as if the whole thing is happening in the body and the consciousness is just centered and looking.

This witnessing has to be carried in all the three steps. And when everything stops, and in the fourth step you have become completely inactive, frozen, then this alertness will come to its peak. [4]

Music to support this meditation and to signal the beginning of each stage has been composed with Osho's guidance. For availability, see back page.

First stage: 15 minutes

Be loose and let your whole body shake, feeling the energies moving up from your feet. Let go everywhere and become the shaking. Your eyes may be opened or closed.

Second stage: 15 minutes

Dance ... any way you feel, and let the whole body move as it wishes.

Kundalini Meditation

Third stage: 15 minutes

Close your eyes and be still, sitting or standing ... witnessing whatever is happening inside and out.

Fourth stage: 15 minutes

Keeping your eyes closed, lie down and be still.

If you are doing the Kundalini Meditation, then allow the shaking, don't do it. Stand silently, feel it coming and when your body starts a little trembling, help it but don't do it. Enjoy it, feel blissful about it, allow it, receive it, welcome it, but don't will it.

If you force it, it will become an exercise, a bodily physical exercise. Then the shaking will be there but just on the surface, it will not penetrate you. You will remain solid, stone-like, rock-like within; you will remain the manipulator, the doer, and the body will just be following. The body is not the question – you are the question.

When I say shake I mean your solidity, your rock-like being should shake to the very foundations so that it becomes liquid, fluid, melts, flows. And when the rock-like being becomes liquid, your body will follow. Then there is no shake, only shaking. Then nobody is doing it, it is simply happening. Then the doer is not. [5]

Osho Meditative Therapies

The ancient methods of meditation were all developed in the East. They never considered the Western man.... I am creating techniques which are not only for the Eastern man, but which are simply for every man – Eastern or Western.

Over a period of 18 months before Osho left His body, He created a new series of "meditative therapies." Uniquely simple and effective, they involve a minimum of interaction among the participants, but the energy of the group helps each individual go more deeply into his or her own process.

The symbol of the mystic rose is that if a man takes care of the seed he is born with, gives it the right soil, gives it the right atmosphere and the right vibrations, moves on a right path where the seed can start growing, then the ultimate growth is symbolized as the mystic rose – when your being blossoms and opens all its petals and releases its beautiful fragrance.

The Mystic Rose Meditation

For those who want to go deeper, I have chosen to create a new meditative therapy. The first part will be laughter – for three hours, people simply laugh for no reason at all. And whenever their laughter starts dying they again say, "Yaa-Hoo!" and it will come back. Digging for three hours you will be surprised how many layers of dust have gathered upon your being. It will cut them like a sword in one blow. For seven days continuously, three hours every day…you cannot conceive how much transformation can come to your being.

And then the second part is tears. The first part removes everything that hinders your laughter – all the inhibitions of past humanity, all the repressions, it cuts them away. It brings a new space within you. But you still have to go a few steps more to reach the temple of your being, because you have suppressed so much sadness, so much despair, so much anxiety, so many tears – they are all there, covering you and destroying your beauty, your grace, your joy.

In old Mongolia they had an ancient idea that every life, whatever pain is suppressed…and pain is suppressed, because nobody wants it. You don't want to be painful, so you suppress it, you avoid, you look somewhere else. But it remains.

And the Mongolian idea was – and I agree with it – that life after life it goes on accumulating in you; it becomes almost a hard shell of pain. If you go in you will find both, laughter and tears. That's why sometimes it happens that by laughing, suddenly you find tears also start coming together with it – very confusing, because ordinarily we think they are contrary. When you are full of tears it is not a time to laugh, or when you are laughing it is not the right season for tears. But existence does not believe in your concepts, ideologies; existence transcends all your concepts, which are dualistic, which are based on duality. Day and night, laughter and tears, pain and blissfulness, they both come together.

When a man reaches into his innermost being he will find the first layer is of laughter and the second layer is of agony, tears.

So for seven days you have to allow yourself to weep, cry, for no reason at all – just the tears are ready to come. You are preventing them; just don't prevent. And whenever you feel they are not coming, just say, "Yaa-Boo!" These are pure sounds, used as a technique to bring all your laughter and all your tears and clean you completely, so that you can become an innocent child.

Finally, the third part is witnessing – the watcher on the hills. Finally, after the laughter and the tears, there is only a witnessing silence. Witnessing on its own is automatically suppressive. Weeping stops when you witness it, it becomes dormant. This meditation gets rid of the laughter and tears beforehand, so that there is nothing to suppress in your witnessing. Then the witnessing simply opens a pure sky. So for seven days you experience simply a clarity.

This is absolutely my meditation.

You will be surprised that no meditation can give you so much as this small strategy. This is my experience of many meditations, that what has to be done is to break two layers in you. Your laughter has been repressed; you have been told, "Don't laugh, it is a serious matter." You are not allowed to laugh in a church, or in a university class….

So the first layer is of laughter, but once laughter is over you will suddenly find yourself flooded with tears, agony. But that too will be a great unburdening phenomenon. Many lives of pain and suffering will disappear. If you can get rid of these two layers you have found yourself.

There is no meaning in the words 'Yaa-Hoo' or 'Yaa-Boo'. These are simply techniques, sounds which can be used for a certain purpose to enter into your own being.

I have invented many meditations, but perhaps this will be the most essential and fundamental one. It can take over the whole world….

Every society has done so much harm by preventing your joys and your tears. If an old man starts crying you will say, "What are you doing? You should feel ashamed; you are not a child, that somebody has taken your banana and you are crying. Have another banana, but don't cry."

Just see – stand on the street and start crying and a crowd will gather to console you: "Don't cry! Whatever has happened forget all about it, it has happened." Nobody knows what has happened, nobody can help you, but everybody will try – "Don't cry!" And the reason is that if you go on crying, then *they* will start crying, because they are also flooded with tears. Those tears are very close to the eyes.

And it is healthy to cry, to weep, to laugh. Now scientists are discovering that crying, weeping, laughter are immensely healthful, not only physically but also psychologically. They are very much capable of keeping you sane. The whole of humanity has gone a little cuckoo for the simple reason that nobody laughs fully, because all around there are people who will say, "What are you doing? Are you a child? – at this age? What will your children think? Keep quiet!"

If you cry and weep without any reason, just as an exercise, a meditation...nobody will believe it. Tears have never been accepted as meditation. And I tell you, they are not only a meditation, they are a medicine also. You will have better eyesight and you will have better inner vision.

I am giving you a very fundamental technique, fresh and unused. And it is going to become worldwide, without any doubt, because its effects will show anybody that the person has become younger, the person has become more loving, the person has become graceful. The person has become more flexible, less fanatic; the person has become more joyful, more a celebrant.

All that this world needs is a good cleansing of the heart of all the inhibitions of the past. And laughter and tears can do both. Tears will take out all the agony that is hidden inside you and laughter will take all that is preventing your ecstasy. Once you have learned the art you will be immensely surprised: why has this not been told up to now? There is a reason: nobody has wanted humanity to have the freshness of a roseflower and the fragrance and the beauty.

I have called this series of lectures *The Mystic Rose*. "Yaa-Hoo!" is the mantra to bring the mystic rose in your very center, to open your center

and release your fragrance, and the Mystic Rose is the fulfillment of your inner being. [1]

Instructions

This meditation in three parts, lasting for 21 days, can also be done alone.

1. Instructions for Laughter

The authentic laughter is not about anything. It is simply arising in you as a flower blossoms in a tree. It has no reason, no rational explanation. It is mysterious; hence the symbol of the mystic rose.

For seven days, begin by shouting Yaa-Hoo! a few times, then just laugh for no reason at all for 45 minutes. You can sit or lie down. Some people find lying on the back helps to relax the stomach muscles and allows energy to move more easily. Some people find that covering themselves with a sheet, or holding their legs in the air helps to bring out the laughing, giggling child in them. The emphasis is on finding your inner laughter, laughter for no reason at all, so your eyes are generally closed. However, some eye contact with your friends to spark off laughter is also fine.

Let your body roll about in a light, playful way, with the innocence of the child within you, and allow yourself to laugh with totality.

At times, you may come up against blocks, which have been there for centuries, preventing your laughter. When this happens, shout Yaa-Hoo! or do gibberish (nonsense sounds) until laughter arises again.

Let-go: At the end of the laughing stage, sit perfectly still, with eyes closed, for a few minutes. The body is frozen, like a statue, gathering all the energy within. Then let-go: relax your body completely and allow it to fall without any effort or control. When you feel ready, sit up again and sit silently, watching for 15 minutes.

2. Instructions for Tears

Once the laughter is over you will find yourself flooded with tears, agony. But that too will be a great unburdening phenomenon. Many lives of pain and suffering will disappear. If you can get rid of those two layers you have found yourself.

For the second week, begin by saying Yaa-Boo softly a few times, then just allow yourself to cry for

45 minutes. You may want to have the room slightly darkened to help you move into your sadness. You can sit or lie down. Close your eyes and move deeply into all the feelings that make you cry.

Allow yourself to cry really deeply, cleansing and unburdening the heart. Feel that the dam of all your pent-up hurts and sufferings is breaking open – let the tears flood out. If you feel blocked or feel sleepy after crying for a while, do gibberish. Rock your body back and forth a little, or say Yaa-Boo again a few times. The tears are there, just don't prevent them.

Let-go: At the end of the crying stage each day, sit perfectly still for a few minutes and then move into let-go, the same as you did after the laughter.

During this week of tears, be open to any situation which might bring tears. Allow yourself to be vulnerable.

3. Instructions for The Watcher on the Hills

For the third week, sit in silence for whatever period of time feels comfortable for you, and then dance to light, heartful music.

You may sit on the floor or use a chair. Your head and back should be as straight as possible, your eyes closed and your breathing natural.

Relax, be aware, become like a watcher on the hills, just witnessing whatever passes by. It is the process of watching which is the meditation; what you are watching is not important. Remember not to become identified with or lost in whatever comes by: thoughts, feelings, body sensations, judgments.

After sitting, play some gentle music of your own choice and dance. Allow the body to find its own movement, and continue watching as you are moving; do not get lost in the music.[2]

4. A Few Points to Help

• *During the entire twenty-one day period, it is best to avoid other cathartic meditations or sessions (e.g. Dynamic or Kundalini Meditations, or sessions like breath, emotional release and bioenergetics.)*

• *If you are doing The Mystic Rose Meditation with friends, do not talk to each other during the meditation.*

• *Many people come to a layer of anger during the week of laughter or during the week of tears. There is no need to stay stuck there. Let it be expressed with gibberish and body movements, then return to the laughter or tears.*

• *Celebrate your laughter, celebrate your tears, celebrate your moments of silent watching!*

No-mind means intelligence. Mind means gibberish, not intelligence, and when I am asking you for gibberish, I am simply asking you to throw out the mind and all its activity so you remain behind – pure, clean, transparent, perceptive.

The No-Mind Meditation

My Beloved Ones, I am introducing you to a new meditation. It is divided in three parts.

The first part is gibberish. The word 'gibberish' comes from a Sufi mystic, Jabbar. Jabbar never spoke any language, he just uttered nonsense. Still he had thousands of disciples because what he was saying was, 'Your mind is nothing but gibberish. Put it aside and you will have a taste of your own being

Use gibberish and go consciously crazy. Go crazy with absolute awareness so that you become the center of the cyclone. Simply allow whatever comes, without bothering whether it is meaningful or reasonable. Just throw out all mind garbage and create the space in which the buddha appears.

In the second part, the cyclone is gone and has taken you also away. The buddha has taken its place in absolute silence and immobility. You are just witnessing the body, the mind and anything that is happening.

In the third part I will say, 'Let go!' Then you relax your body and let it fall without any effort, without your mind controlling. Just fall like a bag of rice.

Each segment will begin with the sound of a drum.[1]

Instructions

Try the meditation for seven days at first, as that will be a long enough period to experience its effects. Allow for approximately 40 minutes of gibberish, followed by 40 minutes of witnessing and Let-Go, but you can continue both stages for a further 20 minutes if you wish.

First stage: Gibberish or Conscious Craziness

Standing or sitting, close your eyes and begin to say nonsense sounds – gibberish. Make any sounds you like, but do not speak in a language, or use words that you know. Allow yourself to express whatever needs to be expressed within you. Throw everything out, go totally mad. Go consciously crazy. The mind thinks in terms of words. Gibberish helps to break up this pattern of continuous verbalization. Without suppressing your thoughts, you can throw them out in this gibberish.

Everything is allowed: sing, cry, shout, scream, mumble, talk. Let your body do whatever it wants: jump, lie down, pace, sit, kick, and so on. Do not let empty spaces happen. If you cannot find sounds to gibber with, just say la la la la, *but don't remain silent.*

If you do this meditation with other people, do not relate or interfere with them in any way. Just stay with what is happening to you, and don't bother about what others are doing.

Second stage: Witnessing

After the gibberish, sit absolutely still and silent and relaxed, gathering your energy inwards, letting your thoughts drift further and further away from you, allowing yourself to fall into the deep silence and peacefulness that is at your center. You may sit on the floor or use a chair. Your head and back should be straight, your body relaxed, your eyes closed and your breathing natural.

Be aware, be totally in the present moment. Become like a watcher on the hills, witnessing whatever passes by. Your thoughts will try to race to the future or back to the past. Just watch them from a distance – don't judge them, don't get caught up in them. Just stay in the present, watching. It is the process of watching which is the meditation, what you are watching is not important. Remember not to become identified with or lost in whatever comes by: thoughts, feelings, body sensations, judgments.

Third stage: Let-Go

Gibberish is to get rid of the active mind, silence is to get rid of the inactive mind, and Let-Go is to enter into the transcendental.

After the witnessing, allow your body to fall back to the ground without any effort or control. Lying back, continue witnessing, being aware that you are not the body nor the mind, that you are something separate from both.

As you travel deeper and deeper inside, you will eventually come to your center. [2]

52

Remember this: regain your childhood. Everyone longs for it, but no one is doing anything to regain it. *Everyone* longs for it! People go on saying that childhood was paradise and poets go on writing poems about the beauty of childhood. Who is preventing you? Regain it! I give you this opportunity to regain it.

Born Again

Be playful. It will be difficult, because you are so much structured. You have an armor around you – it is so difficult to loose it, to relax it. You cannot dance, you cannot sing, you cannot just jump, you cannot just scream and laugh and smile. Even if you want to laugh, you first want something there to be laughed at. You cannot simply laugh. There must be some cause; only then can you laugh. There must be some cause; only then can you cry and weep.

Put aside knowledge, put side seriousness. Be absolutely playful for these days. You have nothing to lose! If you don't gain anything, you will not lose anything. What can you lose in being playful? But I say to you: you will never be the same again.

My insistence on being playful is because of this. I want to throw you back to the very point from where you stopped growing. There has been a point in your childhood when you stopped growing and when you started being false. You may have been angry – a small child in a tantrum, angry – and your father or your mother said, "Don't be angry! This is not good!" You were natural, but a division was created and a choice was there for you: If you want to be natural, then you will not get the love of your parents.

In these eight days I want to throw you back to the point where you started being "good" against being natural. Be playful so your childhood is regained. It will be difficult because you will have to put aside your masks, your faces; you will have to put aside your personality. But remember, the essence can assert itself only when your personality is not there, because your personality has become an imprisonment. Put it aside! It will be painful, but it is worth it because you are going to be reborn out of it. And no birth is without pain. If you are really determined to be reborn, then take the risk.

Instructions

Osho's guidelines for Born Again are as follows:

First stage:

For the first hour you behave like a child, just enter into your childhood. Whatever you wanted to do, do it – dancing, singing, jumping, crying, weeping – anything at all, in any posture. Nothing is prohibited except touching other people. Don't touch or harm anyone else in the group.

Second stage:

For the second hour just sit silently. You will be more fresh, more innocent, and meditation will become easier. [2]

Two hours a day for seven days.

Decide that for these days you will be as ignorant as you were when you were born – just a child, a new babe, knows nothing, asks nothing, discusses nothing, argues nothing. If you can be a little babe, much is possible. Even that which looks impossible is possible. [4]

Dancing as a Meditation

Disappear in the dance

Forget the dancer, the center of the ego; become the dance. That is the meditation. Dance so deeply that you forget completely that 'you' are dancing and begin to feel that you are the dance. The division must disappear; then it becomes a meditation. If the division is there, then it is an exercise: good, healthy, but it cannot be said to be spiritual. It is just a simple dance. Dance is good in itself – as far as it goes, it is good. After it, you will feel fresh, young. But it is not meditation yet. The dancer must go, until only the dance remains.

So what to do? Be totally in the dance, because division can exist only if you are not total in it. If you are standing aside and looking at your own dance, the division will remain: you are the dancer and you are dancing. Then dancing is just an act, something you are doing; it is not your being. So get involved totally, be merged in it. Don't stand aside, don't be an observer.

Participate!

Let the dance flow in its own way; don't force it. Rather, follow it; allow it to happen. It is not a doing but a happening. Remain in the mood of festivity. You are not doing something very serious; you are just playing, playing with your life energy, playing with your bioenergy, allowing it to move in its own way. Just like the wind blows and the river flows – you are flowing and blowing. Feel it.

And be playful. Remember this word 'playful' always – with me, it is very basic. In this country we

Nataraj Meditation

Nataraj is dance as a total meditation. There are three stages, lasting a total of 65 minutes.

call creation God's *leela* – God's play. God has not created the world; it is his play. [1]

Music to support this meditation has been composed with Osho's guidance. For availability, see back page.

First stage: 40 minutes

With eyes closed dance as if possessed. Let your unconscious take over completely. Do not control your movements or be a witness to what is happening. Just be totally in the dance.

Second stage: 20 minutes

Keeping your eyes closed, lie down immediately. Be silent and still.

Third stage: 5 minutes

Dance in celebration and enjoy. [1]

Sufi Whirling is one of the most ancient techniques, one of the most forceful. It is so deep that even a single experience can make you totally different. Whirl with open eyes, just like small children go on twirling, as if your inner being has become a center and your whole body has become a wheel, moving, a potter's wheel, moving. You are in the center, but the whole body is moving.

Whirling Meditation

It is recommended that no food or drink be taken for three hours before whirling. It is best to have bare feet and wear loose clothing. The meditation is divided into two stages, whirling and resting. There is no fixed time for the whirling – it can go on for hours – but it is suggested that you continue for at least an hour to get fully into the feeling of the energy whirlpool.

The whirling is done on the spot in an anti-clockwise direction, with the right arm held high, palm upwards, and the left arm low, palm downwards. People who feel discomfort from whirling anti-clockwise can change to clockwise. Let your body be soft and keep your eyes open, but unfocused so that images become blurred and flowing. Remain silent.

For the first 15 minutes, rotate slowly. Then gradually build up speed over the next 30 minutes until the whirling takes over and you become a whirlpool of energy – the periphery a storm of movement but the witness at the center silent and still.

When you are whirling so fast that you cannot remain upright, your body will fall by itself. Don't make the fall a decision on your part nor attempt to arrange the landing in advance; if your body is soft you will land softly and the earth will absorb your energy.

Once you have fallen, the second part of the meditation starts. Roll onto your stomach immediately so that your bare navel is in contact with the earth. If anybody feels strong discomfort lying this way, he should lie on his back. Feel your body blending into the earth, like a small child pressed to the mother's breasts. Keep your eyes closed and remain passive and silent for at least 15 minutes.

After the meditation be as quiet and inactive as possible.

Some people may feel nauseous during the Whirling Meditation, but this feeling should disappear within two or three days. Only discontinue the meditation if it persists. [2]

Anything Can Be a Meditation

This is the secret: *de-automatize*. If we can de-automatize our activities, then the whole life becomes a meditation. Then any small thing, taking a shower, eating your food, talking to your friend, becomes meditation. Meditation is a quality; it can be brought to *anything*. It is not a specific act. People think that way, they think meditation is a specific act – when you sit facing to the east, you repeat certain mantras, you burn some incense, you do this and that at a particular time in a particular way with a particular gesture. Meditation has nothing to do with all those things. They are all ways to automatize it and meditation is against automatization.

So if you can keep alert, any activity is meditation; any movement will help you immensely. [1]

It is natural and easy to keep alert while you are in movement. When you are just sitting silently, the natural thing is to just fall asleep. When you are lying on your bed it is very difficult to keep alert because the whole situation helps you to fall asleep. But in movement naturally you cannot fall asleep, you function in a more alert way. The only problem is that the movement can become mechanical.

Learn to melt your body, mind and

Running, Jogging, and Swimming

soul. Find ways where you can function as a unity.

It happens many times to runners. You might not think of running as a meditation, but runners sometimes have felt a tremendous experience of meditation. And they were surprised, because they were not looking for it – who thinks that a runner is going to experience

God? But it has happened. And now, more and more, running is becoming a new kind of meditation. It can happen when running.

If you have ever been a runner, if you have enjoyed running in the early morning when the air is fresh and young and the whole world is coming back from sleep, awakening – you were running and your

body was functioning beautifully, the fresh air, the new world born again out of the darkness of the night, everything singing all around, you were feeling so alive …a moment comes when the runner disappears, and there is only running. The body, mind and soul start functioning together; suddenly an inner orgasm is released.

Runners have sometimes come accidentally on the experience of the fourth, *turiya,* although they will miss it – they will think it was just because of running that they enjoyed the moment: that it was a beautiful day, the body was healthy and the world was beautiful, and it was just a certain mood. They will not take note of it – but if they do take note of it, my own observation is that a runner can come close to meditation more easily than anybody else.

Jogging can be of immense help, swimming can be of immense help. All these things have to be transformed into meditations.

Drop the old ideas of meditations – that just sitting underneath a tree in a yoga posture is meditation. That is only one of the ways, and it may be suitable for a few people but it is not suitable for all. For a small child it is not meditation, it is torture. For a young man who is alive and vibrant it is repression, it is not meditation.

Start running in the morning on the road. Start with half a mile and then one mile and come eventually to at least three miles. While running use the whole body; don't run as if you are in a straitjacket. Run like a small child, using the whole body – hands and feet – and run. Breathe deeply and from the belly. Then sit under a tree, rest, perspire and let the cool breeze come; feel peaceful. This will help very deeply.

Sometimes just stand on the earth without shoes and feel the coolness, the softness, the warmth. Whatsoever the earth is ready to give in that moment, just feel it and let it flow through you. And allow your energy to flow into the earth. Be connected with the earth.

If you are connected with the earth, you are connected with life. If you are connected with the earth, you are connected with your body. If you are connected with the earth, you will become very sensitive and centered – and that's what is needed.

Never become an expert in running; remain an amateur so that alertness may be kept. If you feel sometimes that running has become automatic, drop it; try swimming. If that becomes automatic, then try dancing. The point to remember is that the movement is just a situation to create awareness. While it creates awareness it is good. If it stops creating awareness, then it is no more of any use; change to another movement where you will have to be alert again. Never allow any activity to become automatic. [2]

Laughter brings some energy from your inner source to your surface. Energy starts flowing, follows laughter like a shadow. Have you watched it? When you really laugh, for those few moments you are in a deep

Laughing Meditation

meditative state. Thinking stops. It is impossible to laugh and think together. They are diametrically opposite: either you can laugh or you can think. If you really laugh, thinking stops. If you are still thinking, laughter will be just so-so, lagging behind. It will be a crippled laughter.

When you really laugh, suddenly mind disappears. As far as I know, dancing and laughter are the best, natural, easily approachable doors. If you really dance, thinking stops. You go on and on, you whirl and whirl, and you become a whirlpool – all boundaries, all divisions are lost. You don't even know where your body ends and where existence begins. You melt into existence and existence melts into you; there is an overlapping of boundaries. And if you are really dancing – not managing it but allowing it to manage you, allowing it to possess you – if you are possessed by dance, thinking stops.

The same happens with laughter. If you are possessed by laughter, thinking stops.

Laughter can be a beautiful introduction to a non-thinking state. [3]

Instructions for Laughing Meditation

Every morning upon waking, before opening your eyes, stretch like a cat. Stretch every fiber of your body. After three or four minutes, with eyes still closed, begin to laugh. For five minutes just laugh. At first you will be doing it, but soon the sound of your attempt will cause genuine laughter. Lose yourself in laughter. It may take several days before it really happens, for we are so unaccustomed to the phenomenon. But before long it will be spontaneous and will change the whole nature of your day. [4]

The laughing Buddha

There is a story, in Japan, of the laughing Buddha, Hotei. His whole teaching was just laughter. He would move from one place to another, from one marketplace to another marketplace. He would stand in the middle of the market and start laughing – that was his sermon.

His laughter was catching, infectious; a *real* laughter, his whole belly pulsating with the laughter, shaking with laughter. He would roll on the ground with laughter. People who would collect together, they would start laughing, and then the laughter would spread, and tidal waves of laughter, and the whole village would be overwhelmed with laughter.

People used to wait for Hotei to come to their village because he brought such joy, such blessings. He never uttered a single word, never. You asked about Buddha and he would laugh; you asked about enlightenment and he would laugh; you asked about truth and he would laugh. Laughter was his only message. [5]

A man came to me. He had been suffering from chain-smoking for thirty years; he was ill and the doctors said, "You will never be healthy if you don't stop smoking." But he was a chronic smoker; he could not help it. He had tried – not that he had not tried – he had tried hard, and he had suffered much in trying, but only for one day or two days, and then again the urge would come so tremendously, it would simply take him away. Again he would fall into the same pattern.

Smoking Meditation

Because of this smoking he had lost all self-confidence: he knew he could not do a small thing; he could not stop smoking. He had become worthless in his own eyes; he thought himself just the most worthless person in the world. He had no respect for himself. He came to me.

He said, "What can I do? How can I stop smoking?" I said, "Nobody can stop smoking. You have to understand. Smoking is not only a question of your decision now. It has entered into your world of habits; it has taken roots. Thirty years is a long time. It has taken roots in your body, in your chemistry; it has spread all over. It is not just a question of your head deciding; your head cannot do anything. The head is impotent; it can start things, but it cannot stop them so easily. Once you have started and once you have practiced so long, you are a great yogi – thirty years' practicing smoking! It has become autonomous; you will have to de-automatize it."

He said, "What do you mean by 'de-automatization'?"

And that's what meditation is all about, de-automatization.

I said, "You do one thing: forget about stopping. There is no need either. For thirty years you have smoked and lived; of course it was a suffering but you have become accustomed to that too. And what does it matter if you die a few hours earlier than you would have died without smoking? What are you going to do here? What have you done? So what is the point – whether you die Monday or Tuesday or Sunday, this year, that year – what does it matter?"

He said, "Yes, that is true, it doesn't matter." Then I said, "Forget about it; we are not going to stop it at all. Rather, we are going to understand it. So next time, you make it a meditation."

He said, "Meditation out of smoking?"

I said, "Yes. If Zen people can make a meditation out of drinking tea and can make it a ceremony, why not? Smoking can be as beautiful a meditation."

He looked thrilled. He said, "What are you saying?"

He became alive! He said, "Meditation? just tell me – I can't wait!"

I gave him the meditation. I said, "Do one thing. When you are taking the packet of cigarettes out of your pocket, move slowly. Enjoy it, there is no hurry. Be conscious, alert, aware; take it out slowly with full awareness. Then take the cigarette out of the packet with full awareness, slowly – not in the old hurried way, the unconscious way, mechanical way. Then start tapping the cigarette on your packet – but very alertly. Listen to the sound, just as Zen people do when the samovar starts singing and the tea starts boiling … and the aroma. Then smell the cigarette and the beauty of it…."

He said, "What are you saying? The beauty?"

"Yes, it is beautiful. Tobacco is as divine as anything. Smell it; it is God's smell."

He looked a little surprised. He said, "What! Are you joking?"

No, I am not joking. Even when I joke, I don't joke. I am very serious.

"Then put it in your mouth, with full awareness, light it with full awareness. Enjoy every act, every small act, and divide it into as many acts as possible, so you can become more and more aware.

"Then have the first puff: God in the form of smoke. Hindus say, *'Annam Brahm'* – 'Food is God'. Why not smoke? All is God. Fill your lungs deeply – this is a *pranayam.* I am giving you the new yoga for the new age! Then release the smoke, relax, another puff – and go very slowly.

"If you can do it, you will be surprised; soon you will see the whole stupidity of it. Not because others have said that it is stupid, not because others have said that it is bad. You will *see* it. And the seeing will not just be intellectual. It will be from your total being; it will be a vision of your totality. And then one day, if it drops, it drops; if it continues, it continues. You need not worry about it."

After three months he came and he said, "But it dropped."

"Now," I said, "try it on other things too."

This is the secret, *the* secret: de-automatize.

Walking, walk slowly, watchfully. Looking, look watchfully, and you will see trees are greener than they have ever been and roses are rosier than they have ever been. Listen! Somebody is talking, gossiping: listen, listen attentively. When you are talking, talk attentively. Let your whole waking activity become de-automatized. [6]

Breath –
a Bridge to Meditation

If you can do something with the breath, you will suddenly turn to the present.

If you can do something with breath, you will attain to the source of life. If you can do something with breath, you can transcend time and space. If you can do something with breath, you will be in the world and also beyond it. [1]

Vipassana is the meditation that has made more people in the world enlightened than any other, because it is the very essence. All other meditations have the same essence, but in different forms; something non-essential is also joined with them. But vipassana is pure essence. You cannot drop anything out of it and you cannot add anything to improve it.

Vipassana is such a simple thing that even a small child can do it. In fact, the smallest child can do it better than you, because he is not

Vipassana

yet filled with the garbage of the mind; he is still clean and innocent.

Vipassana can be done in three ways – you can choose which one suits you the best.

The first is: awareness of your actions, your body, your mind, your heart. Walking, you should walk with awareness. Moving your hand, you should move with

awareness, knowing perfectly that you are moving the hand. You can move it without any consciousness, like a mechanical thing…you are on a morning walk; you can go on walking without being aware of your feet.

Be alert of the movements of your body. While eating, be alert to the movements that are needed for eating. Taking a shower, be alert to the

coolness that is coming to you, the water falling on you and the tremendous joy of it – just be alert. It should not go on happening in an unconscious state.

And the same about your mind. Whatever thought passes on the screen of your mind, just be a watcher. Whatever emotion passes on the screen of your heart, just remain a witness – don't get involved, don't get identified, don't evaluate what is good, what is bad; that is not part of your meditation.

The second form is breathing, becoming aware of breathing. As the breath goes in, your belly starts rising up, and as the breath goes out, your belly starts settling down again. So the second method is to be aware of the belly: its rising and falling. Just the very awareness of the belly rising and falling…and the belly is very close to the life sources because the child is joined with the mother's life through the navel. Behind the navel is his life's source. So, when the belly rises up, it is really the life energy, the spring of life that is rising up and falling down with each breath. That too is not difficult, and perhaps maybe even easier because it is a single technique.

In the first, you have to be aware of the body, you have to be aware of the mind, you have to be aware of your emotions, moods. So it has three steps. The second approach has a single step: just the belly, moving up and down. And the result is the same. As you become more aware of the belly, the mind becomes silent, the heart becomes silent, the moods disappear.

And the third is to be aware of the breath at the entrance, when the breath goes in through your nostrils.

Feel it at that extreme – the other polarity from the belly – feel it from the nose. The breath going in gives a certain coolness to your nostrils. Then the breath going out…breath going in, breath going out.

That too is possible. It is easier for men than for women. The woman is more aware of the belly. Most of the men don't even breathe as deep as the belly. Their chest rises up and falls down, because a wrong kind of athletics prevails over the world. Certainly it gives a more beautiful form to the body if your chest is high and your belly is almost non-existent.

Man has chosen to breathe only up to the chest, so the chest becomes bigger and bigger and the belly shrinks down. That appears to him to be more athletic.

Around the world, except in Japan, all athletes and teachers of athletes emphasize to breathe by filling your lungs, expanding your chest, and pulling the belly in. The ideal is the lion whose chest is big and whose belly is very small. So be like a lion; that has become the rule for athletic gymnasts, and the people who have been working with the body.

Japan is the only exception where they don't care that the chest should be broad and the belly should be pulled in. It needs a certain discipline to pull the belly in; it is not

natural. Japan has chosen the natural way, hence you will be surprised to see a Japanese statue of Buddha. That is the way you can immediately discriminate whether the statue is Indian or Japanese. The Indian statues of Gautam Buddha have a very athletic body; the belly is very small and the chest is very broad. But the Japanese Buddha is totally different; his chest is almost silent, because he breathes from the belly, but his belly is bigger. It doesn't look very good – because the idea prevalent in the world is so old, but breathing from the belly is more natural, more relaxed.

In the night it happens when you sleep; you don't breathe from the chest, you breathe from the belly. That's why the night is such a relaxed experience. After your sleep, in the morning you feel so fresh, so young, because the whole night you were breathing naturally… you were in Japan!

These are the two points: if you are afraid that breathing from the belly and being attentive to its rising and falling will destroy your athletic form…men may be more interested in that athletic form. Then for them it is easier to watch near the nostrils where the breath enters. Watch, and when the breath goes out, watch.

These are the three forms. Any one will do. And if you want to do two forms together, you can do two forms together; then the effort will become more intense. If you want to do all three forms together, you can do all three forms together. Then the possibilities will be quicker. But it all depends on you, whatever feels easy.

Remember: easy is right.

As meditation becomes settled and mind silent, the ego will disappear. You will be there, but there will be no feeling of 'I'. Then the doors are open.

Just wait with a loving longing, with a welcome in the heart for that great moment – the greatest moment in anybody's life – of enlightenment.

It comes…it certainly comes. It has never delayed for a single moment. Once you are in the right tuning, it suddenly explodes in you, transforms you.

The old man is dead and the new man has arrived. [2]

Sitting

Find a reasonably comfortable and alert position to sit for 40 to 60 minutes. Back and head should be straight, eyes closed and breathing normal. Stay as still as possible, only changing position if it is really necessary.

While sitting, the primary object is to be watching the rise and fall of the belly, slightly above the navel, caused by breathing in and out. It is not a concentration technique, so while watching the breath, many other things will take your attention away. Nothing is a distraction in vipassana, so when something else comes up, stop watching the breath, pay attention to whatever is happening until it's possible to go back to your breath. This may include thoughts, feelings, judgments, body sensations, impressions from the outside world, etc.

It is the process of watching that is significant, not so much what you are watching, so remember not to become identified with whatever comes up; questions or problems may just be seen as mysteries to be enjoyed!

Vipassana walk

This is a slow, ordinary walk based on the awareness of the feet touching the ground.

You can walk in a circle or a line of 10 to 15 steps going back and forth, inside or out of doors. Eyes should be lowered on the ground a few steps ahead. While walking, the attention should go to the contact of each foot as it touches the ground. If other things arise, stop paying attention to the feet, notice what else took your attention and then return to the feet.

It is the same technique as in sitting – but watching a different primary object. You can walk for 20 to 30 minutes. [3]

Shiva said: Radiant one, this experience may dawn between two breaths. After breath comes in (down) and just before turning up (out) – the beneficence.

When your breath comes in, *observe*. For a single moment or a thousandth part of a moment, there is no breathing – before it turns up, before it turns outward. One breath comes in; then there is a certain point and breathing stops. Then the breathing goes out. When the breath goes out, then again for a

Watching the Gap in the Breath

single moment, or a part of a moment, breathing stops. Then breathing comes in.

Before the breath is turning in or turning out, there is a moment when you are not breathing. In that moment the happening is possible, because when you are not breathing you are not in the world. Understand this: when you are not breathing you are dead; you are

still, but dead. But the moment is of such a short duration, you never observe it.

Breath coming in is rebirth; breath going out is death. The outgoing breath is synonymous with death; the incoming breath is synonymous with life. So with each breath you are dying and being reborn. The gap between the two is of a very short duration, but keen, sincere

observation and attention will make you feel the gap. Then nothing else is needed. You are blessed. You have known; the thing has happened.

You are not to train the breath. Leave it just as it is. Why such a simple technique? It looks so simple. Such a simple technique to know the truth? To know the truth means to know that which is neither born nor dies, to know that eternal element which always is. You can know the breath going out, you can know the breath coming in, but you never know the gap between the two.

Try it. Suddenly you will get the point – and you can get it: it is already there. Nothing is to be added to you or to your structure: it is already there. Everything is already there except a certain awareness. So how to do this? First, become aware of the breath coming in. Watch it. Forget everything: just watch breath coming in – the very passage. When the breath touches your nostrils, feel it there. Then let the breath move in. Move with the breath fully conscious. When you are going down, down, down with the breath, do not miss the breath. Do not go ahead; do not follow behind. Just go with it. Remember this: do not go ahead; do not follow it like a shadow. Be simultaneous with it.

Breath and consciousness should become one. The breath goes in; you go in. Only then will it be possible to get the point which is between two breaths. It will not be easy.

Move in with the breath, then move out with the breath: in-out, in-out. Buddha tried particularly to use this method, so this method has become a Buddhist method. In Buddhist terminology it is known as 'Anapanasati Yoga'. And Buddha's enlightenment was based on this technique – only this.

If you go on practicing breath consciousness, breath awareness, suddenly, one day without knowing, you will come to the interval. As your awareness will become keen and deep and intense, as your awareness will become bracketed – the whole world is bracketed out; only your breath coming in or going out is your world, the whole arena for your consciousness – suddenly you are bound to feel the gap in which there is no breath.

When you are moving with breath minutely, when there is no breath, how can you remain unaware? You will suddenly become aware that there is no breath, and the moment will come when you will feel that the breath is neither going out nor coming in. The breath has stopped completely. In that stopping, "the beneficence." [4]

Shiva said: When in worldly activity keep attentive between the two breaths, and so practicing, in a few days be born anew.

Whatsoever you are doing, keep your attention in the gap between the two breaths. But it must be practiced while in activity.

We have discussed the technique that is just similar. Now there is only this difference, that this has to be practiced while in worldly activity. Do not practice it in isolation. This practice is to be done

Watching the Gap in the Marketplace

while you are doing something else. You are eating: go on eating, and be attentive to the gap. You are walking: go on walking and be attentive to the gap. You are going to sleep: lie down, let sleep come. But you go on being attentive to the gap.

Why in activity? Because activity distracts the mind. Activity calls your attention again and again. Do not be distracted. Be fixed at the gap, and do not stop activity; let the activity continue. You will have two layers of existence – doing and being.

We have two layers of existence: the world of doing and the world of being, the circumference and the center. Go on working on the periphery, on the circumference; do not stop it. But go on working attentively on the center also. What will happen?

Your activity will become an acting, as if you are playing a part.

If this method is practiced, your whole life will become a long drama. You will be an actor playing roles, but constantly centered in the gap. If you forget the gap, then you are not playing roles; you have become the role. Then it is not a drama. You have mistaken it as life. That is what we have done.

Everyone thinks he is living life. It is not life. It is just a role – a part which has been given to you by society, by circumstances, by culture, by tradition, by the country, the situation. You have been given a role. You are playing it; you have become identified with it. To break that identification, use this technique.

This technique is just to make yourself a psychodrama – just a play. You are focused in the gap between two breaths, and life moves on, on the periphery. If your attention is at the center, then your attention is not really on the periphery; that is just 'sub-attention'. It just happens somewhere near your attention. You can feel it, you can know it, but it is not significant. It is as if it is not happening to you.

I will repeat this: if you practice this technique, your whole life will be as if it is not happening to you – as if it is happening to someone else. 5

Shiva said: With intangible breath in the center of the forehead, as this reaches the heart at the moment of sleep, have direction over dreams and over death itself.

Take this technique in three parts. One, you must be able to feel the *prana* in breath, the intangible part of it, the invisible part of it, the immaterial part of it. The feeling comes if you are attentive between the two eyebrows. Then it comes easily. If you are attentive in the gap, then too it comes, but a little less easily. If you are aware of the

Dream Mastery

center at your navel where breath comes and touches and goes out, it also comes, but with less ease. The easiest point from which to know the invisible part of breath is to be centered at the third eye. But wherever you are centered, it comes. You begin to feel the prana flowing in.

The ingoing breath and the outgoing breath are the same as vehicles, but the incoming breath is filled with prana and the outgoing breath is empty. You have sucked the prana, and the breath has become empty.

This sutra is very, very significant: "With intangible breath in the center of the forehead, as this reaches the heart at the moment of sleep, have direction over dreams and over death itself." While you are

falling into sleep, this technique has to be practiced – then only, not at any other time. While you are falling asleep, only then. That is the right moment to practice this technique. You are falling asleep. Little by little, sleep is overtaking you. Within moments, your consciousness will dissolve; you will not be aware. Before that moment comes, become aware – aware of

76

the breath and the invisible part, prana, and feel it coming to the heart.

If this happens – that you are feeling invisible breath coming into the heart and sleep overtakes you – you will be aware in dreams. You will know that you are dreaming. Ordinarily we do not know that we are dreaming. While you dream you think that this is reality. That too happens because of the third eye. Have you seen anyone asleep? His eyes move upward and become focused in the third eye.

Because of this focusing in the third eye, you take your dreams as real; you cannot feel they are dreams. They are real. You will know when you get up in the morning, then you will know that "I was dreaming." But this is the later, retrospective realization. You cannot realize in the dream that you are dreaming. If you realize it, then there are two layers: the dream is there, but you are awake, you are aware. For one who becomes aware in dreams, this sutra is wonderful. It says, "Have direction over dreams and over death itself."

If you can become aware of dreams, you can create dreams. Ordinarily you cannot create dreams. How impotent man is! You cannot even create dreams. You *cannot* create dreams! If you want to dream a particular thing, you cannot dream it; it is not in your hands. How powerless man is! Even dreams cannot be created. You are just a victim of dreams, not the creator. A dream happens to you; you cannot do anything. Neither can you stop it nor can you create it.

But if you move into sleep remembering the heart being filled with prana, continuously being touched by prana with every breath, you will become a master of your dreams – and this is a rare mastery. Then you can dream whatsoever dreams you like. Just note while you are falling asleep that "I want to dream this dream," and that dream will come to you. Just say while falling asleep, "I do not want to dream that dream," and that dream cannot enter your mind.

But what is the use of becoming the master of your dreaming? Isn't it useless? No, it is not useless. Once you become master of your dreams you will never dream. It is absurd. When you are master of your dreams, dreaming stops; there is no need for it. And when dreaming stops, your sleep has a different quality altogether, and the quality is the same as of death. 6

*P*atanjali said: The mind also becomes tranquil by alternately expelling and retaining the breath.

Whenever you feel that the mind is not tranquil – tense, worried, chattering, anxious, constantly dreaming

Throwing Things Out

– do one thing: first exhale deeply. Always start by exhaling. Exhale deeply; as much as you can, throw the air out. Throwing out the air, the mood will be thrown out too, because breathing is everything. And then expel the breath as far as possible.

Pull the belly in and retain for a few seconds; don't inhale. Let the air be out, and don't inhale for a few seconds. Then allow the body to inhale. Inhale deeply – as much as you can. Again stop for a few seconds. The gap should be the same as when you retain the breath out – if you retain it out for three seconds, retain the breath in for three seconds. Throw it out and hold for three seconds; take it in and hold for three seconds. But it has to be thrown out completely. Exhale totally and inhale totally, and make a rhythm. Breathe in, hold; breathe out, hold. Breathe in, hold; breathe out, hold. Immediately you will feel a change coming into your whole being. The mood will go; a new climate will enter into you. [7]

Opening the Heart

The heart is the gateless gate to reality. Move from the head to the heart.

We are all hung up in the head. That is our only problem, the *only* one problem. And there is only one solution: get down from the head into the heart and all problems disappear. They are created by the head. And suddenly everything is so clear and so transparent that one is surprised how one was continuously inventing problems.

Mysteries remain but problems disappear. Mysteries abound but problems evaporate. And mysteries are beautiful. They are not to be solved. They have to be lived. [1]

The first point: try to be headless. Visualize yourself as headless; move headlessly. It sounds absurd, but it is one of the most important exercises. Try it, and then you will know. Walk, and feel as if you have no head. In the beginning it will be only 'as if'. It will be very weird. When the feeling comes to you that you have no head, it will be very weird and strange. But by and by you will settle down at the heart.

There is a law. You may have seen that someone who is blind has

From Head to Heart

keener ears, more musical ears. Blind men are more musical; their feeling for music is deeper. Why? The energy that ordinarily moves through the eyes now cannot move through them, so it chooses a different path – it moves through the ears.

Blind men have a deeper sensitivity of touch. If a blind man touches you, you will feel the difference,

because we ordinarily do much work with touch through our eyes: we are touching each other through our eyes. A blind man cannot touch through the eyes, so the energy moves through his hands. A blind man is more sensitive than anyone who has eyes. Sometimes it may not be so, but generally it is so. Energy starts moving from another center if one center is not there.

So try this exercise I am talking about – the exercise in headlessness – and suddenly you will feel a strange thing: it will be as if for the first time you are at the heart. Walk headlessly. Sit down to meditate, close your eyes and simply feel that there is no head. Feel, "My head has disappeared." In the beginning it will be just 'as if', but by and by you will feel that the head has really disappeared. And when you feel that your head has disappeared, your center will fall down to the heart – immediately! You will be looking at the world through the heart and not through the head.

When for the first time Westerners reached Japan, they couldn't believe that the Japanese traditionally have been thinking for centuries that they think through the belly. If you ask a Japanese child – if he is not educated in Western ways – "Where is your thinking?" he will point to his belly.

Centuries and centuries have passed, and Japan has been living without the head. It is just a concept. If I ask you, "Where is your thinking going on?" you will point toward the head, but a Japanese person will point to the belly, not to the head – one of the reasons why the Japanese mind is more calm, quiet and collected.

Now this is disturbed because the West has spread over everything. Now there exists no East. Only in some individuals who are like islands here and there does the East exist. Geographically, the East has disappeared. Now the whole world is Western.

Try headlessness. Meditate standing before your mirror in the bathroom. Look deep into your eyes and feel that you are looking from the heart. By and by the heart center will begin to function. And when the heart functions, it changes your total personality, the total structure, the whole pattern, because the heart has its own way.

So the first thing: try headlessness. Secondly, be more loving, because love cannot function through the head. Be more loving! That is why, when someone is in love, he loses his head. People say that he has gone mad. If you are not in love and mad, then you are not really in love. The head must be lost. If the head is there unaffected, functioning ordinarily, then love is not possible, because for love you need the heart to function – not the head. It is a function of the heart.

It happens that when a very rational person falls in love, he becomes stupid. He himself feels what stupidity he is doing, what silliness. What is he doing! Then he makes two parts of his life; he creates a division. The heart becomes a silent, intimate affair. When he moves out of his house, he moves out of his heart. He lives in the world with the head and only comes down to the heart when he is loving. But it is very difficult. It is *very* difficult, and ordinarily it never happens.

I was staying in Calcutta at a friend's house, and the friend was a justice of the High Court. His wife told me, "I have only one problem to tell you. Can you help me?"

So I said, "What is the problem?"

She said, "My husband is your friend. He loves you and respects you, so if you say something to him it may be helpful."

So I asked her. "What is to be said? Tell me."

She said, "He remains a High Court judge even in bed. I have not known a lover, a friend or a husband. He is a High Court judge twenty-four hours a day."

It is difficult: it is difficult to come down from your pedestal. It becomes a fixed attitude. If you are a businessman, you will remain a businessman in bed also. It is difficult to accommodate two persons within, and it is not easy to change your pattern completely, immediately, anytime you like. It is difficult, but if you are in love you will have to come down from the head.

So for this meditation try to be more and more loving. And when I say be more loving, I mean change the quality of your relationship: let it be based on love. Not only with your wife or with your child or with your friend, but toward life as such, become more loving. That is why Mahavir and Buddha have talked about non-violence: it was just to create a loving attitude toward life.

When Mahavir moves, walks, he remains aware not even to kill an ant. Why? Really, the ant is not concerned. Mahavir is coming down from the head to the heart, creating a loving attitude toward life as such. The more your relationship is based on love – all relationships – the more your heart center will function. It will start working; you will look at the world through different eyes: because the heart has its own way of looking at the world. The mind can never look in that way: that is impossible for the mind. The mind can only analyze! The heart synthesizes; the mind can only dissect, divide. It is a divider. Only the heart gives unity.

When you can look through the heart the whole universe looks like one unity. When you approach through the mind, the whole world becomes atomic. There is no unity: only atoms and atoms and atoms. The heart gives a unitary experience. It joins together and the ultimate synthesis is God. If you can look through the heart, the whole universe looks like one. That oneness is God.

That is why science can never find God. It is impossible, because the method applied can never reach to the ultimate unity. The very method of science is reason, analysis, division. So science comes to molecules, atoms, electrons, and they will go on dividing. They can never come to the organic unity of the whole. The whole is impossible to look at through the head. [2]

83

It is best to do this prayer at night, in a darkened room, going to sleep immediately afterwards; or it can be done in the morning, but it must be followed by fifteen minutes rest. This rest is necessary, otherwise you will feel as if you are drunk, in a stupor.

This merging with energy is prayer. It changes you. And when *you* change, the whole existence changes.

Raise both your hands towards the sky, palms uppermost, head up, just feeling existence flowing in you.

As the energy flows down your arms you will feel a gentle tremor

Prayer Meditation

– be like a leaf in a breeze, trembling. Allow it, help it. Then let your whole body vibrate with energy, and just let whatever happens happen.

You feel again a flowing with the earth. Earth and heaven, above and below, yin and yang, male and female – you float, you mix, you drop yourself completely. You are not. You become one ... merge.

After two to three minutes, or whenever you feel completely

filled, lean down to the earth and kiss the earth. You simply become a vehicle to allow the divine energy to unite with that of the earth.

These two stages should be repeated six more times so that each of the *chakras* can become unblocked. More times can be done, but if you do less you will feel restless and unable to sleep.

Go into sleep in that very state of prayer. Just fall asleep and the energy will be there. You will be flow-

ing with it, falling into sleep. That will help very greatly because then the energy will surround you the whole night and it will continue to work. By the morning you will feel more fresh than you have ever felt before, more vital than you have ever felt before. A new elan, a new life will start penetrating you, and the whole day you will feel full of new energy; a new vibe, a new song in your heart, and a new dance in your step. [3]

Shiva said: In any easy position gradually pervade an area between the armpits into great peace.

A very simple method but it works miraculously – try it. And anyone can try it, there is no danger. In an easy position: the first thing is to be in a relaxed position – easy, whatsoever is easy for you. So don't try some particular position or asana. Buddha sits in a particular posture. It is easy for him. It can also become easy for you if you practice it for a time, but in the very beginning it will not be

The Heart
of Peacefulness

easy for you. And there is no need to practice it: start from any posture that comes easy to you right now. Don't struggle with posture. You can sit in an easy chair and relax. The only thing is your body must be in a relaxed state.

Just close your eyes and feel all over the body. Start from the legs feeling whether there is some ten-

sion. If you feel somewhere there is some tension, do one thing: make it more tense. If you feel that in the leg, in the right leg, there is tension, then make that tension as intense as possible. Bring it to a peak and then suddenly relax so that you can feel how relaxation settles there. Then go all over the body just finding if there is some tension somewhere.

Wherever you feel the tension make it more, because it is easy to relax it when it is intense. In just a mid-state it is very difficult because you cannot feel it.

It is easy to move from one extreme to another, very easy, because the very extreme creates the situation to move to the other. So if you feel some tension in the face then strain all the face muscles as much as possible, create tension and bring it to a peak. Bring it to a point where you feel that now no more is possible – then suddenly relax. So see that all parts of the body, all the limbs, are relaxed.

Be particular about the face muscles, because they carry ninety percent of the tensions – the rest of the body carries only ten percent – because all your tensions are in the mind and the face becomes the storage. So strain your face as much as possible, don't be shy about it. Intensely make it in anguish, anxiety – and then suddenly relax. Do it for five minutes so you can feel now the whole body, every limb, is relaxed.

You can do it lying on the bed, you can do it sitting also – howsoever you feel is easy for you.

The second thing: when you feel that the body has come to an easy posture, don't make much fuss about it. Just feel that the body is relaxed, then forget the body. Because really, remembering the body is a sort of tension. So that's why I say don't make much fuss about it. Relax it and forget it. Forgetting is relaxation, because whenever you remember too much, that very remembering brings a tension to the body.

Then close your eyes and just feel the area between the two armpits: the heart area, your chest. First feel it, just between the two armpits, bring your total attention, total awareness. Forget the whole body, just the heart area between the two armpits, your chest, and feel it filled with great peace.

The moment the body is relaxed, automatically peace happens in your heart. The heart becomes silent, relaxed, harmonious. And when you forget the whole body and bring your attention just to the chest and consciously feel that it is filled with peace, much peace will happen immediately.

There are two areas in the body, particular centers where particular feelings can be created consciously. Between the two armpits is the center of the heart, and the heart center is the source of all peace that happens to you, whenever it happens. Whenever you are peaceful, the peace is coming from the heart. The heart radiates peace. That's why people from all over the world, without any distinction of caste, religion, country, cultured or uncultured, every race, have felt this: that love arises somewhere from the heart. No scientific explanation exists.

So whenever you think of love you think of the heart. Really, whenever you are in love you are relaxed, and because you are relaxed you are filled with a certain peace. And that peace arises from the heart. So peace and love have become joined, associated. Whenever you are in love you are peaceful; whenever you are not in love you are disturbed. Because of peace the heart has become associated with love.

So you can do two things. Either you can search for love, then sometimes you will feel peace. But the path is dangerous, because the other person whom you love has become more important than you. The other is the other, and you are becoming dependent in a way. So love will give you peace sometimes but not always. There will be many disturbances, many moments of anguish and anxiety, because the other has entered and whenever the other enters there is bound to be some disturbance because you can meet with the other only on your surface, and the surface will be disturbed. Only sometimes – when the two of you will be so deeply in love with no conflict – only sometimes you will be relaxed and the heart will glow with peace.

So love can give you only glimpses of peace but never really any establishment, any rootedness in peace. No eternal peace is possible through it, only glimpses. And between two glimpses there will be deep valleys of conflict, violence, hatred, anger.

The other way is not to find peace through love, but to find peace directly. If you can find peace directly – and this is the method – your life will become filled with love. But now the quality of love will be different. It will not be possessive; it will not be centered on one. It will not be dependent and it will not make anyone dependent on you. Your love will become just a lovingness, a compassion, a deep empathy.

And now no one, not even a lover, can disturb you, because your peace is already rooted and your love is coming as a shadow of your inner peace. The whole thing has become reversed: so Buddha is also loving but his love is not an anguish. If you love you will suffer, if you don't love you will suffer. If you don't love you will suffer the absence; if you love you will suffer the presence of love. You are on the surface and whatsoever you do can give you only momentary satisfactions, and then again, the dark valley.

The heart is naturally the source of peace, so you are not creating anything. You are simply coming to a source which is always there. And this imagination will help you become aware that the heart is filled with peace, not that this imagination will create the peace. This is the difference between the tantra attitude and Western hypnosis: hypnotists think that by imagination you are creating it; tantra thinks that you are not creating it – by imagination you are simply becoming attuned to something that is already there. Whatsoever you can create by imagination cannot be permanent. If it is not a reality then it is false, unreal, and you are creating a hallucination.

Try this: whenever you are able to feel the peace between the two armpits filling you, pervading your own heart center, the world will look illusory. This is a sign that you have entered meditation – when the world feels, appears to be illusory. Don't think that the world is illusory; there is no need to think – you will feel it. It will suddenly occur to your mind – "What has happened to the world?" The world has suddenly gone dreamy, a dreamlike existence. It is there, without any substance, just like a film on the screen. It looks so real; it can even be three-dimensional – it just looks like a projected thing. Not that the world is a projected thing, not that it is really unreal – no. The world is real but you create distance, and the distance becomes greater and greater. And you can understand whether the distance is becoming greater and greater or not, by knowing how you are feeling about the world. So that is the criterion. This is not a truth – that the world is unreal – this is a meditative criterion. If the world has become unreal, you have become centered into the being. Now the surface and you are so far away that you can look at the surface as something objective, something other than you. You are not identified.

This technique is very easy and will not take much time if you try it. Even sometimes it happens with this technique that in the very first effort you will feel the beauty and the miracle of it. So try it. But if you are not feeling it in the very first effort, don't be disappointed. Wait, and go on doing it. And it is so easy you can do it any time. Just lying on your bed at night you can do it; just in the morning when you feel that you are now awake you can do it. Do it first and then get up, even ten minutes will be enough, or ten minutes at night just before falling asleep. Make the world unreal, and your sleep will be so deep – you may not have slept like that before. If the world becomes unreal just before falling asleep, dreams will be fewer because if the world has become a dream, dreams cannot continue.

And if the world is unreal, you are totally relaxed, otherwise the reality of the world goes on impinging on you, hammering on you.

As far as I know – I have suggested this technique to many people who suffer from insomnia – it helps deeply. If the world is unreal, tensions dissolve. And if you can move from the periphery, you have already moved to a deep state of sleep – before sleep comes you are already deep into it. And then in the morning it is beautiful because you are so fresh, so young, the whole energy vibrating and just coming from the center back to the periphery.

The moment you become alert that now sleep is finished, don't open your eyes first. First do this: the body is relaxed after the whole night, feeling fresh and alive so do this experiment for ten minutes, then open the eyes. Relax. You are already relaxed; it will not take much time. Just relax. Bring your consciousness to the heart just between the two armpits: feel it filled with deep peace. For ten minutes remain in that peace, and then open the eyes. And the world will look totally different because that peace will be radiated from your eyes also. And the whole day you will feel different – not only will you feel different, you will feel people are behaving differently with you.

To every relationship you contribute something. If your contribution is not there, people behave differently because they feel you are a different person. They may not be aware of it. But when you are filled with peace everyone will behave differently with you. They will be more loving and more kind, less resistant, more open, closer. The magnet is there. The peace is the magnet. When you are peaceful people come nearer to you; when you are disturbed everyone is repelled. This is so physical a phenomenon that you can observe it easily. Whenever you are peaceful you will feel everyone wants to be closer to you because that peace radiates, it becomes vibrations around you. Circles of peace move around you and whosoever comes near feels to be nearer to you – just like the shadow of a tree and you feel to move under the shadow and relax there. 4

Shiva said: Blessed one, as senses are absorbed in the heart, reach the center of the lotus.

So what is to be done in this technique? "As senses are absorbed in the heart..." Try! Many ways are possible. You touch someone: if you are a heart-oriented person the touch immediately goes to your heart, and you can feel the quality. If you take the hand of a person who is head-oriented, the hand will be cold – not just cold, but the very quality will be cold.

Heart Centering

A deadness, a certain deadness, will be in the hand. If the person is heart-oriented, then there is a certain warmth. Then his hand will really melt with you. You will feel a certain thing flowing from his hand to you, and there will be a meeting – a communication of warmth.

This warmth comes from the heart. It can never come from the head because the head is always cool, cold, calculative. The heart is warm, non-calculative. The head always thinks about how to take more, the heart always feels how to give more. That warmth is just a giving – a giving of energy, a giving of inner vibrations, a giving of life. That is why you feel a differ-

ent quality in it. If the person really embraces you, you will feel a deep melting with him.

Touch! Close your eyes; touch anything. Touch your beloved or your lover, touch your child or your mother, or your friend, or touch a tree or a flower, or just touch the earth. Close your eyes and feel a communication from your heart to the earth, or to your beloved. Just feel that your hand is your heart stretched out to touch the earth. Let the feeling of touch be related to the heart.

When you are listening to music, do not listen to it from the head. Let your ears be joined to the heart, not to the head. Just forget your head and feel that you are headless. There is no head at all. It is good to have your own picture in your bedroom without the head. Concentrate on it: you are without the head; do not allow the head to come in. While listening to music, listen to it from the heart. Feel the music coming to your heart; let your heart vibrate with it. Let your senses be joined to the heart, not to the head. Try this with all the senses, and feel more and more that every sense goes into the heart and dissolves into it.

"Blessed one, as senses are absorbed in the heart, reach the center of the lotus." The heart is the lotus. Every sense is just the opening of the lotus, the petals of the lotus. Try to relate your senses to the heart first. Secondly, always think that every sense goes deep down into the heart and becomes absorbed in it. When these two things become established, only then will your senses begin to help you: they will lead you to the heart, and your heart will become a lotus.

This lotus of the heart will give you a centering. Once you know the center of the heart, it is very easy to fall down into the navel center. It is very easy! Really, this sutra does not even mention this; there is no need. If you are really absorbed in the heart totally, and reason has stopped working, then you will fall down. From the heart, the door is opened toward the navel. Only from the head is it difficult to go toward the navel. Or, if you are between the two, between the heart and the head, then too it is difficult to go to the navel. Once you are absorbed in the navel, you have suddenly fallen beyond the heart. You have fallen into the navel center which is the basic one – the original.

If you feel that you are a heart-oriented person, then this method will be very helpful to you. But know well that everyone is trying to deceive himself that he is heart-oriented. Everyone tries to feel that he is a very loving person, a feeling type – because love is such a basic need that no one can feel at ease if he sees that he has no love, no loving heart. So everyone goes on thinking and believing, but belief will not do. Observe very impartially, as if you are observing someone else, and then decide – because there is no need to deceive yourself and it will be of no help. Even if you deceive yourself, you cannot deceive the technique. So when you do this technique, you would feel that nothing is happening. [5]

*A*tisha said: Train in join-ing, sending and taking to-gether. Do this by riding the breath.

Atisha says: start being compas-sionate. And the method is, when you breathe in – listen carefully, it is one of the greatest methods – when you breathe in, think that you are breathing in all the mis-eries of all the people in the world. All the darkness, all the negativity, all the hell that exists anywhere, you are breathing it in. And let it be absorbed in your heart.

Atisha's Heart Meditation

You may have read or heard about the so-called positive thinkers of the West. They say just the oppo-site – they don't know what they are saying. They say "When you breathe out, throw out all your misery and negativity. And when you breathe in, breathe in joy, positivity, happiness, cheerful-ness."

Atisha's method is just the oppo-site: when you breathe in, breathe in all the misery and suffering of all the beings of the world – past, present and future.

And when you breathe out, breathe out all the joy that you have, all the blissfulness that you have, all the benediction that you have. Breathe out, pour yourself into existence. This is the method of compassion: drink in all the suffering and pour out all the blessings.

And you will be surprised if you do it. The moment you take all the suf-ferings of the world inside you, they are no longer sufferings. The heart immediately transforms the energy. The heart is a transforming force: drink in misery, and it is trans-formed into blissfulness…then pour it out.

Once you have learned that your heart can do this magic, this mira-cle, you would like to do it again and again. Try it. It is one of the most practical methods, simple, and it brings immediate results. Do it today, and see. 6

Start with yourself

*A*tisha said: Begin the devel-
opment of taking with yourself.

Atisha says: before you can do this
with the whole existence, you will
have to start first with yourself.
This is one of the fundamental secrets of inner growth. You cannot
do anything with others that you
have not done in the first place with
yourself. You can hurt others if you
hurt yourself, you will be a pain in
the neck to others if you are a pain
in the neck to yourself, you can be
a blessing to others only if you are
a blessing to yourself.

Whatsoever you can do with others,
you must have done to yourself before, because that is the only thing
that you can share. You can share
only that which you have; you cannot share that which you don't
have. Atisha says: "Begin the de-
velopment of taking with yourself."
Rather than starting by taking the
whole misery of the world and absorbing it in the heart, start with
your own misery. Don't go into the
deep sea so fast; learn swimming in
shallow water. And if you immediately start taking the misery of the
whole existence, it will remain simply an experiment in speculation. It

won't be real, it can't be real. It will
be just verbal.

You can say to yourself "Yes, I am
taking the misery of the whole
world" – but what do you know of
the misery of the whole world? You
have not even experienced your
own misery.

We go on avoiding our own misery.
If you feel miserable, you put on
the radio or the TV and you become engaged. You start reading
the newspaper so that you can forget your misery, or you go to the
movies, or you go to your woman
or your man. You go to the club,
you go shopping in the market, just
somehow to keep yourself away
from yourself, so that you need not
see the wound, so that you need not
look at how much it hurts within.

People go on avoiding themselves.
What do they know of misery?
How can they think of the misery
of the whole existence?

First, you have to begin with yourself. If you are feeling miserable, let
it become a meditation. Sit silently,
close the doors. First feel the misery
with as much intensity as possible.
Feel the hurt. Somebody has insulted you: now, the best way to avoid
the hurt is to go and insult him, so
that you become occupied with him.
That is not meditation.

If somebody has insulted you, feel
thankful to him that he has given

you an opportunity to feel a deep
wound. He has opened a wound in
you. The wound may have been
created by many many insults that
you have suffered in your whole
life; he may not be the cause of all
the suffering, but he has triggered a
process.

Just lock your room, sit silently,
with no anger for the person but
with total awareness of the feeling
that is arising in you – the hurt feeling that you have been rejected,
that you have been insulted. And
then you will be surprised that not
only is this man there: all the men
and all the women and all the people that have ever insulted you will
start moving in your memory.

You will start not only remembering them, you will start reliving
them. You will be going into a kind
of primal.

Feel the hurt, feel the pain, don't
avoid it. That's why in many therapies the patient is told not to take
any drugs before the therapy begins, for the simple reason that
drugs are a way to escape from
your inner misery. They don't allow you to see your wounds, they
repress them. They don't allow you
to go into your suffering and unless
you go into your suffering, you
cannot be released from the imprisonment of it.

It is perfectly scientific to drop all

drugs before going into a group – if possible even drugs like coffee, tea, smoking, because these are all ways to escape.

Have you watched? Whenever you feel nervous you immediately start smoking. It is a way to avoid nervousness; you become occupied with smoking. Really it is a regression. Smoking makes you again feel like a child – unworried, non-responsible – because smoking is nothing but a symbolic breast. The hot smoke going in simply takes you back to the days when you were feeding on the mother's breast and the warm milk was going in: the nipple has now become the cigarette. The cigarette is a symbolic nipple.

Through regression you avoid the responsibilities and the pains of being adult. And that's what goes on through many many drugs. Modern man is drugged as never before, because modern man is living in great suffering. Without drugs it would be impossible to live in so much suffering. Those drugs create a barrier; they keep you drugged, they don't allow you enough sensitivity to know your pain.

The first thing to do is close your doors and stop any kind of occupation: looking at the TV, listening to the radio, reading a book. Stop all occupation, because that too is a subtle drug. Just be silent, utterly alone. Don't even pray, because that again is a drug, you are becoming occupied, you start talking to God, you start praying, you escape from yourself.

Atisha is saying: just be yourself. Whatsoever the pain of it and whatsoever the suffering of it, let it be so. First experience it in its total intensity. It will be difficult, it will be heart-rending: you may start crying like a child, you may start rolling on the ground in deep pain, your body may go through contortions. You may suddenly become aware that the pain is not only in the heart, it is all over the body – that it is aching all over, that it is painful all over, that your whole body is nothing but pain.

If you can experience it – this is of tremendous importance – then start absorbing it. Don't throw it away. It is such a valuable energy, don't throw it away. Absorb it, drink it, accept it, welcome it, feel grateful to it. And say to yourself, "This time I'm not going to avoid it, this time I'm not going to reject it, this time I'm not going to throw it away. This time I will drink it and receive it like a guest. This time I will digest it."

It may take a few days for you to be able to digest it, but the day it happens, you have stumbled upon a door which will take you really far, far away. A new journey has started in your life, you are moving into a new kind of being – because immediately, the moment you accept the pain with no rejection anywhere, its energy and its quality changes. It is no longer pain.

In fact one is simply surprised, one cannot believe it, it is so incredible. One cannot believe that suffering can be transformed into ecstasy, that pain can become joy. [7]

Inner Centering

N obody can exist without a center. It has not to be created but only rediscovered. Essence is the center, that which is your nature, that which is God-given. Personality is the circumference, that which is cultivated by society; it is not God-given. It is by nurture, not by nature. [1]

One Sufi mystic who had remained happy his whole life – no one had ever seen him unhappy – he was always laughing. He *was* laughter, his whole being was a perfume of celebration. In his old age, when he was dying – on his deathbed, and still enjoying death, laughing hilariously – a disciple asked, "You puzzle us. Now you are dying. Why are you laughing? What is there funny about it? We are feeling so sad. We wanted to ask you many times in your life why you

Abdullah

are never sad. But now, confronting death, at least one should be sad. You are still laughing! How are you managing it?"

And the old man said, "It is a simple clue. I had asked my master. I had gone to my master as a young man; I was only seventeen, and already miserable. And my master was old, seventy, and he was sitting under a tree, laughing for no reason at all. There was nobody else, nothing had happened, nobody had cracked a joke or anything. And he was simply laughing, holding his belly. And I asked him, 'What is the matter with you? Are you mad or something?'

"He said, 'One day I was also as sad as you are. Then it dawned on me that it is *my* choice, it is *my* life.'

"Since that day, every morning when I get up, the first thing I decide is, before I open my eyes, I say to myself, 'Abdullah' – that was his name – 'what do you want? Misery? Blissfulness? What are you going to choose today?' And it happens that I always choose blissfulness."

It is a choice. Try it. The first moment in the morning when you become aware that sleep has left, ask yourself, "Abdullah, another day! What is your idea? Do you choose misery or blissfulness?"

And who would choose misery? And *why?* It is so unnatural – unless one feels blissful in misery, but then too you are choosing bliss, not misery. [2]

Shiva said: On joyously seeing a long absent friend, permeate this joy.

When you see a friend and suddenly feel a joy rising in your heart, concentrate on this joy. Feel it and become it, and meet the friend while being aware and filled with your joy. Let the friend be just on the periphery, and you remain centered in your feeling of happiness.

This can be done in many other situations. The sun is rising, and suddenly you feel something rising within you. Then forget the sun; let

Finding the Real Source

it remain on the periphery. You be centered in your own feeling of rising energy. The moment you look at it, it will spread. It will become your whole body, your whole being. And don't just be an observer of it; merge into it. There are a few moments when you feel joy, happiness, bliss, but you go on missing them because you become object- centered.

Whenever there is joy, you feel that it is coming from without. You have met a friend – of course, it appears that the joy is coming from your friend, from seeing him. That is not the actual case. The joy is always *within you*. The friend has just become a situation. The friend has helped it to come out, has helped you to see that it is there. And this is not only with joy, but

with everything: with anger, with sadness, with misery, with happiness, with everything, it is so. Others are only situations in which things that are hidden in you are expressed. They are not causes; they are not causing something in you. Whatsoever is happening, it is happening *to you*. It has always been there; it is only that meeting with this friend has become a situation in which whatsoever was hidden has come out in the open – has come out from the hidden sources – it has become apparent, manifest. Whenever this happens remain centered in the inner feeling, and then you will have a different attitude about everything in life.

Even with negative emotions, do this. When you are angry, do not be centered on the person who has aroused it. Let him be on the periphery. You just become anger. Feel anger in its totality; allow it to happen within. Don't rationalize; don't say that this man has created it. Do not condemn the man. He has just become the situation. And feel grateful toward him that he has helped something which was hidden to come into the open. He has hit you somewhere, and a wound was hidden there. Now you know it, so become the wound.

With negative or positive, with any emotion, use this, and there will be a great change in you. If the emotion is negative, you will be freed of it by being aware that it is within you. If the emotion is positive, you will become the emotion itself. If it is joy, you will become joy. If it is anger, the anger will dissolve.

And this is the difference between negative and positive emotions: if you become aware of a certain emotion, and by your becoming aware the emotion dissolves, it is negative. If by your becoming aware of a certain emotion you then become the emotion, if the emotion then spreads and becomes your being, it is positive. Awareness works differently in both cases.

If it is a poisonous emotion, you are relieved of it through awareness. If it is good, blissful, ecstatic, you become one with it. Awareness deepens it. [3]

Shiva said: In moods of extreme desire, be undisturbed.

When desire grips you, you are disturbed. Of course, that is natural. Desire grips you, then your mind starts wavering and many ripples go on, on the surface. The desire pulls you somewhere into the future; the past pushes you somewhere into the future. You are disturbed: you are not at ease. Desire is, therefore, a 'dis-ease'.

This sutra says, "In moods of extreme desire be undisturbed." But

Center of the Cyclone

how to be undisturbed? Desire means disturbance, so how to be undisturbed – and in extreme moments of desire! You will have to do certain experiments; only then will you understand what it means. You are in anger: anger grips you. You are temporarily mad, possessed: you are no more in your senses. Suddenly remember to be undisturbed – as if you are un-

dressing. Inside, become naked, naked from the anger, undressed. Anger will be there, but now you have a point within you which is not disturbed.

You will know that anger is there on the periphery. Like fever, it is there. The periphery is wavering; the periphery is disturbed, but you can look at it. If you can look at it, you will be undisturbed. Become a

witness to it, and you will be undisturbed. This undisturbed point is your original mind. The original mind cannot be disturbed; it is never disturbed. But you have never looked at it. When anger is there, you become identified with the anger. You forget that anger is something other than you. You become one with it, and you start acting through it,

100

you start doing something through it.

Two things can be done. In anger you will be violent to someone, to the object of your anger. Then you have moved to the other. Anger is just in between you and the other. Here I am, there is anger, and there you are – the object of my anger. From anger I can travel in two dimensions. Either I can travel to you: then you become my center of consciousness, the object of my anger. Then my mind becomes focused on you, the one who has insulted me. This is one way that you can travel from anger.

There is another way: you can travel to yourself. You don't move to the person whom you feel has caused the anger. You move to the person who feels to be angry; you move to the subject and not to the object.

Ordinarily, we go on moving to the object. If you move to the object, the dust part of your mind is disturbed, and you will feel, "'I' am disturbed." If you move within to the center of your own being, you will be able to witness the dust part: you will be able to see that the dust part of the mind is disturbed, but "I am not disturbed". And you can experiment upon this with any desire, any disturbance.

A sexual desire comes to your mind; your whole body is taken by it: you can move to the sexual object, the object of your desire. The object may be there, it may not be there. You can move to the object in imagination also, but then you will get more and more disturbed. The further away you go from your center, the more you will be disturbed. Really, the distance and disturbance are always in proportion. The more distant you are from your center, the more you are disturbed; the nearer you are to the center, the less you are disturbed. If you are just at the center, there is no disturbance.

In a cyclone, there is a center which is undisturbed – in the cyclone of anger, the cyclone of sex, the cyclone of any desire. Just in the center there is no cyclone, and a cyclone cannot exist without a silent center. The anger also cannot exist without something within you which is beyond anger.

Remember this: nothing can exist without its opposite. The opposite is needed there. Without it, there is no possibility of it existing. If there were no center within you which remains unmoved, no movement would be possible there. If there were no center within you which remains undisturbed, no disturbance could happen to you. Analyze this and observe this. If there were no center of absolute undisturbance in you, how could you feel that you are disturbed? You need a comparison. You need two points to compare.

Suppose a person is ill: he feels illness because somewhere within him, a point, a center of absolute health exists. That is why he can compare. You say that your head is aching: how is it that you know about this ache, this headache? If you were the headache, you could not know it. You must be someone else, something else – the observer, the witness, who can say, "My head is aching."

This sutra says, "In moods of extreme desire, be undisturbed." What can you do? This technique is not for suppression. This technique is not saying that when there is anger, suppress it and remain undisturbed – no! If you suppress, you will create more disturbance. If the anger is there and an effort to suppress is there, it will double the disturbance. When anger is there, close your doors, meditate on the anger, allow the anger to be. You remain undisturbed, and don't suppress it.

It is easy to suppress; it is easy to express. We do both. We express if the situation allows, and if it is convenient and not dangerous for you. If you can harm the other and the other cannot harm you, you will express the anger. If it is dangerous, if the other can harm you more, if your boss or whoever you are angry at is more strong, you will suppress it.

Expression and suppression are easy: witnessing is difficult. Witnessing is neither. It is not suppressing, it is not expressing. It is not expressing because you are not expressing it to the object of anger. It is not being suppressed either. You are allowing it to be expressed – expressed in a vacuum. You are meditating on it.

Stand before a mirror and express your anger – and be a witness to it. You are alone, so you can meditate on it. Do whatsoever you want to do, but in a vacuum. If you want to beat someone, beat the empty sky. If you want to be angry, be angry; if you want to scream, scream. But do it alone, and remember yourself as a point which is seeing all this, this drama. Then it becomes a psychodrama, and you can laugh at it and it will be a deep catharsis for you. Afterwards you will feel relieved of it – and not only relieved of it: you will have gained something through it. You will have matured; a growth will have come to you. And now you will know that even while you were in anger there was a center within you which was undisturbed. Now try to uncover

this center more and more, and it is easy to uncover it in desire.

This technique can be very useful, and much benefit can happen to you through it. But it will be difficult because when you become disturbed, you forget everything. You may forget that you have to meditate. Then try it in this way: don't wait for the moment when anger happens to you. Don't wait for that moment! Just close the door to your room, and think of some past experience of anger when you went mad. Remember it, and re-enact it. That will be easy for you. Re-enact it again; do it again; relive it. Don't just remember it: relive it.

Remember that someone had insulted you and what was said and how you reacted to him. React again; replay it.

This re-enacting something from the past will do much. Everyone has scars in his mind, unhealed wounds. If you re-enact them, you will be unburdened. If you can go to your past and do something which has remained incomplete, you will be unburdened from your past. Your mind will become fresher; the dust will be thrown away.

Remember in your past something which you feel has remained suspended. You wanted to kill someone, you wanted to love someone, you wanted this and that, and that

has remained incomplete. That incomplete thing goes on hovering around the mind like a cloud.

"In moods of extreme desire, be undisturbed": Gurdjieff used this technique a great deal. He created situations, but to create situations a school is needed. You cannot do that alone. Gurdjieff had a small school in Fontainebleau, and he was a taskmaster. He knew how to create situations. You would enter the room where a group was sitting, and something would be done so that you would get angry. And it would be done so naturally that you would never imagine that some situation was being created for you. But it was a device. Someone would insult you by saying something, and you would get disturbed. Then everyone would help the disturbance and you would become mad. And when you were right at the point where you could explode, Gurdjieff would shout, "Remember! Remain undisturbed!" You can help. Your family can become a school; you can help each other. Friends can become a school and they can help each other. You can decide with your family. The whole family can decide that now a situation has to be created for the father or for the mother, and then the whole family works to create the situation. When the father or mother goes completely mad, then everyone starts laughing and says, "Remain completely undisturbed." You can help each other, and the experience is simply wonderful. Once you know a cool center within you in a hot situation, you cannot forget it. And then in any hot situation you can remember it, reclaim it, regain it.

In the West now one technique, a therapeutic technique, is used: it is called "psychodrama." It helps, and it is also based on techniques like this. In psychodrama you just enact, you just play a game.

In the beginning it is a game, but sooner or later you become possessed. And when you become possessed your mind starts functioning, because your mind and your body function automatically. They function automatically!

So if you see an actor acting in a psychodrama who, in a situation of anger, really becomes angry, you may think that he is simply acting, but it is not so. He might have really become angry; it may not be acting at all now. He is possessed by the desire, by the disturbance, by the feeling, by the mood, and if he is really possessed, only then does his acting look real.

Your body cannot know whether you are playing or whether you are doing it for real. You may have ob-served yourself at some time in your life that you were just playing at being angry, and you didn't know when the anger became real. Or, you were just playing and you were not feeling sexual: you were playing with your wife or with your girlfriend, or with your husband, and then suddenly it became real. The body took over.

The body can be deceived. The body cannot know whether it is real or unreal, particularly with sex. If you imagine it, your body thinks it is real. Once you start do-ing something, the body thinks it is real and it starts behaving in a real way.

Psychodrama is a technique based on such methods. You are not an-gry: you are simply acting angry – and then you get into it. But psy-chodrama is beautiful because you know that you are simply acting. And then on the periphery anger be-comes real, and just behind it you are hidden and looking at it. Now you know that you are not disturbed, but the anger is there, the distur-bance is there. The disturbance is there, and yet the disturbance is not.

This feeling of two forces working simultaneously gives you a tran-scendence, and then in real anger also you can feel it. Once you know how to feel it, you can feel it in real situations also. Use this technique. This will change your life totally. Once you know how to remain undisturbed, the world is not mis-ery for you. Then nothing can cre-ate any confusion in you, nothing can hurt you, really. Now there is no suffering for you, and once you know it you can do another thing.

Once you can detach your center from the periphery, you can do it. Once the center is detached com-pletely, if you can remain undis-turbed in anger, in desire, you can play with desires, with anger, with disturbances.

This technique is to create a feeling of two extremes within you. They are there: two polar opposites are there. Once you become aware of this polarity, you become for the first time a master of yourself. Oth-erwise others are your masters; you are just a slave. Your wife knows, your son knows, your father knows, your friends know that you can be pushed and pulled. You can be disturbed, you can be made hap-py and unhappy. If someone else can make you happy and unhappy, you are not a master. You are just a slave. The other has a hold. Just by a single gesture, he can make you unhappy; just by a small smile he can make you happy. So you are just at the mercy of someone else; the other can do anything to you.

And if this is the situation, then all your reactions are simply reactions, not actions.

This knowledge of the center or this grounding in the center makes you a master. Otherwise you are a slave, and a slave of so many – not only of one master, but of many. Everything is a master, and you are a slave to the whole universe. Obviously, you will be in trouble. With so many masters pulling you in so many directions and dimensions, you are never together; you are not in a unity. And pulled in so many dimensions, you are in anguish. Only a master of oneself can transcend anguish. [4]

Shiva said: Oh, lotus-eyed one, sweet of touch, when singing, seeing, tasting, be aware you are and discover the ever-living.

This technique says while doing anything – singing, seeing, tasting – be aware that you *are* and discover the ever-living: and discover within yourself the current, the energy, the life, the ever-living. But we are not aware of ourselves. Gurdjieff used self-remembering as a basic technique in the West.

Feel 'I Am'

The self-remembering is derived from this sutra. The whole Gurdjieffian system is based on this one sutra: Remember yourself, whatsoever you are doing. It is very difficult. It looks very easy, but you will go on forgetting. Even for three or four seconds you cannot remember yourself. You will have a feeling that you are remembering, and suddenly you will have moved to some other thought. Even with this thought that "Okay, I am remembering myself," you will have missed, because this thought is not self-remembering. In self-remembering there will be no thought; you will be completely empty. And self-remembering is not a mental process. It is not that you say, "Yes, I am." Saying "Yes, I am," you have missed. This is a mind thing; this is a mental process: "I am."

Feel "I am," not the words "I am." Don't verbalize. Just feel that you are. Don't think. Feel! Try it. It is difficult, but if you go on insisting it happens. While walking, remember you are, and have the feeling of your being, not of any thought, not of any idea. Just feel. I touch your hand or I put my hand on your head: don't verbalize. Just feel the touch, and in that feeling feel not only the touch, but feel also the touched one. Then your consciousness becomes double-arrowed.

You are walking under trees: the trees are there, the breeze is there, the sun is rising. This is the world all around you; you are aware of it. Stand for a moment and suddenly remember that you are, but don't verbalize. Just feel that you are. This nonverbal feeling, even if for only a single moment, will give you a glimpse – a glimpse which no LSD can give you, a glimpse which is of the real. For a single moment you are thrown back to the center of

your being. You are behind the mirror; you have transcended the world of reflections; you are existential. And you can do it at any time. It doesn't need any special place or any special time. And you cannot say, "I have no time." When eating you can do it, when taking a bath you can do it, when moving or sitting you can do it – anytime. No matter what you are doing, you can suddenly remember yourself, and then try to continue that glimpse of your being.

It will be difficult. One moment you will feel it is there, the next moment you will have moved away. Some thought will have entered, some reflection will have

come to you, and you will have become involved in the reflection. But don't be sad and don't be disappointed. This is so because for lives together we have been concerned with the reflections. This has become a robot-like mechanism. Instantly, automatically, we are thrown to the reflection. But if even for a single moment you have the glimpse, it is enough for the beginning. And why is it enough? Because you will never get two moments together. Only one moment is with you always. And if you can have the glimpse for a single moment, you can remain in it. Only effort is needed – a continuous effort is needed.

Gurdjieff tried from one corner. Just try to remember you are. Raman Maharshi tried from another corner. He made it a meditation to ask, to inquire, "Who am I?" And don't believe in any answers that the mind can supply. The mind will say, "What nonsense are you asking? You are this, you are that, you are a man, you are a woman, you are educated or uneducated, rich or poor." The mind will supply answers, but go on asking. Don't accept any answer because all the answers given by the mind are false.

Who Am I?

They are from the unreal part of you. They are coming from words, they are coming from scriptures, they are coming from conditioning, they are coming from society, they are coming from others. Go on asking. Let this arrow of "Who am I?" penetrate deeper and deeper. A moment will come when no answer will come.

That is the right moment. Now you are nearing the answer. When no answer comes, you are near the answer because mind is becoming silent – or, you have gone far away from the mind. When there will be no answer and a vacuum will be created all around you, your questioning will look absurd. Whom are you questioning? There is no one to answer you. Suddenly, even your questioning will stop. With the questioning, the last part of the mind has dissolved because this question was also of the mind. Those answers were of the mind and this question was also of the mind. Both have dissolved, so now *you are.*

Try this. There is every possibility, if you persist, that this technique can give you a glimpse of the real – and the real is ever-living. 5

Shiva said: Each thing is perceived through knowing. The self shines in space through knowing. Perceive one being as knower and known.

Whenever you know something, it is known through knowing. The object comes to your mind through the faculty of knowledge. You look at a flower. You know this is a rose flower. The rose flower is there and you are inside. Something from you comes to the rose flower, something from you is projected on the rose flower. Some energy

To the Very Center of Being

moves from you, comes to the rose, takes its form, color and smell, and comes back and informs you that this is a rose flower.

All knowledge, whatsoever you know, is revealed through the faculty of knowing. Knowing is your faculty. Knowledge is gathered through this faculty. But knowing reveals two things: the known and the knower. Whenever you are

knowing a rose flower, your knowledge is half if you forget the knower who is knowing it. So while knowing a rose flower there are three things: the rose flower – the known; the knower – you; and the relationship between the two – knowledge.

So knowledge can be divided into three points: knower, known and knowing.

Knowing is just like a bridge between two points – the subject and the object. Ordinarily your knowledge reveals only the known; the knower remains unrevealed. Ordinarily your knowledge is one-arrowed: it points to the rose but it never points to you. Unless it starts pointing to you, that knowledge will allow you to know about the world, but it will not allow you to know about yourself.

All the techniques of meditation are to reveal the knower. George Gurdjieff used a particular technique just like this. He called it self-remembering. He said that whenever you are knowing something, always remember the knower. Don't forget it in the object. Remember the subject. Just now you are listening to me. When you are listening to me, you can listen in two ways. One: your mind can be focused towards me – then you forget the listener. Then the speaker is known but the listener is forgotten.

Gurdjieff said that while listening, know the speaker and also know the listener. Your knowledge must be double-arrowed, pointing to two points – the knower and the known. It must not only flow in one direction towards the object. It must flow simultaneously towards two directions – the known and the knower. This he called self-remembering.

Buddha called it *samyak smriti* – right-mindfulness. He said that your mind is not in a right-mindfulness if it knows only one point. It must know both. And then a miracle happens: if you are aware of both the known and the knower, suddenly you become the third – you are neither. Just by endeavoring to be aware of both the known and the knower, you become the third, you become a witness. A third possibility arises immediately – a witnessing self comes into being – because how can you know both? If you are the knower, then you remain fixed to one point. In self-remembering you shift from the fixed point of the knower. Then the knower is your mind and the known is the world, and you become a third point, a consciousness, a witnessing self.

This third point cannot be transcended, and that which cannot be transcended is the ultimate. That which can be transcended is not worthwhile, because then it is not your nature – you can transcend it.

You are sitting near a rose flower: look at it. The first thing to do is be totally attentive, give total attention to the rose, so that the whole world disappears and only the rose remains there – your consciousness is totally attentive to the being of the rose. If the attention is total then the world disappears, because the more the attention is concentrated on the rose, the more everything else falls away. The world disappears; only the rose remains. The rose becomes the world.

This is the first step – to concentrate on the rose. If you cannot concentrate on the rose, it will be difficult to move to the knower, because then your mind is always diverted. So concentration becomes the first step towards meditation. Only the rose remains; the whole world has disappeared. Now you can move inwards; now the rose becomes the point from where you can move. Now see the rose, and start becoming aware of yourself – the knower.

In the beginning you will miss. When you shift to the knower, the rose will drop out of consciousness. It will become faint, it will go away, it will become distant. Again you will come to the rose, and you will forget the self. This hide-and-seek play will go on, but if you persist, sooner or later a moment will come when suddenly you will be in-between. The knower, the mind, and the rose will be there, and you will be just in the middle, looking at both. That middle point, that balancing point, is the witness.

Once you know that, you have become both. Then the rose – the known, and the knower – the mind, are just two wings of you. Then the object and the subject are just two wings; you are the center of both. They are extensions of you. Then the world and the divine are both extensions of you. You have come to the very center of being. And this center is just a witness. [6]

Looking Within

These techniques are concerned with the practice of looking. Before we enter these techniques, something has to be understood about the eyes, because these techniques depend on that. The first thing: eyes are the most non-bodily part of the human body, the least bodily. If matter can become non-matter, then such is the case with eyes. Eyes are material, but simultaneously they are also non-material. Eyes are a meeting point of you and your body. Nowhere else in the body is the meeting so deep.

The human body and you are much separated. A great distance is there, but at the point of the eyes you are nearest to your body and the body is nearest to you. That is why eyes can be used for the inner journey. A single jump from the eyes can lead you to the source. That is not possible from the hand, not possible from the heart, not possible from anywhere else in the body. From elsewhere you will have to travel long; the distance is great. But from the eyes a single step is enough to enter into yourself.

Eyes are very liquid, moving, in constant movement, and that movement has its own rhythm, its own system, its own mechanism. Your eyes are not moving at random, anarchically. They have a rhythm of their own and that rhythm shows many things. If you have a sexual thought in the mind, your eyes move differently – with a different rhythm. Just by looking at your eyes and the movement, one can say what type of thought is moving inside. When you feel hungry and a thought of food is inside, eyes have a different movement.

So remember this, that eye movements and thinking are joined together. That is why, if you stop your eyes and their movements, your thought process will stop immediately. Or if your thought process stops your eyes will stop automatically. And one point more: the eyes move continuously from one object to another. From A to B, from B to C, they go on moving. Movement is their nature. It is just like a river flowing: movement is their nature!

And because of that movement, they are so alive! Movement is also life.

You can try to stop your eyes at a particular point, at a particular object, and not allow them to move, but movement is their nature. You cannot stop movement, but you can stop your eyes: understand the distinction. You can stop your eyes at a particular fixed point – at a dot on the wall. You can stare at the dot; you can stop your eyes. But movement is their nature. So they may not move from object A to object B because you have forced them to remain at A, but then a very strange phenomenon happens.

Movement is bound to be there; that is their nature. If you do not allow them movement from A to B, they will move from outwards to inwards. Either they can move from A to B, or if you do not allow this outward movement they will move inwards. Movement is their nature; they need movement. If you suddenly stop and do not allow them to move outwards, they will start moving inwards.

So there are two possibilities of movement. One is from object A to object B – this is an outward movement; this is how it is happening naturally. But there is another possibility which is of tantra and yoga – not allowing movement from one outside object to another and stopping this movement. Then the eyes jump from an outside object to the inner consciousness. They begin to move inwards. Remember these points; then it will be easy to understand the techniques. [1]

Shiva said: Eyes closed, see your inner being in detail. Thus see your true nature.

"Eyes closed" – close your eyes. But this closing is not enough. Total closing means to close your eyes and stop their movements. Otherwise the eyes will continue to see something which is of the outside. Even with closed eyes you will see things – images of things. Actual things are not there, but images, ideas, collected memories – they will start flowing. They are also from outside, so your eyes are

Seeing Within

still not totally closed. "Totally" closed eyes means nothing to see. Understand the difference. You can close your eyes; that is easy. Everyone closes them every moment. In the night you close your eyes, but that will not reveal the inner nature to you. Close your eyes so that nothing remains to be seen – no outside object, no inside image of any outside object, just a blank darkness as if you have suddenly gone blind – not blind only to reality, but to the dream reality also.

One has to practice it. A long period will be needed; it cannot be done suddenly. You will need a long training. Close your eyes. Anytime you feel it is easy and you have time, close your eyes and then inwardly stop all movements of the eyes. Do not allow any movement.

Feel! Do not allow any movement. Stop all movements of the eyes. Feel as if they have become stones, and then remain in that "stony" state of the eyes. Do not do anything; just remain there. Suddenly someday, you will become aware that you are looking inside yourself.

You have seen your body only from the outside. You have seen your body in a mirror or you have seen your hands from the outside. You do not know what the inside of your body is. You have never entered into your own self; you have never been at the center of your body and being to look around at what is there from the inside.

Close your eyes, see your inner being in detail and move from limb to limb inside. Just go to your toe. Forget the whole body: move to the toe. Stay there and have a look. Then move through the legs, come on upwards, go to every limb. Then many things happen. *Many* things happen!

Then your body becomes such a sensitive vehicle, you cannot even imagine it. Then if you touch someone, you can move into your hand totally and that touch will become transforming. That is what is meant by a teacher's touch, a master's touch: he can move to any limb totally, and then he is concentrated there. If you can move to any part of your body totally, that part becomes alive – so much alive that you cannot imagine what happens to that part. Then you can

move to the eyes totally. If you can move to your eyes totally and then look in someone's eyes, you will penetrate him; you will go to his very depths.

Close your eyes; see your inner being in detail. The first, outer part of it is to look at your body from inwardly – from your inner center. Stand there and have a look. You will be separated from the body because the looker is never the looked at. The observer is different from the object.

If you can see your body totally from the inside, then you can never fall into the illusion that you are the body. Then you will remain different – totally different: inside it but not it, in the body but not the body. This is the first part. Then you can move. Then you are free to move. Once freed from the body, freed from the identity, you are free to move. Now you can move into your mind – deep down. This is the inner cave of the mind.

If you enter this cave of the mind, you will become separate from the mind also. Then you will see that the mind is also an object which

you can look at, and that which is entering the mind is, again, separate and different. This entering into the mind is what is meant by "seeing your inner being in detail." Body and mind both should be entered and looked at from within. Then you are simply a witness, and this witness cannot be penetrated.

That is why it is your innermost core: that is you. That which can be penetrated, that which can be seen, is not you. When you have come to that which cannot be penetrated, that in which you cannot move, which cannot be observed, then only have you come to the real self. You cannot witness the witnessing source, remember; that is absurd.

If someone says that "I have witnessed my witness," that is absurd. Why is it absurd? Because if you have witnessed your witnessing self, then the witnessing self is not the witnessing self. That who has witnessed it is the witness. That which you can see, you are not; that which you can observe, you are not; that which you can become aware of, you are not. [2]

114

S hiva said: Look upon a bowl without seeing the sides or the material. In a few moments become aware.

Look at anything. A bowl or any object will do, but look with a different quality. "Look upon a bowl without seeing the sides or the material." Look upon any object, but with these two conditions. Do not look at the sides: look at the object as a whole. Ordinarily, we look at parts. It may not be done so consciously, but we look at parts. If I look at you, first I see your face,

Looking as a Whole

then your torso and then your whole body. Look at an object as a whole; do not divide it in parts. Why? Because when you divide in parts, the eyes have an opportunity to move from one part to another. Look at a thing as a whole. You can do it.

Try it. First look at a thing from one fragment to another. Then suddenly look at this thing as a whole; do not divide it. When you look at a thing as a whole, the eyes have no need to move. In order not to give any opportunity for movement, this has been made a condition: look at an object totally, taken as a whole; secondly, without seeing the material. If the bowl is of wood, do not see the wood: just see the bowl, the form. Do not see the substance.

It may be of gold, it may be of silver. Observe it. Do not look at the material of which it is made. Just look at the form. The first thing is to look at it as a whole. Secondly, look at it as a form, not as a substance. Why? Because substance is the material part, form is the spiritual part, and you are to move from the material to the non-material. It will be helpful.

Try it. You can try it with anyone. Some man or some woman is standing: look and take the man or woman wholly into your look, totally into it. It will be a weird feeling in the beginning because you are not habituated, but it is very beautiful in the end. And then, do not think about whether the body is beautiful or not, white or black, man or woman. Do not think; just look at the form. Forget the substance and just look at the form.

In a few moments become aware. Go on looking at the form as a whole. Do not allow the eyes any movement. Do not start thinking about "the material." What will happen? You will suddenly become aware of your self. Looking at something, you will become aware of your self. Why? Because for the eyes there is no possibility to move outwards. The form has been taken as a whole, so you cannot move to the parts. The material has been dropped; pure form has been taken. Now you cannot think about gold, wood, silver, etc.

Remain with the whole and the form. Suddenly you will become aware of yourself because now the eyes cannot move. And they need movement; that is their nature: so your look will move toward you. It will come back, it will return home, and suddenly you will become aware of your self. This becoming aware of one's self is one of the most ecstatic moments possible. When for the first time you become aware of your self, it has such beauty and such bliss that you cannot compare it with anything else you have known. [3]

Lu-tsu said: When the light is made to move in a circle, all the energies of heaven and earth, of the light and the dark, are crystallized.

Your consciousness is flowing outward – this is a fact, there is nothing to believe in it. When you look at an object, your consciousness flows towards the object.

For example, you are looking at me. Then you forget yourself, you become focused on me. Then your energy flows towards me, then your eyes are arrowed towards me.

Inner Circle

This is extroversion. You see a flower and you are enchanted, and you become focused on the flower. You become oblivious of yourself, you are only attentive to the beauty of the flower.

This we know – every moment it is happening. A beautiful woman passes by and suddenly your energy starts following her. We know this outward flow of light. This is only half of the story. But each time the light flows out, you fall into the background, you become oblivious of yourself.

The light has to flow back so that you are both the subject and the object at the same time, simultaneously, so that you see yourself. Then self-knowledge is released. Ordinarily, we live only in this half way – half-alive, half-dead, that's the situation. And slowly slowly, light goes on flowing outward and never returns. You become more and more empty inside, hollow. You become a black hole.

The Taoist experience is that this energy that you spend in your extroversion can be more and more crystallized rather than spent if you learn the secret science of turning it backwards. It is possible; that is the whole science of all methods of concentration.

Just standing before a mirror some day, try one small experiment. You are looking at the mirror, your own face in the mirror, your own eyes in the mirror. This is extroversion: you are looking into the mirrored face – your own face, of course, but it is an object outside you. Then, for a moment, reverse the whole process. Start feeling that you are being looked at by the reflection in the mirror – not that you are looking at the reflection but the reflection is looking at you – and you will be in a very strange space. Just try it for a few minutes; you will be very alive, and something of immense power will start entering you. You may even become frightened because you have never known it; you have never seen the complete circle of energy.

Although it is not mentioned in Taoist scriptures this seems to me the most simple experiment any-body can do – and very easily. Just standing before the mirror in your bathroom, first look into the reflection: you are looking and the reflection is the object. Then change the whole situation, reverse the process. Start feeling that you are the reflection and the reflection is looking at you. Immediately you will see a change happening, a great energy moving towards you.

In the beginning it may be frightening because you have never done it and you have never known it; it will look crazy. You may feel shaken, a trembling may arise in you, or you may feel disoriented, because your whole orientation up to now has been extroversion. Introversion has to be learned slowly, slowly. But the circle is complete. If you do it for a few days you will be surprised how much more alive you feel the whole day – just a few minutes standing before the mirror and letting the energy come back to you so the circle is complete – and whenever the circle is complete there is a great silence. The incomplete circle creates restlessness, when the circle is complete it creates rest. It makes you centered, and to be centered is to be powerful. The power is yours.

This is just an experiment; you can try it in many ways.

Looking at a rose flower, first look at it for a few moments, a few minutes, and then start the reverse process: the rose flower is looking at you. You will be surprised how much energy the rose flower can give to you. The same can be done with trees and the stars and with people. The best way to do it is with the woman or man you love. Just look into each other's eyes. First begin looking at the other and then start feeling the other returning the energy to you; the gift is coming back. You will feel replenished, you will feel showered, bathed, basked in a new kind of energy. You will come out of it rejuvenated, vitalized. [4]

118

Meditations on Light

I n your heart a flame is burning.
Your body is just a light around the flame. [1]

Do this at least twice a day – the best time is early in the morning, just before you get out of bed. The moment you feel you are alert, awake, do it for twenty minutes. Do it *first* thing in the morning! – don't get out of bed. Do it there, then and there, immediately! – because when you are coming out of sleep you are very very delicate, receptive. When you are coming out of sleep you are very fresh, and the impact will go very deep. When you are just coming out of sleep you are less in the mind than ever. Hence some gaps

Golden Light Meditation

are there through which the method will penetrate into your innermost core. And early in the morning, when you are awakening and the whole earth is awakening, there is a great tide of awakening energy all over the world. Use that tide; don't miss that opportunity.

All ancient religions used to pray early in the morning when the sun rose, because the rising of the sun is the rising of all the energies in existence. In that moment you can simply ride on the rising energy wave; it will be easier. By the evening it will be difficult, energies will be falling back; then you will be fighting against the current. In the morning you will be going with the current.

So the best time to begin is in the early morning, *immediately,* just when you are half-asleep, half-awake. And the process is so simple. It needs no posture, no *yogasana,* no bath is needed, nothing.

You simply lie down, as you are lying down in your bed, on your back. Keep your eyes closed.

When you breathe in, just visualize great light entering from your head into your body, as if a sun has risen just close to your head – golden light pouring into your head. You are just hollow and the golden light is pouring into your head, and going, going, going, deep, deep, and going out through your toes. When you breathe in, do it with this visualization.

And when you breathe out, visualize another thing: darkness entering through your toes, a great dark river entering through your toes, coming up, and going out through the head. Do slow, deep breathing so you can visualize. Go very slowly. And just out of sleep you can have very deep and slow breaths because the body is rested, relaxed.

Let me repeat: breathing in, let golden light come into you through your head, because it is there that the Golden Flower is waiting. That golden light will help. It will cleanse your whole body and will make it absolutely full of creativity. This is male energy.

Then when you exhale, let darkness, the darkest you can conceive, like a dark night, river-like, come from your toes upward – this is feminine energy: it will soothe you, it will make you receptive, it will calm you, it will give you rest – and let it go out of the head. Then inhale again, and golden light enters in.

Do it for twenty minutes early in the morning.

And then the second best time is when you are going back to sleep, in the night.

Lie down on the bed, relax for a few minutes. When you start feeling that now you are wavering between sleep and waking, just in that middle, start the process again, and continue for twenty minutes. If you fall asleep doing it, that is the best, because the impact will remain in the subconscious and will go on working.

After a three-month period you will be surprised: the energy that was constantly gathering at the *muladhar,* at the lowest, the sex center, is no more gathering there. It is going upwards. 2

Shiva said: Waking, sleeping, dreaming, know you as light.

While "waking," moving, eating, working, remember yourself as light, as if in your heart a flame is burning, and your body is nothing but the aura around the flame. Imagine it: in your heart a flame is burning, and your body is nothing but a light aura around the flame; your body is just a light around the flame. Allow it to go deep within your mind and your consciousness. Imbibe it.

Heart of Light

It will take time, but if you go on thinking about it, feeling it, imagining it, within a certain period you will be able to remember it the whole day. While awake, moving on the street, you are a flame moving. No one else will be aware of it in the beginning, but if you continue it, after three months others will also become aware. Only when others become aware can you then be at ease. Don't say anything to anyone. Simply imagine a flame, and your body as just the aura around it – not a physical body, but an electric body, a light body. Go on doing it.

If you persist, within three months, or somewhere nearabout then, others will become aware that something has happened to you. They will feel a subtle light around you. When you come near them, they will feel a different warmth. If you touch them, they will feel a fiery touch. They will become aware that something strange is happening to you. Don't tell anyone. When others become aware, then you can feel at ease, and then you can enter the second step, not before it.

The second step is to take it into

dreaming. Now you can take it into dreaming. It has become a reality. Now it is not an imagination. Through imagination you have uncovered a reality. It is real. Everything consists of light. You are light – unaware of the fact – because every particle of matter is light.

The scientists say it consists of electrons; it is the same thing. Light is the source of all. You are also condensed light: through imagination you are simply uncovering a reality. Imbibe it – and when you have become so filled with it, you can carry it into dreams, not before.

Then, while falling asleep, go on thinking of the flame, go on seeing it, feeling you are the light. Remembering it…remembering… remembering you fall into sleep, and the remembrance continues. In the beginning you will start having some dreams in which you will feel you have a flame within, that you are light. By and by, in the dreams also you will move with the same feeling. And once this feeling enters the dreams, dreams will start disappearing. There will be fewer and fewer dreams and more and more deep sleep.

When in your dreaming, this reality is revealed – that you are light, a flame, a burning flame – all dreams will disappear. Only when dreams disappear can you carry this feeling into sleep, never before. Now you are at the door. When dreams have disappeared and you remember yourself as a flame, you are at the door of sleep. Now you can enter with the feeling. And once you enter sleep with the feeling that you are a flame, you will be aware in it – the sleep will now happen only to your body, not to you.

Yoga and Tantra divide the life of man's mind into three divisions – the life of the mind, remember. They divide mind into three divisions: waking, sleeping, dreaming. These are not the divisions of your consciousness, these are the divisions of your mind, and consciousness is the fourth.

They have not given any name to it in the East; they call it simply the fourth, turiya. The first three have names; these are the clouds. They can be named – a waking cloud, a sleeping cloud, a dreaming cloud. They are all clouds, and the space in which they move – the sky – is unnamed, left simply as the fourth.

This technique is to help you go beyond these three states. If you can be aware that you are a flame, a light, that sleep is not happening to you, you are conscious. You are carrying a conscious effort; now you are crystallized around that flame. The body is asleep, you are not.

This is what Krishna says in the Gita: that yogis never sleep. While others are asleep, they are awake. Not that their bodies never sleep, their bodies sleep – but only bodies. Bodies need rest, consciousness needs no rest; because bodies are mechanisms, consciousness is not a mechanism. Bodies need fuel, they need rest. That's why when they are born, they are young, then they become old, and then they die. Consciousness is never born, never becomes old, never dies. It needs no fuel, it needs no rest. It is pure energy, perpetual eternal energy. If you can carry this image of flame and light through the doors of sleep, you will never sleep again, only the body will rest. And while the body is sleeping, you will know it. Once this happens, you have become the fourth. Now the waking and the dreaming and the sleeping are parts of the mind. They are parts, and you have become the fourth – one who goes through all of them and is none of them. [3]

Shiva said: Kind Devi, enter etheric presence pervading far above and below your form.

This method can be done only if you have done "Touching as a Feather". It can be done separately also, but then it will be very difficult. But if you do the other first, then it is good to do the second and very easy.

Whenever it happens that you feel light, levitating, as if you can fly, suddenly you will become aware that around your body form there

Seeing Etheric Presence

is a bluish light. But that you can see only when you feel that you can levitate, that your body can fly, that it has become light, completely free of any burden, completely free of any gravitation towards the earth.

Whenever you feel this weightlessness, just with closed eyes become aware of the form of your body. Just with closed eyes, feel your toes and their form, and the legs and their form, and then the form of the whole body. If you are sitting in *siddhasana,* just like a Buddha, then feel the form while sitting like a Buddha. Inside just try to feel the form of your body. It will become apparent, it will appear before you, and you will simultaneously become aware that just around the form there is a bluish light.

Do it with closed eyes in the beginning. And when this light goes on spreading and you feel an aura, a bluish aura, all around the form, then sometimes while doing it at night with no light in a dark room, open your eyes and you will see it exactly around your body – a bluish form, just light, blue light, all around your body. If you actually want to see it, not with closed eyes, but with open eyes, do it in a dark room with no light at all.

This bluish form, this bluish light, is the presence of the etheric body. You have many bodies. This technique is concerned with the etheric body, and through the etheric body you can enter into the highest ecstasy. There are seven bodies, and every body can be used to enter into the divine; every body is just a door.

This technique uses the etheric body, and the etheric body is the easiest to realize. The deeper the body, the more difficult; but the etheric body is just near you, just near the physical. It is just near. The second form is of the etheric – just around you, just around your body. It penetrates your body and it is also around your body just like a hazy light, a blue light, hanging all around like a loose robe.

Whenever someone loves you, whenever someone touches you with deep love, he touches your etheric body. That's why you feel it as such a soothing thing. It has even been photographed. Two lovers in deep love, making love: if their intercourse can continue beyond a certain limit, beyond forty minutes, and there is no ejaculation, around both the bodies, deep in love, a blue light appears. It has even been photographed.

First you will have to become aware of the form that surrounds your physical form, and when you have become aware, then help it to grow, help it to increase and expand. What can you do?

Just sitting silently, looking at it; not doing anything, just looking at the bluish form around you; not doing anything, just looking at it – you will feel it is increasing, spreading, becoming bigger and bigger. Because when you are not doing anything, the whole energy goes to the etheric. Remember this. When you are doing anything, the energy is taken out of the etheric.

When you are not doing anything, your energy is not moving out. It goes to the etheric. It is accumulated there. Your etheric body becomes an electric reservoir. And the more it grows, the more you become silent. The more you become silent, the more it grows. And once you know how to give energy to the etheric body and how not to waste it unnecessarily, you have come to realize; you have come to know about a secret key. [4]

Shiva said: Feel the cosmos as a translucent ever-living presence.

This technique is based on inner sensitivity. First grow in sensitivity. Just close your doors, make the room dark, and light a small candle. Sit near the candle with a very loving attitude – rather, with a prayerful attitude. Just pray to the candle, "Reveal yourself to me." Take a bath, throw cold water on your eyes, then sit in a very prayerful mood before the candle. Look at it and forget

Translucent Presence

everything else. Just look at the small candle – the flame and the candle. Go on looking at it. After five minutes you will feel that many things are changing in the candle. They are not changing in the candle – remember. Your eyes are changing.

With a loving attitude, with the whole world closed out, with total concentration, with a feeling heart, just go on looking at the candle and the flame. Then you will discover new colors around the flame, new shades which you were never aware were there. They are there: the whole rainbow is there. Wherever light is, the rainbow is there because light is all color. You need a subtle sensitivity. Just feel it and go on looking at it. Even if tears start flowing, go on looking at it.

Those tears will help your eyes to be more fresh.

Sometimes you may feel that the flame, the candle, has become mysterious. It is not the ordinary candle you brought with you. It has taken on a new glamour. A subtle divineness has come into it. Go on doing this. You can also do this with many other things. Sensitivity must grow. Your every sense must become more alive. Then you can experiment with this technique. "Feel the cosmos as a translucent ever-living presence." Everywhere light is – in many, many shapes, forms, light is happening everywhere. Look at it! And light *is* everywhere, because the whole phenomenon is based on the foundation of light. Look at a leaf or a flower or a rock, and sooner or later you will feel rays coming out of it. Just wait patiently. Don't be in a hurry because nothing is revealed when you are in a hurry. In a hurry you are dull.

Wait silently with anything, and you will discover a new phenomenon which was always there, but to which you were not alert – not aware of it.

"Feel the cosmos as a translucent ever-living presence," and your mind will become completely silent as you feel the presence of the ever-living existence. You will be just a part in it, just a note in the great symphony. No burden, no tension: the drop has fallen into the ocean. But great imagination will be needed in the beginning, and if you are also trying other sensitivity

training it will be helpful.

You can try many ways. Just take someone's hand into your hand. Close your eyes and feel the life in the other. Feel it, and allow it to move toward you. Feel your own life and allow it to move toward the other. Sit near a tree and touch the bark of the tree. Close your eyes and feel the life arising in the tree, and you change immediately.

If this method is done for three months, you will be living in a different world because now you will be different. [5]

Meditations on Darkness

Just like the seed that starts its life in the darkness of the soil, or the child that starts its life in the darkness of the womb, all beginnings are in the dark, because darkness is one of the most essential things for anything to begin.

The beginning is mysterious, hence darkness is needed. And the beginning is so delicate, that's also why darkness is needed. The beginning is also very intimate, that's also why darkness is needed. Darkness has depth and a tremendous power to nourish. The day tires you; the night rejuvenates.

The morning will come, the day will follow, but if you are afraid of the darkness then the day will never come. If one wants to skip darkness then the day is impossible. One has to go through the dark night of the soul to reach to the dawn. Death is first, then life is.

In the ordinary sequence of things birth is first, then is life, but in the inner world, in the inner journey, it is just the opposite: death is first, then is life. [1]

*S*hiva said: In rain during a black night, enter that blackness as the form of forms.

How can you enter blackness? Three things.

Step 1:

Stare into blackness. Difficult. It is easy to stare at a flame, at any source of light, because it is there as an object, pointed; you can direct your attention to it. Darkness is not an object; it is everywhere,

Inner Darkness

it is all around. You cannot see it as an object. Stare into the vacuum. All around it is there; you just look into it. Feel at ease and look into it. It will start entering your eyes. And when the darkness enters your eyes, you are entering into it.

Remain with open eyes when doing this technique in the dark night. Don't close your eyes, because with closed eyes you have a different darkness that is your own,

mental; it is not real. Really, it is a negative part; it is not positive darkness.

Here is light: you close your eyes and you can have a darkness, but that darkness is simply the negative of the light. Just as when you look at the window and then you close your eyes, you have a negative figure of the window. All our experience is of light, so when we close our eyes we have a negative experience of light which we call

darkness. It is not real, it won't do.

Open your eyes, remain with open eyes in darkness, and you will have a different darkness – the positive darkness that is there. Stare into it. Go on staring into darkness. Your tears will start, your eyes will get sore, they will hurt. Don't get worried, just go on. And the moment the darkness, the real darkness which is there, enters in your eyes, it will give you a

131

very deep soothing feeling. When real darkness enters in you, you will be filled by it.

And this entering of darkness will empty you of all negative darkness. This is a very deep phenomenon. The darkness that you have within is a negative thing; it is against the light. It is not the absence of light; it is against the light. It is not the darkness that Shiva is speaking of as the form of all forms – the real darkness that's there.

We are so afraid of it that we have created many sources of light just as protection, and we live in a lighted world. Then we close our eyes and the lighted world reflects negatively inside. We have lost contact with the real darkness that is there – the darkness of the Essenes, or the darkness of Shiva. We have no contact with it. We have become so much afraid of it that we have turned ourselves completely away. We are standing with our backs to it.

So this will be difficult, but if you can do it, it is miraculous, it is magical. You will have a different being altogether. When darkness enters you, you enter into it. It is always reciprocal, mutual. You cannot enter into any cosmic phenomenon without the cosmic phenomenon entering into you. You cannot rape it, you cannot force any entry. If you are available, open, vulnerable,

and if you give way for any cosmic realm to enter in you, then only will you enter into it. It is always mutual. You cannot force it; you can only allow it.

It is difficult to find real darkness in cities now; difficult in our houses to find real darkness. With the unreal light we have made everything unreal. Even our darkness is polluted, it is not pure. So it is good to move to some remote place only to feel darkness. Just go to a very remote village where there is no electricity, or move to a mountain peak. Just be there for one week to experience pure darkness.

You will come back a different man, because in those seven days of absolute darkness, all the fears, all the primitive fears, will come up. You will have to face monsters, you will have to face your own unconscious. The whole humanity will…it will be as if you are passing through the whole passage that has passed, and deep from your unconscious many things will arise. They will look real. You may get afraid, scared, because they will be so real – and they are just your mental creations.

You have to come to terms with your unconscious. And this meditation on darkness will absorb all your madness completely. Try it. Even in your home you can try it.

Every night, for one hour remain with darkness. Don't do anything, just stare into darkness. You will have a melting feeling, and you will feel that something is entering you and you are entering into something.

Staying, living with darkness for three months, for one hour a day, you will lose all feeling of individuality, of separation. Then you will not be an island; you will become the ocean. You will be one with darkness. And darkness is so oceanic: nothing is so vast, nothing is so eternal. And nothing is so near you, and of nothing are you so scared and afraid. It is just by the corner, always waiting.

Step 2:

Lie down and feel as if you are near your mother. The darkness is the mother, the mother of all. Think: when there was nothing, what was there? You cannot think of anything other than darkness. If everything disappears, what will still be there? Darkness will be there.

Darkness is the mother, the womb, so lie down and feel that you are lying in the womb of your mother. And it will become real, it will become warm, and sooner or later you will start feeling that the darkness, the womb, is enveloping you from everywhere, you are in it.

Step 3:

Moving, going to work, talking, eating, doing whatsoever, carry a patch of darkness within you. The darkness that has entered in you, just carry it. As we were discussing about the method of carrying a flame, carry darkness. As I said to you, if you carry a flame and feel you are light, your body will start radiating a certain strange light and those who are sensitive will start feeling it; the same will happen with darkness.

If you carry darkness within you, your whole body will become so relaxed and calm, so cool, that it will be felt. And as when you carry light within you some people will become attracted to you, when you carry darkness within you, some people will simply escape from you. They will become afraid and scared. They will not be able to bear so silent a being; it will become unbearable to them.

Carrying darkness within for the whole day will help you very much, because then when you contemplate and meditate on darkness in the night, the inner darkness that you have carried the whole day will help you to meet – the inner will come to meet the outer.

And just by remembering that you are carrying darkness – you are filled with darkness, every pore of the body, every cell of the body is filled with darkness – you will feel so relaxed. Try it. You will feel so relaxed. Everything in you will be slowed down. You will not be able to run, you will walk, and that walk will be slowed down also. You will walk slowly, just as a pregnant woman walks. You will walk slowly, very carefully. You are carrying something.

And quite the opposite will happen when you are carrying a flame: your walk will become faster; rather, you would like to run. There will be more movement, you will become more active. Carrying darkness you will be relaxed. Others will start feeling that you are lazy.

In the days when I was at the university, I was doing this experiment for two years. I became so lazy that even to get out of bed in the morning was difficult. My professors became very much disturbed about it, and they thought something had gone wrong with me – either I was ill, or I had become absolutely indifferent. One professor who loved me very much, the head of my department, became so worried that on my examination days he would come to fetch me from the hostel in the morning just to lead me to the examination hall so that I would be there on time. Every day he would see that I had entered the hall, and only then would he feel okay and go home.

Try it. It is one of the most beautiful experiences in life to carry darkness in your womb, to become dark. Walking, eating, sitting, doing whatsoever, remember, the darkness is filled in you; you are filled with it. And then see how things change. You cannot get excited, you cannot be very active, you cannot be tense. Your sleep will become so deep that dreams will disappear and the whole day you will move as if intoxicated. [2]

Shiva said: When a moonless rainy night is not present, close eyes and find blackness before you. Opening eyes, see blackness. So faults disappear forever.

This is a little bit more difficult. In the previous meditation, you carry the real darkness within. In this one you carry the false out – go on carrying it. Close your eyes, feel darkness; open your eyes, and with open eyes see the darkness out. This is how you throw the inner false darkness out – go on throwing

Carry Out Inner Darkness

it. It will take at least three to six weeks, and then one day suddenly you will be able to carry the inner darkness out. The day you can carry the inner darkness out, you have come upon the real inner darkness. The real can be carried; the false cannot be carried.

And it is a very magical experience. If you can carry the inner darkness out, even in a lighted room you can carry it out, and a patch of darkness spreads before you. The experience is very weird, because the room is lighted. Or even in sunlight...if you have come to the inner darkness you can bring it out. Then a patch of darkness comes before your eyes. You can go on spreading it.

Once you know that it can happen, you can have darkness, dark as the darkest night, in the full sunny day. The sun is there, but you can spread the darkness. The darkness is always there; even while the sun is there the darkness is there. You cannot see it; it is covered by the sunlight. Once you know how to uncover it, you can uncover it.

That's the method. First feel it inside; feel it deeply so you can perceive it out. Then open the eyes suddenly and feel it out. It will take time.

And if you can bring the inner darkness outside, faults disappear forever, because if the inner darkness is felt, you have become so cool, so silent, so unexcitable, that faults cannot remain with you.

Remember this: faults can exist only if you are prone to be excited, if you tend to be excited. They don't exist in themselves; they exist in your capacity to get excited. Someone insults you, and you have no darkness within to absorb the insult: you become inflamed, you get angry, you get fiery, and then everything is possible. You can be violent, you can kill, you can do what only a madman can do. Anything is possible – you are now mad. Someone praises you: you again go mad to the other extreme.

All around you there are situations, and you are not capable of absorbing. Insult a buddha: he can absorb it, he can simply swallow it, digest it. Who digests that insult? An inner pool of darkness, silence. You throw anything poisoned; it is absorbed. No reaction comes out of it. Try this, and when someone insults you, just remember that you are filled with darkness, and suddenly you will feel there is no reaction. You pass through a street; you see a beautiful woman or a man – you get excited. Feel that you are filled with darkness; suddenly the passion will disappear. You try it. This is absolutely experimental, there is no need to believe it.

When you feel that you are filled with passion or desire or sex, simply remember the inner darkness. For a single moment close your eyes and feel darkness and see – the passion has disappeared, the desire is no more there. The inner darkness has absorbed it. You have become an infinite vacuum into which anything can fall and it will not return. You are now like an abyss. [3]

Moving Energy Upwards

The first thing is to feel one's energy. The first thing is not the question, "How to use it?" The first thing is: how to feel it and how to feel it intensely, passionately, totally. And the beauty is that once you have felt your energy, out of that very feeling the insight arises: how to use it.

The energy starts directing you. It is not that *you* direct the energy: on the contrary, the energy starts moving on its own accord and you simply follow it. Then there is spontaneity and then there is freedom. [1]

Shiva said: Consider your essence as light rays rising from center to center up the vertebrae, and so rises 'living-ness' in you.

Many yoga methods are based on this. First understand what it is, then the application. The verte-brae, the spine is the base of both your body and mind. Your mind, your head, is the end part of your spine. The whole body is rooted in the spine. If the spine is young, you are young. If the spine is old, you are old. If you can keep your

The Ascent of Life Energy 1

spine young, it is difficult to be-come old. Everything depends on your spine. If your spine is alive, you will have a very brilliant mind. If the spine is dull and dead, you will have a very dull mind. The whole of yoga tries in many ways to make your spine alive, brilliant, filled with light, young and fresh. The spine has two ends. The be-ginning is the sex center and the

end is *sahasrar* (the seventh center at the top of the head). The begin-ning of the spine is attached to the earth, and sex is the most earthly thing in you. From the beginning center in your spine you are in con-tact with nature, with what has been called *prakrati* – the earth, the material. From the last center, or the second pole, *sahasrar,* in the head, you are in contact with the

divine. These are the two poles of your existence: first is sex and the other is the *sahasrar*. There is no word for 'sahasrar' in English. These are the two poles – either your life will be sex-oriented or sahasrar-oriented. Either your ener-gy will be flowing down from the sex center back to the earth, or your energy will be released from the sa-hasrar into the cosmos. From the sahasrar you flow into the Brahman, into the absolute existence. From sex you flow down into the relative existence. These are the two flows, the two possibilities. Unless you start flowing upward, your misery will never end. You may have glimpses of happiness, but only glimpses – and very illusory ones.

When the energy starts moving upward, you will have more and more real glimpses. And once it reaches the sahasrar and is released from there, you will have absolute bliss with you – that is nirvana. Then there is no glimpse: you become the bliss itself. So the whole thing for yoga and tantra is how to move energy upward through the vertebrae, through the spinal column, how to help it move against gravity. Sex is very easy because it follows gravitation. The earth is pulling everything down, back; your sex energy is pulled by the earth. You may not have heard it, but astronauts have felt this – the moment they move beyond the earth's gravity, they don't feel much sexuality. As the body loses weight, sexuality dissolves, disappears.

The earth is pulling your life energy down and this is natural, because the life energy comes from the earth. You eat food and you are creating life energy within you; it comes from the earth, and the earth

is pulling it back. Everything goes to its source. And if it continues to move in this way, life energy going back again and again, you are moving in a circle; you will go on moving for lives and lives. You can go on moving this way infinitely unless you take a jump just like the astronauts. Like the astronauts you have to take a jump and move beyond the circle. Then the pattern of earth's gravitation is broken. It can be broken!

The techniques for how it can be broken are here – for how the energy can move vertically and rise up within you, reaching new centers; for how new energies can be revealed within you, making you a new person with every move. And the moment the energy is released from your sahasrar, the opposite pole of sex, you are no more man. Then you don't belong to this earth; you have become divine. That is what is meant when we say Krishna is God or Buddha is God. Their bodies are just like yours. Their bodies will have to fall ill and they will have to die. Everything happens in their bodies as it happens to you. Only one thing is *not* happening in their bodies which *is* happening to you – the energy has broken the gravitation pattern.

That you cannot see; it is not visible to your eyes. But sometimes when

you are sitting by the side of a buddha, you can feel this. Suddenly you feel an upsurge of energy within you, and your energy starts moving upward. Only then do you know that something has happened. Just by being in contact with a buddha your energy begins to move upward toward the sahasrar. A buddha is so powerful that even the earth is less powerful, it cannot pull your energy downwards. Those who have felt this around a Jesus, a Buddha, a Krishna, have called them God. They have a different source of energy which is stronger than the earth.

How can the pattern be broken? This technique is very useful for breaking the pattern. First understand something basic. One, if you have observed at all, you must have observed that your sex energy moves with imagination. Just through imagination your sex center starts functioning. Really, without imagination it cannot function. That is why if you are in love with someone it functions better: because with love imagination enters. If you are not in love it is very difficult. It will not function.

Since the sex center functions through imagination, you can get erections and ejaculations even in dreams – they are real; dreams are just imagination. It has been observed that every man, if physically fit, will have at least ten erections in the night. With every movement of the mind, with only a slight thought of sex, an erection will come. Your mind has many energies, many faculties, and one is will. But you cannot will sex. For sex, will is impotent. If you try to love someone, you will feel you have gone impotent. So never try.

Will never functions with sex; only imagination will function. Imagine, and the center will start to function. Why am I emphasizing this fact? – because if imagination helps the energy to move, then you can move it upward or downward just by imagination. You cannot move your blood by imagination; you cannot do anything else in the body by imagination. But sex energy can be moved by imagination, you can change its direction.

This sutra says, "Consider your essence as light rays..." Think of yourself, your being, as light rays ..."from center to center up the vertebrae," up your spine, "and so rises 'livingness' in you."

Yoga has divided your spine into seven centers. The first is the sex center and the last is sahasrar, and between these two there are five centers. Some systems divide into nine, some into three, some into four: division is not very meaningful. You can make your own division. Just five centers are enough to work with: the first is the sex center, the second is just behind the navel, the third is just behind the heart, the fourth is behind your two eyebrows, just in between, in the middle of the forehead. And the fifth, sahasrar, is just on the peak of your head. These five will do.

This sutra says, "Consider yourself": which means imagine yourself – close your eyes and imagine yourself just as if you are light. This is not just imagination. In the beginning it is, but it is a reality also because everything consists of light. Science says now that everything consists of light; science says that everything consists of electricity. Tantra has always said that everything consists of light particles – and you also. That is why the Koran says that God is light. You are light!

Imagine first that you are just light rays; then move your imagination to the sex center. Concentrate your attention there and feel that light rays are rising upward from the sex center, as if the sex center has become a source of light and light rays are moving in an upsurge – upward toward the navel center.

Division is needed because it will be difficult for you to connect your sex center with the sahasrar. So smaller divisions will be of help. If you can connect, no divisions are needed. You can just drop all divisions from your sex center onwards, and the energy, the life force will rise up as light toward the sahasrar. But divisions will be more helpful because your mind can conceive of smaller fragments more easily.

So just feel that the energy, the light rays, are rising up from your sex center to your navel like a river of light. Immediately you will feel a warmth rising in you. Soon your navel will become hot. You can feel the hotness; even others can feel that hotness. Through your imagination the sex energy will have started to rise. When you feel that now the second center at the navel has become a source of light, that the rays are coming and being collected there, then start to move to the heart center. As the light reaches the heart center, as the rays are coming, your heartbeat will be changed. Your breathing will become deeper, and a warmth will come to your heart. Go on upwards.

And as you feel warmth, just side by side you will feel a 'livingness', a new life coming to you, an inward light rising up. Sex energy has two parts: one is physical and one is psychic. In your body everything has two parts. Just like your body and mind, everything within you has two parts – one material and the other spiritual. Sex energy has two parts. The material part is semen. It cannot rise upwards; there is no passage for it. Because of this, many physiologists of the West say that tantra and yoga methods are nonsense and they deny them completely. How can sex energy rise up? There is no passage and sex energy cannot rise. They are right and still wrong. Semen, the material part, cannot rise, but that is not the whole of it – it is only the body of sex energy; it is not the sex energy. The sex energy is the psychic part of it, and the psychic part can rise. And for that psychic part, the spinal passage is used – the spinal passage and its centers. But that has to be felt and your feelings have gone dead.

I remember somewhere that a certain psychotherapist wrote about a patient, a woman. He was telling her to feel something but the psychotherapist felt that whatever she did she was not feeling, but thinking about feeling, and that is a different thing. So the therapist put his hand on the woman's hand and pressed it, telling her to close her eyes and relate what she felt. She said immediately, "I feel your hand."

But the therapist said, "No, this is not your feeling. This is just your thinking, your inference. I have put my hand in your hand; you say you are feeling my hand. But you are not. This is inference. What do you feel?" So she said, "I feel your fingers."

The therapist again said, "No, this is not feeling. Don't infer anything. Just close your eyes and move to the place where my hand is; then tell me what you feel." Then she said, "Oh! I was missing the whole thing. I feel pressure and warmth."

When a hand touches you, a hand is not felt. Pressure and warmth are felt. The hand is just inference, it is intellect, not feeling. Warmth and pressure, that is feeling. Now she was feeling. We have lost feeling completely. You will have to develop feeling. Only then can you do such techniques. Otherwise, they will not function. You will just intellectualize. You will just think that you are feeling, and nothing will happen. That is why people come to me and say, "You tell us this technique is so significant, but nothing happens." They have tried, but they are missing a dimension – the feeling dimension. So first you will have to develop that, and there are some methods which you can try.

The feeling center must start functioning; only then will these techniques be of any help. Otherwise you will go on thinking that energy is rising, but there will be no feeling. And if there is no feeling, imagination is impotent, futile. Only a feeling imagination will give you a result. You can do many other things and there is no need to make a specific effort to do them. When you go to sleep just feel your bed, feel the pillow – the coldness. Just turn on to it: play with the pillow.

Close your eyes and listen to the noise of the air conditioner, or of the traffic or of the clock or anything. Just listen. Don't label, don't say anything. Don't use the mind. Just live in the sensation. In the morning, in the first moment of waking, when you feel that now sleep has gone, don't start thinking. For a few moments you can again be a child – innocent, fresh. Don't start thinking. Don't think about what you are going to do and when you are starting for the office and what train you are going to catch. Don't start thinking. You will have enough time for all that nonsense. Just wait.

For a few moments just listen to the noises. A bird is singing or the wind is passing through the trees or a child is crying or the milkman has come and is making sounds or the milk is being poured. With anything that happens, feel it. Be sensitive to it, open to it. Allow it to happen to you and your sensitivity will grow.

Create sensitivity and feeling. Then it will be easy for you to do these techniques, and then you will feel 'livingness' arising in you. Don't leave this energy anywhere. Allow it to come to the sahasrar. Remember this: whenever you do this experiment, don't leave it in the middle. You have to complete it. Take care that no one disturbs you. If you leave this energy somewhere in the middle, it can be harmful. It has to be released. So bring it to the head and feel as if your head has become an opening.

In India we have pictured the sahasrar as a lotus – as a thousand-petaled lotus. 'Sahasrar' means thousand-petaled, an opening of a thousand petals. Just conceive of the lotus with a thousand petals, opened, and from every petal this light energy is moving into the cosmos. Again, this is a love act – not with nature now, but with the ultimate. Again, it is an orgasm.

There are two types of orgasms: one is sexual and the other spiritual. The sexual comes from the lowest center and the spiritual from the highest center. From the highest you meet the highest and from the lowest you meet the lowest. Even while actually in the sex act, you can do this exercise: both the partners can do this. Move the energy upwards, and then the sex act becomes tantra *sadhana:* it becomes meditation.

But don't leave the energy somewhere in the body at some center. Someone may come and you will have some business, or some phone call will come and you will have to stop. So do it at such a time that no one will disturb you, and don't leave the energy in any center. Otherwise that center where you leave the energy will become a wound, and you may create many mental illnesses. So be aware; otherwise don't do this. This method needs absolute privacy and no disturbance, and it must be done completely. The energy must come to the head, and it should be released from there.

You will have various experiences. When you will feel that the rays are starting to come up from the sex center, there will be erections or sensations at the sex center. Many, many people come to me very afraid and scared. They say that whenever they start meditation, when they start to move deep, there is an erection. They wonder, "What is this?" They are afraid because they think that in meditation sex should not be there. But you don't know life's functioning. It is a good sign. It shows that energy is now there alive. Now it needs movement. So don't become scared and don't think that something is wrong. It is a good sign.

When you start meditation the sex center will become more sensitive, alive, excited, and in the beginning the excitement will be just the same as any sexual excitement – but only in the beginning. As your meditation becomes deeper, you will feel energy flowing up. As the energy flows, the sex center becomes silent, less excited.

When the energy really moves to the sahasrar, there will be no sensation at the sex center. It will be totally still and silent. It will have become completely cool, and the warmth will have come to the head. And this is physical. When the sex center is excited, it becomes hot. You can feel that hotness; it is physical. When the energy moves, the sex center will become cooler and cooler and cooler, and the hotness will come to the head. You will feel dizzy.

When the energy comes to the head, you will feel dizzy. Sometimes you may even feel nausea because for the first time energy has come to the head and your head is not acquainted with it. It has to become tuned. So don't become afraid.

Sometimes you may become unconscious immediately, but don't be afraid. This happens. If so much energy moves suddenly and explodes in the head, you may become unconscious. But that unconsciousness cannot remain for more than one hour. Within one hour the energy automatically falls back or is released. I say one hour, but in fact it is exactly 48 minutes.

It cannot be more that that. It never has been in thousands of years of experiments, so don't be afraid. If you do become unconscious, it is okay. After that unconsciousness you will feel so fresh that it is as if you have been in sleep for the first time, in the deepest sleep.

Yoga calls it by a special name: 'yoga tandra' – yogic sleep. It is very deep: you move to your deepest center. But don't be afraid. And if your head becomes hot, it is a good sign. Release the energy. Feel as if your head is opening like a lotus flower, as if energy is being released into the cosmos. As the energy is released, you will feel a coldness coming to you. You have never felt the coldness that comes after this hotness. But do the technique completely; never do it incompletely. [2]

*S*hiva said: Or in the spaces between, feel this as lightning.

This is a very similar method with a slight difference: "Or in the spaces between, feel this as lightning." Between one center and another, as the rays are coming, you can feel it like lightning – just a jump of light. For some people the second will be more suitable and for others the first. This is why there is a modification. There are people who cannot imagine things gradually and there are people who

The Ascent of Life Energy 2

cannot imagine in jumps. If you can think and imagine gradually, then the first method is good. But if you try the first method and you suddenly feel that from one center the rays jump directly to the second, then don't do the first method. The second is better for you. "Feel this as lightning" – like a spark of light jumping from one center to the next. And the second is more

real because light really jumps. There is no gradual step-by-step growth. Light is a jump.

For women the first technique will be easier and for men the second. The feminine mind can conceive of gradualness more easily and the male jumps more easily. The male mind is 'jumpy': it jumps from one thing to another. There is a subtle uneasiness in the male mind. The

female mind has a gradual process. It is not jumpy. That is why female and male logic are very different. A man goes on jumping from one thing to another, and for women this in inconceivable. For them there must be growth – gradual growth. But choose. Try these, and choose whichever you feel is good for you.

Two or three things more about

this method. With lightning you may feel such hotness that it may seem unbearable. If you feel that, don't try it. Lightning can give you much heat. If you feel this, that it is unbearable, then don't try this. Then with the first method, if you are at ease, then it is good. Otherwise – with uneasiness – don't try it. Sometimes the explosion can be so great that you may become afraid of it, and once afraid you will never be able to do it again. Then fear enters.

So one has to be aware always not to become afraid of anything. If you feel that fear will come and it is too much for you, don't try it. Then the first method with light rays is best. If you feel that even with light rays too much hotness is coming to you, and it depends because people differ, then conceive of the rays as cool, imagine them as cool. Then instead of feeling warmth you will feel a coldness with everything. That too will be effective. So you can decide: try and decide. Remember, with this technique, and with others also, if you feel very uneasy or anything unbearable, don't do it. There are other methods, and this one may not be for you. With unnecessary disturbance inside, you will create more problems than you will solve. [3]

Listening to the Soundless Sound

T he meditations concerned with ear energy are feminine meditations, passive – you have just to listen, not to do anything. Listening to the birds, the wind passing through the pine trees, or to some music, or to the noise of the traffic – just listening, doing nothing – great silence comes in, and great peace starts falling and showering on you. It is easier through the ear than through the eye. It is easier through the ear because the ear is passive, non-aggressive. It cannot do anything to existence, it can only let it happen. The ear is a door: it allows. [1]

Nadabrahma is an old Tibetan technique which was originally done in the early hours of the morning. It can be done at any time of the day, alone or with others, but have an empty stomach and remain inactive for at least 15 minutes afterwards. For music to support the meditation, see back page.

First Stage: 30 minutes

Sit in a relaxed position with eyes closed and lips together. Start humming, loudly enough to be heard by others and create a

Nadabrahma Meditation

vibration throughout your body. You can visualize a hollow tube or an empty vessel, filled only with the vibrations of the humming. A point will come when the humming continues by itself and you become the listener. There is no special breathing and you can alter the pitch or move your body smoothly and slowly if you feel it.

Second Stage: 15 minutes

The second stage is divided into two 7 1/2 minute sections. For the first half, move the hands, palms up, in an outward circular motion. Starting at the navel, both hands move forwards and then divide to make two large circles mirroring each other left and right. The

movement should be so slow that at times there will appear to be no movement at all. Feel that you are giving energy outwards to the universe.

After 7 1/2 minutes turn the hands, palms down, and start moving them in the opposite direction. Now the hands will come together towards the navel and divide outwards to the sides of the body. Feel that you are taking energy in. As in the first stage, don't inhibit any soft, slow movements of the rest of your body.

Third Stage: 15 minutes

Sit or lie absolutely quiet and still. [2]

Nadabrahma
for couples

*T*he Master has given a beautiful variation of this technique for couples.
Partners sit facing each other, covered by a bedsheet and holding each other's crossed hands. It is best to wear no other clothing. Light the room only by four small candles and burn a particular incense, kept only for this meditation.
Close your eyes and hum together for thirty minutes. After a short while the energies will be felt to meet, merge and unite. [3]

Shiva said: Intone a sound as AUM slowly. As sound enters soundfulness, so do you.

"Intone a sound as AUM slowly": for example, take AUM. This is one of the basic sounds. A-U-M: these three sounds are combined in it. A-U-M are three basic sounds. *All* sounds are made of them or derived from them; all sounds are combinations of these three sounds. So these three are basic. They are as basic as the claim of physics that the electron, neutron

Aum

and proton are basic. This has to be deeply understood.

The intoning of a sound is a very subtle science. First you have to intone it loudly, outwardly. Then others can hear it, and it is good to start loudly. Why? Because you can also hear it clearly when you intone it loudly: because whatsoever you say, it is to others – and this has become a habit.

Whenever you are talking you are talking to others, and you hear yourself talk only when you are talking to others. So start from the natural habit.

Intone the sound 'Aum', then by and by, feel attunement with the sound. When you intone the sound Aum, be filled with it. Forget everything else. Become the Aum, become the sound. And it is very

easy to become the sound because sound can vibrate through your body, through your mind, through your whole nervous system. Feel the reverberation of Aum. Intone it and feel it as if your whole body is being filled with it, every cell is vibrating with it.

Intoning is also "in-tuning." Tune yourself with the sound, become the sound. And then, as you feel a deep harmony between you and the sound and you develop a deep affection for it (and the sound is so beautiful and so musical – Aum), then the more you intone it the more you will feel yourself filled with a subtle sweetness. There are sounds which are bitter, there are sounds which are very hard. Aum is a very sweet sound, the purest. Intone it and be filled with it.

And when you begin to feel harmonious with it, you can drop intoning loudly. Then close your lips and intone it inwardly, but inwardly also first try loudly. Intone inwardly, but loudly so that the sound spreads all over your body, touches every part, every cell of your body. You will feel vitalized by it, you will feel rejuvenated, you will feel a new life entering you because your body is a musical instrument. It needs harmony, and when the harmony is disturbed you are disturbed.

That is why, when you hear music, you feel good. Why do you feel good? What is music but just some harmonious sounds! Why do you feel such a well-being when there is music around you? And when there is chaos, noise, why do you feel so disturbed? You yourself are deeply musical. You are an instrument, and that instrument re-echoes things.

Intone 'Aum' inside, and you will feel that your whole body dances with it. You will feel that your whole body is undergoing a cleansing bath; every pore is being cleansed. But as you feel it more intensely and as it penetrates you more, go on becoming more and more slow because the slower the sound, the deeper it can go. It is just like homeopathy. The smaller the dose, the deeper it penetrates – because if you want to go deeper, you have to go more subtly, more subtly, more subtly.

Crude, coarse sounds cannot enter your heart. They can enter your ears, but they cannot enter your heart. The passage is very narrow and the heart is so delicate, that only very slow, very rhythmic, very atomic sounds are allowed to enter it. And unless a sound enters your heart, the mantra is not complete. The mantra is complete only when the sound enters your heart – the deepest, most central core of your being. Then go on being more slow, more slow, more slow.

And there are also other reasons for making these sounds slower and more subtle: the more subtle a sound is, the more intense an awareness you will need to feel it inside. The more coarse the sound, the less need there is of any awareness. The sound is enough to hit you; you will become aware of it. But then it is violent.

If a sound is musical, harmonious, subtle, then you will have to listen to it inside and you will have to be very alert to listen to it. If you are not alert, you will go to sleep and miss the whole point. That is the problem with mantra, with any chanting, with any use of sound: it can create sleep. It is a subtle tranquilizer. If you continuously repeat any sound without being alert about it, you will fall asleep because then the repetition becomes mechanical. 'Aum-Aum-Aum' becomes mechanical, and then repetition creates boredom.

So two things have to be done: sound has to be slowed down and you have to become more alert. The more sound becomes subtle, the more alert you are. To make you more alert the sound has to be made more subtle, and a point comes when sound enters soundlessness, or soundfulness, and you enter total awareness. When the sound enters soundlessness or soundfulness, by that time your alertness must have touched the peak. When the sound reaches the valley, when it goes to the downmost, deepest center in the valley, your alertness has gone to the very peak, to the Everest. And there, sound dissolves into soundfulness or soundlessness, and you dissolve into total awareness. [4]

Every night before you go to sleep, you can do a small technique that will help tremendously. Put the lights out, sit in your bed ready to sleep, but sit for fifteen minutes. Close your eyes and then start any monotonous nonsense sound, for example: la, la, la – and wait for the mind to supply new sounds. The only thing to be remembered is that those sounds or words should not be of any language that you know. If you know English, German, and Italian, then they should not be of Italian, German, or English. Any other language that you

Devavani

don't know is allowed – Tibetan, Chinese, Japanese. But if you know Japanese then it is not allowed, then Italian is wonderful. Speak any language that you don't know. You will be in a difficulty for a few seconds only for the first day, because how do you speak a language you don't know? It can be spoken, and once it starts, any sounds, nonsense words, just to put the conscious off and allow the unconscious to speak ....

When the unconscious speaks, the unconscious knows no language. It is a very, very old method. It comes from the Old Testament. It was called in those days *glossolalia,* and a few churches in America still use it. They call it 'talking in tongues'. And it is a wonderful method, one of the most deep and penetrating into the unconscious. You start with 'la, la, la,' and then you can go on with anything that comes. Just for the first day you

will feel it a little difficult. Once it comes, you know the knack of it. Then for fifteen minutes, use the language that is coming to you, and use it as a language; in fact you are talking in it. This fifteen minutes will relax the conscious mind so deeply and then you just simply lie down and go to sleep. Your sleep will become deeper. Within weeks you will feel a depth in your sleep, and in the morning you will feel completely fresh. [5]

Devavani is the Divine Voice which moves and speaks through the meditator, who becomes an empty vessel, a channel. This meditation is a Latihan of the tongue.

It relaxes the conscious mind so deeply that, when done last thing at night, it is sure to be followed by a profound sleep.

There are four stages of 15 minutes each.

Keep your eyes closed throughout.

Instructions for Devavani Meditation

First stage: 15 minutes
Sit quietly, preferably with gentle music playing.

Second stage: 15 minutes
Start making nonsense sounds, for example "la...la...la," and continue until unfamiliar word-like sounds arise. These sounds need to come from the unfamiliar part of the brain used as a child, before words were learned. Allow a gentle conversational intonation; do not cry or shout, laugh or scream.

Third stage: 15 minutes
Stand up and continue to speak, allowing your body to move softly in harmony with the sounds. If your body is relaxed the subtle energies will create a Latihan outside your control.

Fourth stage: 15 minutes
Lie down, be silent and still. [6]

154

Shiva said: While listening to stringed instruments, hear their composite central sound; thus omnipresence.

You are hearing an instrument – a sitar, or anything. Many notes are there. Be alert and listen to the central core, the backbone of it around which all the notes are flowing, the deepest current which holds all the notes together – that which is central, just like your backbone. The whole body is held by the backbone. Listening to the music, be alert, penetrate the music, and find the backbone of it –

Music as Meditation

the central thing which goes on flowing, holding everything together. Notes come and go and disappear, but the central core flows on. Become aware of it.

Basically, originally, music was used for meditation; in particular, Indian music developed as a method for meditation, Indian dancing developed as a method of meditation. For the doer it was a deep meditation, and for the audience also it was a deep meditation. A dancer or a musician can be a technician. If there is no meditation in it, he is a technician. He can be a great technician. He can be a great technician, but then the soul is not there – only the body. The soul comes only when the musician is a deep meditator.

And music is just the outward thing. While playing on his sitar, one is not *only* playing on his sitar: he is also playing on his alertness inside. The sitar goes on outwardly and his intense awareness moves inside. The music flows outwardly, but he is aware, constantly alert of the innermost core of it. And that gives samadhi! That becomes ecstasy! That becomes the highest peak!

But what are you doing when you listen to music? You are not meditating. On the contrary, you are using music as something like alcohol. You are using it to be relaxed, you are using it for self-forgetfulness.

This is the misfortune, the misery: the techniques which were developed for awareness are being used for sleep. And this is how man goes on doing mischief with himself.

This sutra says while listening to stringed instruments, hear their complete central sound, their composite central sound; "thus omnipresence." And then you will know what *is* to be known or what is worth knowing. You will become omnipresent.

With that music, finding the composite central core, you will become awake, and with that awakening you will be everywhere.

Right now, you are "somewhere" – a point which we call 'ego'.

That is the point where you are. If you can become awake, this point will disappear. You will not be anywhere then: you will be *everywhere* – as if you have become the all. You will have become the ocean, you will have become the infinite. The finiteness is with the mind; the infiniteness enters with meditation. [7]

Shiva said: Bathe in the center of sound, as in the continuous sound of a waterfall, or by putting the fingers in the ears, hear the sound of sounds.

This technique can be done in many ways. One way is to begin by just sitting anywhere. Sounds are always present. It may be in a market or it may be at a Himalayan retreat: sounds are there. Sit silently, and with sound there is something very special. Whenever there are sounds, you are the center. All the

The Center of Sound

sounds come to you from everywhere, from all directions.

With sight, with eyes, this is not so. Sight is linear. I see you, then there is a line toward you. Sound is circular; it is not linear. So all sounds come in circles and you are the center. Wherever you are, you are always the center of sound. For sounds, you are always "God," the center of the whole universe.

Every sound is coming to you, moving toward you, in circles.

This technique says, "Bathe in the center of sound." Wherever you are, if you are doing this technique, just close your eyes and feel the whole universe filled with sound. Feel as if every sound is moving toward you and you are the center. Even this feeling that you are the center will give you a very deep

peace. The whole universe becomes the circumference, and you are the center and everything is moving toward you, falling toward you.

"As in the continuous sound of a waterfall" – if you are sitting by the side of a waterfall, close your eyes, and feel the sound all around you, falling on you, from every side, creating a center in you from every side. Why this emphasis on feeling that you are in the center? Because in the center there is no sound. The center is without sound; that is why you can hear sounds. Otherwise, you could not hear them. A sound cannot hear another sound. Because you are soundless at your center, you can hear sounds. The center is absolute silence: that is why you can hear sounds entering you, coming to you, penetrating you, encircling you.

If you can find out where the center is, where in you the field is to which every sound is coming, suddenly sounds will disappear and you will enter into soundlessness. If you can feel a center where every sound is being heard, there is a sudden transference of consciousness. One moment you will be hearing the whole world filled with sounds, and another moment your awareness will suddenly turn in and you will hear the soundlessness, the center of life.

Once you have heard that, then no sound can disturb you. It comes to you, but it never reaches you. It comes to you, it is always coming to you, but it *never* reaches you. There is a point where no sound enters. That point is *you.*

Do it in a market: there is no other place like a market. It is so much filled with sounds – mad sounds.

But do not start thinking about sounds – that this is good and this is bad and this is disturbing and that is very beautiful and harmonious. You are not supposed to think about sounds. You are simply supposed to think of the center. You are not supposed to think about every sound moving toward you – whether it is good, bad, beautiful. You are just to remember that you are the center and all the sounds are moving toward you – every sound, whatsoever the sort.

Sounds are not heard in the ears. They are *not* heard in the ears; ears cannot hear them. They only do a transmission work, and in the transmission they cut out much which is useless for you. They choose, they select, and then those sounds enter you. Now find out within where your center is. Ears are not the center. You are hearing from somewhere deep down. The ears are simply sending you selected sounds. Where are you? Where is your center?

If you are working with sounds, then sooner or later you will be surprised – because the center is not in the head. The center is *not* in the head! It appears in the head because you have never heard sounds: you have heard words. With words the head is the center; with sounds it is not the center. That is why in Japan

they say that man thinks not through the head, but through the belly – because they were working with sounds since long ago.

You have seen in every temple a gong. That was placed there to create sounds around a seeker. Someone would be meditating, and the gong would be sounded or a bell would be rung. The very disturbance seems to have been created by the sound of the bell. Someone is meditating, and this bell or gong seems disturbing. This seems disturbing! In a temple, every visitor who comes will hit the gong or ring the bell. With someone meditating there, this would seem to be a constant disturbance. It is not – because the person is waiting for this sound.

So every visitor is helping. Again and again the bell is hit, and the sound is created and the meditator again enters himself. He looks at the center where this sound goes deep. There is one hit on the bell: the visitor has done that. Now the second hit will be inside the meditator, somewhere inside. Where is it? The sound always hits at the belly, at the navel, never in the head. If it hits in the head, you can understand well that it is not sound: it is words. Then you have started thinking about the sound. Then the purity is lost.

"Bathe in the center of sound, as in the continuous sound of a waterfall, or, by putting the fingers in the ears, hear the sound of sounds." You can create the sound just by using your finger, or with anything which closes your ears forcibly. Then a certain sound is heard. What is that sound and why do you hear it when the ears are closed, when the ears are plugged?

Just as there are negatives of photographs, there are negative sounds. Not only can the eyes see the negative: the ears can even hear the negative. So when you close your ears, you hear the negative world of sounds. All the sounds have stopped. Suddenly a new sound is heard. This sound is the absence of sound. A gap has come in. You are missing something, and then you hear this absence. "Or, by putting the fingers in the ears, hear the sound of sounds" – that negative sound is known as the sound of sounds – because it is not really a sound, but its absence. Or, it is a natural sound because it is not created by anything.

"Putting the fingers in the ears, hear the sound of sounds" – this absence of sound is a very subtle experience. What will it give to you? The moment there are no sounds, you fall back upon yourself. With sounds we move away; with sounds we move to the other. Try to understand this: with sounds we are related to the other, we communicate with the other.

If sound is the vehicle to move to the other, then soundlessness becomes the vehicle to move to oneself. With sound you communicate with the other, with soundlessness you fall down into your own abyss, into yourself. That is why so many techniques use soundlessness to move within.

Become absolutely dumb and deaf – even if only for a few moments. And you cannot go anywhere else than to yourself: so suddenly you will find that you are standing within; no movement will be possible.

That is why silence was practiced so much. In it, all the bridges for moving to the other are broken.

"Or, by putting the fingers in the ears, hear the sound of sounds" – in one technique two opposites have been shown. "Bathe in the center of sound, as in the continuous sound of a waterfall" – this is one extreme; "or, by putting the fingers in the ears, hear the sound of sounds": this is another extreme. One part is to hear the sounds coming to your center, another part is to stop all sounds and feel the soundless center. These both have been given in one technique for a special purpose – so that you can move from one to another.

The "or" is not a choice to do this or that. Do both! That is why both have been given in one technique. First do one for a few months, then do the other for a few months. You will be more alive, and you will know two extremes. And if you can move to the two extremes easily, you can remain young forever. [8]

Shiva said: In the beginning and gradual refinement of the sound of any letter, awake.

How can you do it? Go to a temple. A bell is there or a gong. Take the bell in your hand and wait. First become totally alert. The sound is going to be there and you are not to miss the beginning. First become totally alert, as if your life depends on this, as if someone is going to kill you this very moment and you will be awake. Be alert –

The Beginning and End of Sound

as if this is going to be your death. And if there is thought, wait, because thought is sleepiness. With thought you cannot be alert. When you are alert, there is no thought. So wait! When you feel that now the mind is without thought, that there is no cloud and you are alert, then move with the sound.

Look when the sound is not there, then close your eyes. Then look when the sound is created, struck; then move with the sound. The sound will become slower and slower, subtler and subtler and subtler, and then it will not be there. Then go on with the sound. Be aware, alert. Move with the sound to the very end. See both the poles of the sound, both the beginning and the end.

Try it with some outer sound like a gong or a bell or anything, then close your eyes. Utter any letter in-side – Aum or any other – and then do the same experiment with it. It is difficult; that is why we do it outwardly first. When you can do it outwardly, then you will be able to do it inwardly. Then do it. Wait for the moment when the mind is vacant, then create the sound inside. Feel it, move with it, go with it, until it disappears completely.

It will take time until you can do

160

this. A few months will be needed, at least three months. In these three months, you will become more and more alert, more and more alert. The pre-sound state and the after-sound state have to be watched. Nothing is to be missed. Once you become so alert that you can watch the beginning and the end of a sound, through this process you will have become a totally different person. [9]

Finding the Space Within

E mptiness is your innermost center. All activity is on the periphery: the innermost center is just a zero. [1]

*S*hiva said: In summer when you see the entire sky end-lessly clear, enter such clarity.

Meditate on the sky: a summer sky with no clouds, endlessly empty and clear, nothing moving in it, in its total virginity. Contemplate on it, meditate on it, and enter this clarity. Become this clarity, this space-like clarity.

To meditate on the sky is beautiful. Just lie down so you forget the earth; just lie down on your back on any lonely beach, on any

Enter the Clear Sky

ground, and just look at the sky. A clear sky will be helpful – un-clouded, endless. Just looking, staring at the sky, feel the clarity of it – the uncloudedness, the bound-less expanse – and then enter that clarity, become one with it. Feel as if you have become the sky, the space.

This technique – to look into the clarity of the sky and to become one with it – is one of the most practiced. Many traditions have used this. And particularly for the modern mind it will be very useful, because nothing is left on earth to meditate on – only the sky. If you look all around, everything is man-made, everything is limited, with a boundary, a limitation. Only the sky is still, fortunately, open to meditate on.

Try this technique, it will be help-ful, but remember three things. One: don't blink – stare. Even if your eyes start to feel pain and tears come down, don't be wor-ried. Even those tears will be a part of unloading; they will be helpful. Those tears will make your eyes more innocent and fresh-bathed. You just go on star-ing.

The second point: don't think about the sky, remember. You can start thinking about the sky. You can remember many poems, beautiful poems about the sky – then you will miss the point. You are not to think *about* it – you are to enter it, you are to be one with it – because if you start thinking about it, again a barrier is created. You are missing the sky again, and you are enclosed in your own mind again. Don't think about the sky. Be the sky. Just stare and move into the sky, and allow the sky to move into you. If you move into the sky, the sky will move into you immediately.

How can you do it? How will you do it – this moving into the sky? Just go on staring further and further away. Go on staring – as if you are trying to find the boundary. Move deep. Move as much as you can. That very movement will break the barrier. And this method should be practiced for at least forty minutes; less than that will not do, will not be of much help.

When you really feel that you have become one, then you can close the eyes. When the sky has entered in you, you can close the eyes. You will be able to see it within also. So only after forty minutes, when you feel that the oneness has happened and there is a communion and you have become part of it and the mind is no more, close the eyes and remain in the sky within.

The clarity will help the third point: "enter such clarity." The clarity will help – the uncontaminated, unclouded sky. Just be aware of the clarity that is all around you. Don't think about it; just be aware of the clarity, the purity, the innocence. These words are not to be repeated. You have to feel them rather than think. And once you stare into the sky the feeling will come, because it is not on your part to imagine these things – they are there. If you stare they will start happening to you.

If you meditate on open unclouded sky, suddenly you will feel that the mind is disappearing, the mind is dropping away. There will be gaps. Suddenly you will become aware that it is as if the clear sky has entered in you also. There will be intervals. For a time, thoughts will cease – as if the traffic has ceased and there is no one moving.

In the beginning it will be only for moments, but even those moments are transforming. By and by the mind will slow down, bigger gaps will appear. For minutes together there will be no thought, no cloud. And when there is no thought, no cloud, the outer sky and the inner become one, because only the thought is the barrier; only the thought creates the wall. Only be-cause of thought the outer is outer and the inner is inner. When thought is not there, the outer and the inner lose their boundaries, they become one. Boundaries never really existed there. They appeared only because of the thought, the barrier.

But if it is not summer what will you do? If the sky is clouded, not clear, then close your eyes and just enter the inner sky. Just close your eyes, and if you see some thoughts, just see them as if they are clouds floating in the sky. Be aware of the background, the sky, and be indifferent to thoughts.

We are too much concerned with thoughts and never aware of the gaps. One thought passes, and before another enters there is a gap – in that gap the sky is there. Then, whenever there is no thought, what is there? The emptiness is there. So if the sky is clouded – it is not summertime and the sky is not clear – close your eyes, focus your mind on the background, the inner sky in which thoughts come and go. Don't pay much attention to thoughts; pay attention to the space in which they move.

For example, we are sitting in this room. I can look at this room in two ways. Either I can look at you, so that I am indifferent to the space you are in, the roominess, the room you are in – I look at you, I focus my mind on you who are here, and not on the room in which you are – or, I can change my focus: I can look into the room, and I become indifferent to you. You are there, but my emphasis, my focus, is on the room. Then the total perspective changes. Just do this in the inner world. Look at the space. Thoughts are moving in it: be indifferent to them, don't pay any attention to them. They are there; note it down that they are there, moving. The traffic is moving in the street. Look at the street and be indifferent to the traffic. Don't look to see who is passing; just know that something is passing and be aware of the space in which it is passing. Then the summer sky happens within. [2]

Shiva said: Beloved, at this moment let mind, knowing, breath, form be included.

This technique is a little difficult, but if you can do it, then it is very wonderful, beautiful. Sitting, don't divide. Sitting in meditation, be inclusive of all – your body, your mind, your breath, your thinking, your knowing, everything. Be inclusive of all. Don't divide, don't create any fragmentation. Ordinarily we are fragmenting; we go on fragmenting. We say, "The body is not me." There are techniques

Include Everything

which can use that also, but this technique is totally different, rather it is the opposite.

Don't divide. Don't say, "I am not the body." Don't say, "I am not the breath." Don't say, "I am not the mind." Just say, "I am all" – and be all. Don't create any fragmentation within you. This is a feeling. With closed eyes include everything that exists in you. Don't get yourself

centered anywhere – be uncentered. The breath comes and goes, the thought comes and moves. The form of your body will go on changing. You have not observed this.

If you sit with closed eyes, you will feel that sometimes your body is big, sometimes your body is small; sometimes it is very heavy, sometimes just light, as if you can fly.

You can feel this increasing and decreasing of the form. Just close your eyes and sit and you will feel that sometimes the body is very big – filling the whole room; sometimes it is so small – just atomic. Why does this form change? As your attention changes, the form of the body changes. If you are inclusive, it will become big; if you exclude – "this is not I,

168

this is not I" – then it will become very minute, very small, atomic.

Include everything in your being and don't discard anything. Don't say, "This is not I." Say, "I am," and include everything in it. If you can do this just sitting, wonderful, absolutely new happenings will happen to you. You will feel there is no center; in you there is no center. And with the center gone, there is no self, there is no ego; only consciousness remains – consciousness like a sky covering everything. And when it grows, not only your own breath will be included, not only your own form will be included; ultimately the whole universe becomes inclusive to you.

The basic point is to remember inclusiveness. Don't exclude. This is the key for this sutra – inclusiveness, include. Include and grow. Include and expand. Try it with your body, and then try it with the outside world also.

Sitting under a tree, look at the tree, then close your eyes and feel that the tree is within you. Look at the sky, then close your eyes and feel that the sky is within you. Look at the rising sun, then close your eyes and feel that the sun is rising within you. Feel more inclusive.

A tremendous experience will happen to you. When you feel that the tree is within you, immediately you will feel more young, more fresh. And this is not imagination, because the tree and you both belong to the earth. You are both rooted in the same earth and ultimately rooted in the same existence. So when you feel that the tree is within you, the tree *is* within you – this is not imagination – and immediately you will feel the effect. The tree's aliveness, the greenery, the freshness, the breeze passing through it, will be felt within you in your heart. Include more and more existence and don't exclude.

So remember this: make it a style of life to include – not only meditation, but a style of life, a way of living. Try to include more and more. The more you include, the more you expand, the more your boundaries recede to the very corners of existence. One day only you are; the whole existence is included. This is the ultimate of all religious experience. [3]

Y ou cannot find a better situation in which to meditate than while flying at a high altitude. The higher the altitude, the easier is the meditation. Hence, for centuries, meditators have been moving to the Himalayas to find a high altitude.

A Meditation for the Jet-Set

When gravitation is less and the earth is very far away, many pulls of the earth are far away. You are far away from the corrupted society that man has built. You are surrounded by clouds and the stars and the moon and the sun and the vast space. So do one thing: start feeling one with that vastness, and do it in three steps. The first step is: for a few minutes just think that you are becoming bigger…you are filling the whole plane. Then the second step: start feeling that you are becoming even bigger, bigger than the plane, in fact the plane is now inside you. And the third step: feel that you have expanded into the whole sky. Now these clouds that are moving, and the moon and the stars – they are moving in you; you are huge, unlimited.

This feeling will become your meditation, and you will feel completely relaxed and non-tense. [4]

Patanjali says: On attaining the utmost purity of the nirvichara stage of samadhi, there is a dawning of the spiritual light.

Your innermost being is of the nature of light. Consciousness is light, consciousness is the *only* light. You are existing very unconsciously: doing things, not knowing why; desiring things, not knowing why; asking things, not knowing why; drifting in an unconscious sleep.

Feel the Absence of Things

You are all sleepwalkers. Somnambulism is the only spiritual disease – walking and living in sleep. Become more conscious.

Start being conscious with objects. Look at things with more alertness. You pass by a tree; look at the tree with more alertness. Stop for a while, look at the tree; rub your eyes, look at the tree with more alertness. Collect your awareness, look at the tree, and watch the difference. Suddenly when you are alert, the tree is different: it is more green, it is more alive, it is more beautiful. The tree is the same, only you have changed.

Look at a flower as if your whole existence depends on this look. Bring all your awareness to the flower and suddenly the flower is transfigured – it is more radiant, it is more luminous. It has something of the glory of the eternal, as if the eternal has come into the temporal in the shape of a flower.

Look at the face of your husband, your wife, your friend, your beloved, with alertness; meditate on it, and suddenly you see not only the body, but that which is beyond the body, which is coming out of the body. There is an aura of the spiritual around the body. The face of the beloved is no more the face of your beloved; the face of the beloved has become the face of the divine. Look at your child. With full alertness, awareness, watch him playing and suddenly the object is transfigured.

For example, a bird sings in the tree: be alert, as if in that moment you exist and the song of the bird – the whole doesn't exist, doesn't matter. Focus your being towards the song of the bird and you will see the difference. The traffic noise exists no more, or exists at the very periphery of existence, far away, distant. The small bird and its song fill your being completely – only you and the bird exist. And then when the song has stopped, listen to the absence of the song. Then the object becomes subtle.

Remember always: when a song stops it leaves a certain quality to the atmosphere – the absence. It is no more the same. The atmosphere has changed completely because the song existed and then the song disappeared. Now the absence of the song – watch it, the whole existence is filled by the absence of the song. It is more beautiful than any song because it is the song of silence. A song uses sound, and when the sound disappears the absence uses the silence. After a bird has sung, the silence is deeper. If you can watch it, if you can be alert, you are now meditating on a very subtle object, a *very* subtle object.

A person moves, a beautiful person moves – watch the person. And when he has left, watch the absence; he has left something. His energy has changed the room; it is no more the same room.

If you have a good nose – very few people have; humanity has almost lost the nose completely. Animals are better; their smell is far more sensitive, more capable than man's. Something has happened to man's nose, something has gone wrong; very few people have a capable nose, but if you have – then be near a flower, let the smell fill you. Then, by and by, move away from the flower, very slowly, but continue being attentive to the smell, the fragrance. As you move away, the fragrance will become more and more subtle, and you will need more awareness to feel it. Become the nose. Forget about the whole body, bring all your energy to the nose, as if only the nose exists. If you lose track of the smell by and by, go a few steps further ahead. Again catch hold of the smell, then move back, move backward. By and by, you will be able to smell a flower from a very, very great distance – nobody else will be able to smell that flower from there. Then go on moving. In a very simple way you are making the object subtle. Then a moment will come when you will not be able to smell the smell: now smell the absence. Now smell the absence where the fragrance was just a moment before, and it is no longer there. That is the other part of its being, the absent part, the dark part. If you can smell the absence of the smell, if you can feel it, that it makes a difference – it *makes* a difference – then the object has become very subtle.

You can do it with incense. Burn incense, meditate on it, feel it, smell it, be filled with it, and then move backwards, away from it. And go on, go on meditating on it and let it become more and more subtle. A moment comes when you can feel the absence of a certain thing. Then you have come to a very deep awareness.

But when the object completely disappears, and the presence of the object disappears, and the absence of the object disappears, thought disappears and the idea of no-mind disappears, only then have you attained to the utmost. Now this is the moment when suddenly grace descends on you. This is the moment when flowers shower. This is the moment when you are connected with the source of life and being. This is the moment when you are no more a beggar; you have become the emperor. This is the moment when you are crowned. Before it you were on a cross; this is the moment the cross disappears and you are crowned. [5]

Tilopa said: Like a hollow bamboo rest at ease with your body.

This is one of Tilopa's special methods. Every master has his own special method through which he has attained, and through which he would like to help others. This is Tilopa's specialty: "Like a hollow bamboo rest at ease with your body."

A bamboo – inside completely hollow. When you rest, you just feel that you are like a bamboo – inside completely hollow and

Hollow Bamboo

empty. And in fact this is the case: your body is just like a bamboo, and inside it is hollow. Your skin, your bones, your blood, all are part of the bamboo, and inside there is space, hollowness.

When you are sitting with a completely silent mouth, inactive, tongue touching the roof and silent, not quivering with thoughts, mind watching passively, not wait-ing for anything in particular, feel like a hollow bamboo – and suddenly infinite energy starts pouring within you, you are filled with the unknown, with the mysterious, with the divine. A hollow bamboo becomes a flute and the divine starts playing it. Once you are empty then there is no barrier for the divine to enter in you.

Try this; this is one of the most beautiful meditations, the meditation of becoming a hollow bamboo. You need not do anything else. You simply become this – and all else happens. Suddenly you feel something is descending in your hollowness. You are like a womb and a new life is entering in you, a seed is falling. And a moment comes when the bamboo completely disappears. [6]

Entering into Death

L ife is a pilgrimage towards death. From the very beginning, death is coming. From the moment of birth,
death has started coming towards you; you have started
moving towards death.

And the greatest calamity that has happened to the
human mind is that it is against death. Being against
death means you will miss the greatest mystery. And being against death also means that you will miss life itself
– because they are deeply involved in each other; they
are not two. Life is growing, death is the flowering of it.
The journey and the goal are not separate – the journey
ends in the goal. [1]

Shiva said: Focus on fire rising through your form, from the toes up, until the body burns to ashes but not you.

Buddha liked this technique very much; he initiated his disciples into this technique.

Whenever someone was initiated by Buddha, the first thing was this: he would tell him just to go to the burning place and observe a body being burned, a dead body being burned. For three months he was not to do anything, but just sit there and watch.

Entering into Death

Buddha said, "Don't think about it. Just look at it." And it is difficult not to come upon the thought that sooner or later your body is going to be burned. Three months is a long time, and continuously, day and night, whenever there was a body to be burned, the seeker was to meditate. Sooner or later he would start seeing his own body on the burning pyre. He would start seeing himself being burned.

If you are very much afraid of death you cannot do this technique, because the very fear will protect you. You cannot enter into it. Or, you can just imagine on the surface, but your deep being will not be in it. Then nothing will happen to you.

Remember, whether you are afraid or not, death is the only certainty.

In life, nothing is certain except death. Everything is uncertain; only death is a certainty. All else is accidental – it can happen, it may not happen – only death is not accidental. And look at the human mind. We always talk about death as if it is an accident. Whenever someone dies we say his death was untimely. Whenever someone dies we start talking as if it has been an accident. Only death is not an accident – only death. Everything else is accidental. Death is absolutely certain. You have to die.

And when I say you have to die, it seems in the future, very far away. It is not so – you have already died. The moment you were born, you died. With birth, death has become a fixed phenomenon. One part of it has already happened – the birth; now only the second, later part has to happen. So you are already dead, half-dead, because once one is born, one has come into the realm of death, entered into it. Now nothing can change it, now there is no way to change it. You have entered into it. You are half-dead with birth.

Secondly: death is not going to happen in the end; it is already happening. It is a process. Just as life is a process, death is a process. We create the dualism – but life and death are just like your two feet, your two legs. Life and death are both one process. You are dying every moment.

Let me put it this way: whenever you inhale, it is life, and whenever you exhale, it is death.

The first thing a child does is to inhale. A child cannot exhale. The first thing is inhalation. He cannot exhale, because there is no air within his chest; he has to inhale. The first act is inhalation. And the old man, while dying, will do the last act, which will be exhalation. Dying, you cannot inhale – or can you? When you are dying, you cannot inhale. The last act cannot be inhalation; the last act will be exhalation. The first act is inhalation and the last is exhalation. Inhalation is birth and exhalation is death. But every moment you are doing both – inhaling, exhaling. Inhalation is life, exhalation is death.

You may not have observed, but try to observe it. Whenever you exhale, you are more at peace. Exhale deeply and you will feel a certain peace within. Whenever you inhale, you become intense, you become tense. The very intensity of inhalation creates a tension. And the normal, ordinary emphasis is always on inhalation. If I tell you to take deep breaths, you will always start with inhalation.

Really, we are afraid of exhaling. That's why breathing has become shallow. You never exhale, you go on inhaling. Only the body goes on exhaling, because the body cannot exist with inhalation alone. It needs both: life and death.

Step 1:

Try one experiment. The whole day, whenever you remember, exhale deeply and don't inhale. Allow the body to inhale; you simply exhale deeply. You will feel a deep peace, because death is peace, death is silence. And if you can pay attention, more attention, to exhalation, you will feel egoless. With inhalation you will feel more egoistic; with exhalation you will feel more egoless. Pay more attention to exhalation. The whole day, whenever you remember, exhale deeply and don't inhale. Allow the body to inhale; you don't do anything.

This emphasis on exhalation will help you very much to do this experiment, because you will be ready to die. A readiness is needed, otherwise the technique will not be of much help. And you can be ready only if you have tasted death in a certain way. Exhale deeply and you will have a taste of it. It is beautiful.

Death is just beautiful, because nothing is like death – so silent, so relaxing, so calm, so unperturbed. But we are afraid of death. And why are we afraid of death? Why is there so much fear of death? We are afraid of death not because of death – because we don't know it. How can you be afraid of something you have never encountered? How can you be afraid of something that you don't know? At least you must know it to be afraid of it. So really you are not afraid of death; the fear is something else. You have never really lived – that creates the fear of death.

The fear comes because you are not living, so you are afraid – "I have not lived yet, and if death happens, then what? Unfulfilled, unlived, I will die." The fear of death comes only to those who are not really alive. If you are alive, you will welcome death. Then there is no fear. You have known life; now you would like to know death also. But we are so afraid of life itself that we have not known it, we have not entered deep into it. That creates the fear of death.

If you want to enter this technique you must be aware of this deep fear. And this deep fear must be thrown away, purged, only then can you enter the technique. This will help: pay more attention to exhalation. The whole day you will feel relaxed, and an inner silence will be created.

Step 2:

You can deepen this feeling more if you do another experiment. Just exhale deeply for fifteen minutes a day. Sit in a chair or on the ground, exhale deeply, and while exhaling close the eyes. When the air goes out, you go in. And then allow the body to inhale, and when the air goes in, open the eyes and you go

out. It is just the opposite: when the air goes out, you go in; when the air goes in, you go out.

When you exhale, space is created within, because breath is life. When you exhale deeply, you are vacant, life has gone out. In a way you are dead, for a moment you are dead. In that silence of death, enter within. Air is moving out: you close your eyes and move within. The space is there and you can move easily.

Before doing the following technique, do this experiment for fifteen minutes so that you are ready – not only ready, but welcoming, receptive. The fear of death is not there, because now death appears like relaxation, death appears like a deep rest.

Step 3:

Just lie down. First conceive of yourself as death; the body is just like a corpse. Lie down, and then bring your attention to the toes. With closed eyes move inward. Bring your attention to the toes and feel that the fire is rising from there upward, everything is being burned. As the fire rises, your body is disappearing. Start from the toes and move upwards.

Why start from the toes? It will be easier, because the toes are very far away from your I, from your ego.

Your ego exists in the head. You cannot start from the head, it will be very difficult, so start from the faraway point – the toes are the most faraway point from the ego. Start the fire from there. Feel that the toes are burned, only ashes remain, and then move slowly, burning everything that the fire comes across. Every part, the legs, the thighs, will disappear.

Just go on seeing that they have become ashes. The fire is rising upward, and the parts it has passed are no longer there; they have become ashes. Go on upward, and lastly the head disappears. You will remain just a watcher on the hill. The body will be there – dead, burned, ashes – and you will be the watcher, you will be the witness. This witness has no ego.

This technique is very good to reach the egoless state. Why? – because so many things are implied in it. It appears simple; it is not so simple. The inner mechanism is very complex. First thing: your memories are part of the body. Memory is matter; that's why it can be recorded – it is recorded in the brain cells. They are material, part of the body. Your brain cells can be operated on, and if certain brain cells are removed, certain memories will disappear from you.

Remember, this is the point to

understand: if the memory is still there, then the body remains and you have been playing tricks. If you go really deep into feeling that the body is dead, burning, and the fire has completely destroyed it, you will not have any memory in that moment. In that moment of watching, there will be no mind. Everything will have stopped – no movement of thought, just watching, just seeing what has happened.

And once you know this, you can remain in this state continuously. Once you have known that you can separate yourself from the body – this technique is just a method to separate yourself from the body, just to create a gap between you and the body, just for a few moments to be out of the body. If you can do this, then you can remain in the body and you will not be in the body. You can go on living as you were living before, but you will not be the same again.

This technique will take at least three months. Go on doing it. It is not going to happen in one day, but if you go on doing it for one hour every day, within three months, one day suddenly your imagination will have helped and the gap will be created, and you will actually see the body gone to ashes. Then you can watch.

In that watching you will realize a deep phenomenon – that the ego is a false entity. It was there because you were identified with the body; with the thoughts, with the mind. You are neither – neither the mind nor the body. You are different from all that surrounds you; you are different from your periphery. [2]

Celebrating Death

I have heard about three monks. No name is mentioned, because they never told their names to anybody, they never answered anything. So in China they are only known simply as 'the three laughing monks'.

They did only one thing: they would enter a village, stand in the marketplace, and start laughing. Suddenly people would become aware, and they would laugh with their whole being. Then others would also get the infection, and then a crowd would gather, and just looking at them the whole crowd would start laughing. What is happening? Then the whole town would get involved, and they would move to another town. They were loved very much. That was their only sermon, the only message – that laugh. And they would not teach, they would simply create the situation.

Then it happened that they became famous all over the country – 'the three laughing monks'. The whole of China loved them, respected them. Nobody had preached that way – that life must be just a laughter and nothing else. And they were not laughing at anybody in particu-

lar, but simply laughing, as if they had understood the cosmic joke. They spread so much joy all over China without using a single word. People would ask their names, but they would simply laugh, so that became their name – 'the three laughing monks'.

Then they became old, and in one village one of the three monks died. The whole village was very expectant, very filled with expectations, because now at least when one of them has died, they must weep. This would be something worth seeing, because no one could even conceive of these people weeping.

The whole village gathered. The two monks were standing by the side of the corpse of the third and laughing, such a belly laugh. So the villagers asked, "At least explain this!"

So for the first time they spoke, and they said, "We are laughing because this man has won. We were always wondering who would die first, and this man has defeated us. We are laughing at our defeat, at his victory. And then, he lived with us for many years, and we laughed together and we enjoyed each other's togetherness, presence. There can be no other way of giving him the last send-off. We can only laugh."

The whole village was sad, but

when the dead monk's body was put on the funeral pyre, then the village realized that not only these two were joking – the third who was dead was also laughing. Because the third man who was dead had told his companions, "Don't change my dress!" It was conventional that when a man died, they changed the dress and gave a bath to the body, so he had said, "Don't give me a bath, because I have never been unclean. So much laughter has been in my life that no impurity can accumulate near me, can even come to me. I have not gathered any dust; laughter is always young and fresh. So don't give me a bath and don't change my clothes."

So, just to pay him respect, they had not changed his clothes. And when the body was put on the fire, suddenly they became aware that he had hidden many things under his clothes and those things started ... Chinese fireworks!! So the whole village laughed, and those two said, "You rascal! You have died, but again you have defeated us. Your laughter is the last."

There is a cosmic laughter, when the whole joke of this cosmos is understood. That is the highest, only a buddha can laugh like that. These three monks must have been three buddhas. [3]

Watching with the Third Eye

It is one of the contributions of the East to the world: the understanding that between these two eyes, there is a third eye inside which normally remains dormant.

One has to work hard, bring his whole sexual energy upward, against gravitation, and when the energy reaches the third eye, it opens. Many methods have been tried to do that, because when it opens there is suddenly a flash of light, and things which have never been clear to you suddenly become clear.

When I emphasize watching, witnessing…that is the finest method to bring the third eye into action, because that watching is inside. These two eyes cannot be used, they can only look outward. They have to be closed. And when you try to watch inside, that certainly means there is something like an eye which sees. Who sees your thoughts? Not these eyes. Who sees that anger is arising in you? That place of seeing is called symbolically 'the third eye'. [1]

This technique consists of four stages of 15 minutes each. The first two stages prepare the meditator for the spontaneous Latihan of the third stage. Osho has said that if the breathing is done correctly in the first stage the carbon dioxide formed in the bloodstream will make you feel as high as Gourishankar (Mt. Everest).

Music for this technique has been composed with Osho's guidance. For availability see back page.

Gourishankar Meditation

First stage: 15 minutes

Sit with closed eyes. Inhale deeply through the nose, filling the lungs. Hold the breath for as long as possible, then exhale gently through the mouth and keep the lungs empty for as long as possible. Continue this breathing cycle throughout the first stage.

Second stage: 15 minutes

Return to normal breathing and with a gentle gaze look at a candle flame or a flashing blue light. Keep your body still.

Third stage: 15 minutes

With closed eyes, stand up and let your body be loose and receptive. The subtle energies will be felt to move the body outside your normal control. Allow this Latihan to happen. Don't you do the moving: let moving happen, gently and gracefully.

Fourth stage: 15 minutes

Lie down with closed eyes, silent and still.

The first three stages should be accompanied by a steady rhythmic beat, preferably combined with a soothing background music. The beat should be seven times the normal heartbeat and, if possible, the flashing light should be a synchronized strobe. [1]

This is another powerful, cathartic technique that creates a circle of energy that results in a natural centering. See back page for music to support the meditation.

First stage: 15 minutes

With open eyes run on the spot, starting slowly and gradually, getting faster and faster. Bring your knees up as high as possible. Breathing deeply and evenly will move the energy within. Forget

Mandala Meditation

the mind and forget the body. Keep going.

Second stage: 15 minutes

Sit with your eyes closed and mouth open and loose. Gently rotate your body from the waist, like a reed blowing in the wind. Feel the wind blowing you from side to side, back and forth,

around and around. This will bring your awakened energies to the navel center.

Third stage: 15 minutes

Lie on your back, open your eyes and, with the head still, rotate them in a clockwise direction. Sweep them fully around in the sockets as if you are following the

second hand of a vast clock, but as fast as possible. It is important that the mouth remains open and the jaw relaxed, with the breath soft and even. This will bring your centered energies to the third eye.

Fourth stage: 15 minutes

Close your eyes and be still. [2]

186

Shiva said: Attention between eyebrows, let mind be before thought. Let form fill with breath essence to the top of the head and there shower as light.

This was the technique given to Pythagoras. Pythagoras went with this technique to Greece. And, really, he became the fountainhead, the source, of all mysticism in the West. He is the father of all mysticism in the West.

This technique is one of the very deep methods. Try to understand

Finding the Witness

this: "Attention between the eyebrows..." Modern physiology, scientific research, says that between the two eyebrows is the gland which is the most mysterious part in the body. This gland, called the pineal gland, is the third eye of the Tibetans – *Shivanetra:* the eye of Shiva, of tantra. Between the two eyes there is a third eye existing, but ordinarily it is non-functioning.

You have to do something about it to open it. It is not blind. It is simply closed. This technique is to open the third eye.

"Attention between the eyebrows..." Close your eyes, then focus both of your eyes just in the middle of the two eyebrows. Focus just in the middle, with closed eyes, as if you are looking with your two eyes. Give total attention to it.

This is one of the simplest methods of being attentive. You cannot be attentive to any other part of the body so easily. This gland absorbs attention like anything. If you give attention to it, both your eyes become hypnotized with the third eye. They become fixed; they cannot move. If you are trying to be attentive to any other part of the body, it is difficult. This third eye catches attention, forces attention. It is magnetic for attention. So all the methods all over the world have used it. It is the simplest to train attention because not only are you trying to be attentive: the gland itself helps you; it is magnetic. Your attention is brought to it forcibly. It is absorbed.

It is said in the old tantra scriptures that attention is food for the third eye. It is hungry; it has been hungry for lives and lives. If you pay attention to it, it becomes alive. It becomes alive! The food is given to it. And once you know that attention is food, once you feel that your attention is magnetically drawn, attracted, pulled by the gland itself, attention is not a difficult thing then. One has only to know the right point. So just close your eyes, let your two eyes move just in the middle, and feel the point. When you are near the point, suddenly your eyes will become fixed. When it will be difficult to move them, then know you have caught the right point.

"Attention between the eyebrows, let mind be before thought…" If attention is between the eyebrows, for the first time you will come to experience a strange phenomenon. For the first time you will feel thoughts running before you; you will become the witness. It is just like a film screen: thoughts are running and you are a witness. Once your attention is focused at the third eye center, you become immediately the witness of thoughts.

Ordinarily you are not the witness: you are identified with thoughts. If anger is there, you become anger. If a thought moves, you are not the witness – you become one with the thought, identified, and you move with it. You become the thought; you take the form of the thought. When sex is there you become sex; when anger is there you become anger; when greed is there you become greed. Any thought moving becomes identified with you. You do not have any gap between you and the thought.

But focused at the third eye, suddenly you become a witness. Through the third eye, you become the witness. Through the third eye, you can see thoughts running like clouds in the sky or people moving on the street.

Try to be a witness. Whatsoever is happening, try to be a witness. You are ill, the body is aching and painful, you have misery and suffering, whatsoever: be a witness to it. Whatsoever is happening, do not identify yourself with it. Be a witness – an observer. Then if witnessing becomes possible, you will be focused in the third eye.

Secondly, vice versa is also the case. If you are focused in the third eye, you will become a witness. These two things are part of one. So the first thing: by being centered in the third eye there will be the arising of the witnessing self. Now you can encounter your thoughts. This will be the first thing. And the second thing will be that now you can feel the subtle, delicate vibration of breathing. Now you can feel the form of breathing, the very essence of breathing.

First try to understand what is meant by 'the form', by 'the essence of breathing'. While you are breathing, you are not only breathing air. Science says you are breathing only air – just oxygen, hydrogen, and other gases in their combined form of air. They say you are breathing "air!" But tantra says that air is just the vehicle, not the real thing. You are breathing *prana* – vitality. Air is just the medium; prana is the content. You are breathing prana, not only air.

By being focused in the third eye, suddenly you can observe the very essence of breath – not breath, but the very essence of breath, prana. And if you can observe the essence of breath, prana, you are on the point from which the jump, the breakthrough happens. [3]

188

*S*hiva said: Touching eye-
balls as a feather, lightness
between them opens into
heart and there permeates the
cosmos.

Use both your palms, put them on
your closed eyes, and allow the
palms to touch the eyeballs – but
just like a feather, with no pressure.
If you press you miss the point,
you miss the whole technique.
Don't press; just touch like a feather. You will have to adjust, because
in the beginning you will be pressing. Put less and less pressure until

Touching as a Feather

you are just touching with no pressure at all – just your palms touch
the eyeballs. Just a touch, just a
meeting with no pressure, because
if the pressure is there, then the
technique will not function. So –
like a feather.

Why? – because a needle can do
something which a sword cannot
do. If you press, the quality has
changed – you are aggressive. And

the energy that is flowing through
the eyes is very subtle: a small
pressure and it starts fighting and a
resistance is created. If you press,
then the energy that is flowing
through the eyes will start a resistance, a fight; a struggle will ensue.
So don't press; even a slight pressure is enough for the eye energy to
judge.

It is very subtle, it is very delicate.

Don't press – like a feather, just
your palm is touching, as if not
touching. Touching as if not touching, no pressure; just a touch, a
slight feeling that the palm is
touching the eyeball, that's all.

What will happen? When you simply touch without any pressure,
the energy starts moving within. If
you press, it starts fighting with
the hand, with the palm, and

189

moves out. Just a touch and the energy starts moving within. The door is closed; simply the door is closed and the energy falls back. The moment energy falls back, you will feel a lightness coming all over your face, your head. This energy moving back makes you light.

And just between these two eyes is the third eye, the wisdom-eye, the *prajna-chakshu*. Just between the two eyes is the third eye. The energy falling back from the eyes hits the third eye. That's why one feels light, levitating, as if there is no gravitation. And from the third eye the energy falls on the heart. It is a physical process: just drip, drip, it drops, and you will feel a very light feeling entering in your heart. The heartbeats will slow down, the breathing will slow down. Your whole body will feel relaxed.

Even if you are not entering deep meditation, this will help you physically. Any time during the day, relax on a chair – or if you don't have a chair, when just sitting in a train – close your eyes, feel a relaxed being in the whole of your body, and then put both your palms on your eyes. But don't press – that's the very significant thing. Just touch like a feather.

When you touch and don't press, your thoughts will stop immediately. In a relaxed mind thoughts cannot move; they get frozen. They need frenzy and fever, they need tension to move. They live through tension. When the eyes are silent, relaxed, and the energy is moving backwards, thoughts will stop. You will feel a certain quality of euphoria, and that will deepen daily.

So do it many times in the day. Even for a single moment, touching will be good. Whenever your eyes feel exhausted, dry of energy, exploited – after reading, seeing a film, or watching TV – whenever you feel it, just close the eyes and touch. Immediately there will be the effect. But if you want to make it a meditation, then do it for at least forty minutes. And the whole thing is not to press. It is easy for a single moment to have a feather-like touch; it is difficult for forty minutes. Many times you will forget and you will start pressing.

Don't press. For forty minutes, just remain aware that your hands have no weight; they are just touching. Go on being aware that you are not pressing, only touching. This will become a deep awareness, just like breathing. As Buddha says to breathe with full awareness, the same will happen with touching, because you have to be constantly mindful that you are not pressing. Your hand should just be a feather, a weightless thing, simply touching.

Your mind will be totally there, alert, near the eyes, and the energy will be flowing constantly. In the beginning it will be just dropping in drops. Within months you will feel it has become a river-like thing, and within a year you will feel it has become a flood. And when it happens – "touching eye-balls as a feather, lightness between them" – when you touch you will feel lightness. You can feel it right now. Immediately, the moment you touch, a lightness comes. And that "lightness between them opens into the heart"; that lightness penetrates, opens into the heart. In the heart, only lightness can enter; nothing heavy can enter. Only very light things can happen to the heart.

This lightness between the two eyes will start dropping into the heart, and the heart will open to receive it – "and there permeates the cosmos." As the falling energy becomes a stream and then a river and then a flood, you will be washed completely, washed away. You will not feel that you are. You will feel simply the cosmos is. Breathing in, breathing out, you will feel you have become the cosmos. The cosmos comes in and the cosmos goes out. The entity that you have always been, the ego, will not be there. 4

Lu-tsu said: One should look at the tip of one's nose.

Why? – because this helps, it brings you in line with the third eye. When both your eyes are fixed on the tip of the nose it does many things. The basic is that your third eye is exactly in line with the tip of the nose – just a few inches above, but in the same line. And once you are in the line of the third eye, the attraction of the third eye, the pull, the magnetism, of the third eye is so great that if you

Looking at the Tip of the Nose

have fallen in line with it, you will be pulled even against yourself. You just have to be exactly in line with it so that the attraction, the gravitation, of the third eye starts functioning. Once you are exactly in line with it there will be no need to make any effort.

Suddenly you will find the gestalt has changed, because the two eyes create the duality of the world and thought, and the single eye between the two eyes creates the gaps. This is a simple method of changing the gestalt.

The mind can distort it – the mind can say, "Okay, now look at the tip of the nose. Think of the tip of the nose, concentrate on it." If you concentrate too much on the tip of the nose you will miss the point, because you have to be there at the tip of the nose but very relaxed so that the third eye can pull you. If you are too concentrated on the tip of the nose, rooted, focused, fixed there, your third eye will not be able to pull you in, because your third eye has never functioned before. Its pull cannot be very great in the beginning. Slowly slowly it grows more and more. Once it starts functioning and the dust that has gathered around it disappears with use, and the mechanism is humming well, then even if you are fixed on the tip of the nose you will be pulled in. But not in the beginning. You have to be very very light, not a burden, without any stress and strain. You have to be simply there, present, in a kind of let-go ... .

If one is not guided by the nose, either one opens wide the eyes and looks into the distance, so that the nose is not seen, or the lids shut too much, so that the eyes close, and again the nose is not seen.

Another function of looking very lightly at the tip of the nose is this: that it doesn't allow you to open your eyes wide. If you open your eyes wide the whole world becomes available, and there are a thousand and one distractions. A beautiful woman passes by and you start following – at least in the mind. Or somebody is fighting; you are not concerned, but you start thinking. "What is going to happen?" Or somebody is crying and you become curious. A thousand and one things are continuously moving around you. If the eyes are wide open, you become masculine energy, yang.

If the eyes are completely closed you fall into a kind of reverie, you start dreaming; you become feminine energy, yin. To avoid both just look at the tip of the nose – a simple device, but the result is almost magical.

And this is not only so with the Taoists. Buddhists know it, Hindus know it. Down the ages all the meditators have somehow stumbled upon the fact that if your eyes are just half open, in a very miraculous way you escape two pitfalls. One is being distracted by the outside world, the other is being distracted by the inside dream world. You remain exactly on the boundary of the inner and the outer. And that's the point: to be on the boundary of the inner and the outer means you are neither male nor female in that moment. Your vision is free of duality; your vision has transcended the division in you. Only when you are beyond the division in you do you fall into the line of the magnetic field of the third eye.

The main thing is to lower the eyelids in the right way, and then to allow the light to stream in of itself.

That is very important to remember: you are not to pull the light in, you are not to force the light in. If the window is open, the light comes in of its own accord. If the door is open, the light floods in. You need not bring it in, you need not push it in, you need not drag it in. And how can you drag light in? How can you push light in? All that is needed is that you should be open and vulnerable to it.

One looks with both eyes at the tip of the nose.

Remember, you have to look with both eyes at the tip of the nose so that at the tip of the nose, your two eyes lose their duality. So, on the tip of the nose the light that is streaming out from your eyes becomes one; it falls on a single point. Where your two eyes meet, that is the place where the window opens. And then all is well. Then let it be, then simply enjoy, then simply celebrate, delight, rejoice. Then nothing has to be done.

One looks with both eyes at the tip of the nose, sits upright....

It is helpful to sit upright. When your spine is straight, the energy from your sex center also becomes available to the third eye. Just simple devices, nothing complex about them ... it is just that when your two eyes meet at the tip of the nose, you are available to the third eye. Make your sex energy also available to the third eye. Then the effect will be double, the effect will be forceful, because your sex center has all the energy that you have. When the spine is erect, straight, the sex center is also available to the third eye. It is better to attack the third eye from both dimensions, to try to penetrate the third eye from both directions.

One...sits upright and in a comfortable position.

The master is making things very clear. Upright, certainly, but don't make it uncomfortable; otherwise again you will be distracted by your discomfort. That is the meaning of a yoga posture. The Sanskrit word *asana* means a comfortable posture. Comfort is the basic quality of it. If it is not comfortable then your mind will be distracted by the discomfort. It has to be comfortable.

It does not necessarily mean the middle of the head.

And by centering it is not meant that you have to be centered in the middle of the head.

The center is omnipresent; everything is contained in it; it is connected with the release of the whole process of creation.

And when you have reached the third eye point and you are centered there and the light is flooding in, you have reached the point from which the whole creation has arisen. You have reached the formless, the unmanifest. Call it God if you will. This is the point, this is the space, from which all has arisen. This is the very seed of the whole existence. It is omnipotent, it is omnipresent, it is eternal.

Fixating contemplation is indispensable.

What is contemplation? A moment of no-thought. A state of no-thought, an interval. And it is always happening, but you are not alert about it; otherwise there is no problem in it. One thought comes, then another comes, and between these two thoughts there is always a small gap. And that gap is the door to the divine, that gap is contemplation. If you look into that gap deeply, it starts becoming bigger and bigger.

The mind is like a road full of traffic; one car passes by, then another car passes by, and you become so concerned with the cars that you don't see the gap that is always there between two cars. Otherwise they would collide. They don't collide; something is there between them that keeps them separate. Your thoughts don't collide, they don't run over each other, into each other. They don't even overlap in any way. Each thought has its own boundary, each thought is definable, but the procession of thoughts is so fast, so speedy, that you cannot see the gap unless you are really waiting for it, searching for it.

Contemplation means changing the gestalt. Ordinarily we look at thoughts: one thought, another thought, another thought. When you change the gestalt you look at one interval, another interval, another interval. Your emphasis is no longer on the thoughts but on the interval.

One must not stay sitting rigidly if worldly thoughts come up, but one must examine where the thought is, where it began, and where it fades out.

This is not going to happen in the first try. You will be looking at the tip of the nose and thoughts will come. They have been coming for so many lives, they cannot leave you alone so easily. They have become part of you, they have become almost built-in. You are living almost a programmed life.

This happens: when people sit silently in meditation more thoughts come than ordinarily, than usually come – unusual explosions. Millions of thoughts rush in, because they have some investment in you – and you are trying to get out of their power? They will give you a hard time. So thoughts are bound to come. What are you going to do with thoughts? You cannot just go on sitting there, you will have to do something. Fighting is not going to help because if you start fighting you will forget to look at the tip of the nose, the awareness of the third eye, the circulation of the light; you will forget all and you will be lost in the jungle of thoughts. If you start chasing thoughts you are lost, if you follow them you are lost, if you fight them you are lost. Then what is to be done?

And this is the secret. Buddha has also used the same secret. In fact, the secrets are almost the same because man is the same – the lock is the same, so the key has to be the same. This is the secret: Buddha calls it *sammasati,* right remembrance. Just remember: this thought has come, see where it is, with no antagonism, with no justification, with no condemnation. Just be objective as a scientist is objective. See where it is, from where it is coming, where it is going. See the coming of it, see the staying of it, see the going of it. And thoughts are very mobile; they don't stay long. You simply have to watch the arising of the thought, the staying of the thought, and the going of the thought. Don't try to fight, don't try to follow, just be a silent observer. And you will be surprised: the more settled observation becomes, the less thoughts will come. When observation is perfect, thoughts disappear. There is only a gap left, an interval left.

But remember one more point: the mind can again play a trick.

Nothing is gained by pushing reflection further.

That's what Freudian psychoanalysis is: the free association of thoughts. One thought comes, and then you wait for another thought, and then another, and the whole chain…. That's what all kinds of psychoanalysis do – you start moving backwards into the past. One thought is connected with another, and so on and so forth, *ad infinitum.* There is no end to it. If you go into it you will be moving into an eternal journey that will be a sheer wastage. Mind can do that. So beware of it.

You cannot go with mind beyond mind, so don't try the futile, the unnecessary; otherwise one thing will lead you to another and so on and so forth, and you will completely forget what you were trying to do there. The tip of the nose will disappear, the third eye will be forgotten, the circulation of the light will be miles away from you.

So these two things have to be remembered, these are two wings. One: when there is an interval, no thought is coming, contemplate. When a thought comes then just look at these three things: where the thought is, from where it has come, where it is going. For a moment stop looking into the gap, look at the thought, watch the thought, say good-bye to it. When it leaves,

again immediately move back to contemplation.

When the flight of the thoughts keeps extending further, one should stop and begin contemplating. Let one contemplate and then start fixating again.

So, whenever the thought comes, fixate. Whenever the thought goes, contemplate.

That is the double method of making fast the enlightenment. It means the circulation of the light. The circulation is fixation. The light is contemplation.

Whenever you contemplate you will see light flooding in, and whenever you fixate you will create the circulation, you will make the circulation possible. Both are needed.

The light is contemplation. Fixation without contemplation is circulation without light.

That's what has happened; that calamity has happened to hatha yoga. They fixate, they concentrate, but they have forgotten the light. They have completely forgotten about the guest. They only go on preparing the house, they have become so engrossed in preparing the house that they have forgotten the purpose for which they are preparing the house, for whom. The hatha yogi continuously prepares his body, purifies his body, does yoga postures, breathing exercises, and goes on doing it *ad nauseam.* He has completely forgotten what he is doing it for. And the light is standing there but he won't allow it because the light can come in only when he is completely in a let-go.

Fixation without contemplation is circulation without light.

This is the calamity that happens to the so-called yogis. The other kind of calamity happens to psychoanalysts, philosophers.

Contemplation without fixation is light without circulation.

They think about the light, but they have not made the preparation for it to flood in; they only *think* of light. They think of the guest, they imagine a thousand and one things about the guest, but their house is not ready. Both miss.

Take note of that!

Don't fall into either of these two fallacies. If you can remain alert, it is a very simple process and immensely transforming. In a single moment, a man who understands rightly can enter into a separate kind of reality. [5]

Just Sitting

Y ou are simply sitting there, doing nothing ... and all is silence and all is peace and all is bliss. You have entered God, you have entered truth. [1]

The Zen people say just sit, don't do anything. The *most* difficult thing in the world is just to sit doing nothing. But once you have got the knack of it, if you go on sitting for a few months doing nothing for a few hours every day, slowly, slowly many things will happen. You will feel sleepy, you will dream. Many thoughts will crowd your mind, many things. The mind will say, "Why are you wasting your time? You could have earned a little money. At least you could have gone to a film, entertained your-

Zazen

self, or you could have relaxed and gossiped. You could have watched the TV or listened to the radio, or at least you could have read the newspaper you have not seen. Why are you wasting your time?" Mind will give you a thousand and one arguments, but if you just go on listening without being bothered by the mind...it will do all kinds of tricks; it will hallucinate, it will dream, it will become sleepy. It will do all that is possible to drag you out of just sitting. But if you go on, if you persevere, one day the sun rises.

One day it happens, you are not feeling sleepy, the mind has become tired of you, is fed up with you, has dropped the idea that you can be trapped, is simply finished with you! There is no sleep, no hal- lucination, no dream, no thought. You are simply sitting there, doing nothing ... and all is silence and all is peace and all is bliss. You have entered God, you have entered truth. 2

You can sit anywhere, but what- soever you are looking at should not be too exciting. For example things should not be moving too much. They become a distraction.

You can watch the trees – that is not a problem because they are not moving and the scene remains constant. You can watch the sky or just sit in the corner watching the wall.

The second thing is, don't look at anything in particular – just emptiness, because the eyes are there and one has to look at something, but you are not looking at anything in particular. Don't focus or concentrate on anything – just a diffuse image. That relaxes very much.

And the third thing, relax your breathing. Don't do it, let it happen. Let it be natural and that will relax even more.

The fourth thing is, let your body remain as immobile as possible. First find a good posture – you can sit on a pillow or mattress or whatsoever you feel to, but once you settle, remain immobile, because if the body does not move, the mind automatically falls silent. In a moving body, the mind also continues to move, because body-mind are not two things. They are one ... it is one energy.

In the beginning it will seem a little difficult but after a few days you will enjoy it tremendously. You will see, by and by, layer upon layer of the mind starting to drop. A moment comes when you are simply there with no mind. [3]

Instructions

Sit facing a plain wall, approximately at your arm's length away. Eyes should be half-open allowing the gaze to rest softly on the wall. Keep your back straight, and rest one hand inside the other with thumbs touching to form an oval. Stay as still as possible for 30 minutes.

While sitting, just allow a choiceless awareness, not directing the attention anywhere in particular, but remaining as receptive and alert as possible, moment to moment. [4]

200

Buddha was to give a special talk one day, and thousands of followers had come from miles around.

When Buddha appeared he was holding a flower. Time passed, but Buddha said nothing. He just looked at the flower. The crowd grew restless, but Mahakashyap, who could restrain himself no longer, laughed.

Buddha beckoned him over, handed him the flower, and said to the crowd: "I have the eye of the true teaching. All that can be given with words I have given to you;

The Laughter of Zen

but with this flower, I give to Mahakashyap the key to this teaching."

This story is one of the most significant ones, because from this was passed the tradition of Zen. Buddha was the source, and Mahakashyap was the first, the original master of Zen. Buddha was the source, Mahakashyap was the first master, and this story is the source

from where the whole tradition – one of the most beautiful and alive that exists on earth, the tradition of Zen – started.

Try to understand this story. Buddha came one morning, and as usual a crowd had gathered. Many people were waiting to listen to him. But one thing was unusual – he was carrying a flower in his hand. Never before had he carried

anything in his hand. People thought that someone must have presented it.

Buddha came; he sat under the tree. The crowd waited and waited and he would not speak. He wouldn't even look at them. He just went on looking at the flower. Minutes passed, then hours, and the people became very restless.

It is said that Mahakashyap couldn't

contain himself – he laughed loudly. Buddha called him, gave him the flower and said to the gathered crowd, "Whatsoever can be said through words, I have said to you, and that which cannot be said through words, I give to Mahakashyap. The key cannot be communicated verbally. I hand over the key to Mahakashyap."

But for Zen this is the origin. Mahakashyap became the first holder of the key. Then six holders in succession existed in India, up to Bodhidharma. He was the sixth holder of the key, and then he searched and searched all over India, but he couldn't find a man of the capability of Mahakashyap – a man who could understand silence. He had to leave India just in search of a man to whom the key could be given; otherwise the key would be lost.

Buddhism entered China with Bodhidharma in search of a man to whom the key could be given, a man who could understand silence, who could talk heart to heart without being obsessed in the mind, who had no head.

This communication beyond words is possible only from heart to heart. So, for nine years, Bodhidharma searched in China, and then he could find only one man.

A Chinese became the seventh master. And up to now it has been traveling. The key is still there; somebody is still holding it. The river has not dried.

We require even a Buddha to talk, because that's all we understand. This is foolish. You should learn to be silent with a Buddha, because only then can he enter you. Through words he can knock at your door, but can never enter; through silence he can enter you, and unless he enters, nothing will happen to you. His entry will bring a new element to your world; his entry into the heart will give you a new beat and a new pulse, a new release of life, but only his entry.

Mahakashyap laughed at the foolishness of man. They were restless and thinking: When will Buddha stand up and drop this whole silence so that we can go home? He laughed.

Laughter started with Mahakashyap, and has been going on and on in Zen tradition. There is no other tradition which can laugh. In Zen monasteries, they have been laughing and laughing and laughing.

Mahakashyap laughed, and this laughter carried many dimensions in it. One dimension was at the foolishness of the whole situation, at a Buddha silent and nobody understanding him, everybody expecting him to speak. His whole life Buddha had been saying that the truth cannot be spoken, and still everybody expected him to speak.

The second dimension – he laughed at Buddha also, at the whole dramatic situation he had created, sitting there with a flower in his hand, looking at the flower, creating so much uneasiness, restlessness, in everybody. At this dramatic gesture of Buddha, he laughed and he laughed.

The third dimension – he laughed at his own self. Why couldn't he understand up to now? The whole thing was easy and simple. And the day you understand, you will laugh, because there is nothing to be understood. There is no difficulty to be solved. Everything has always been simple and clear. How could you miss it?

With Buddha sitting silent, the birds singing in the trees, the breeze passing through the trees, and everybody restless, Mahakashyap understood.

What did he understand? He understood that there is nothing to be understood, there is nothing to be said, there is nothing to be explained. The whole situation is simple and transparent. Nothing is hidden in it. There is no need to search, because all that is, is here and now, within you.

He laughed at his own self also, at the whole absurd effort of many lives just to understand this silence – at so much thinking.

Buddha called him, gave him the flower and said: "Hereby, I give you the key."

What is the key? Silence and laughter is the key – silence within, laughter without. And when laughter comes out of silence, it is not of this world, it is divine.

When laughter comes out of silence you are not laughing at anybody's cost. You are simply laughing at the whole cosmic joke. And it really is a joke. That's why I go on telling jokes to you, because jokes carry more than any scriptures. It is a joke because inside you, you have everything, and you are searching everywhere. What else should a joke be?

You are a king, and acting like a beggar in the streets; not only acting, not only deceiving others, but deceiving yourself that you are a beggar. You have the source of all knowledge and are asking questions; you have the knowing self and think that you are ignorant; you have the deathless within you and are afraid and fearful of death and disease. This really is a joke, and if Mahakashyap laughed, he did well. Mahakashyap has remained silent, and silently the inner river has been flowing. To others the key has been given, and the key is still alive, still opens the door.

These two are the parts. The inner silence – the silence so deep that there is no vibration in your being; you are, but there are no waves; you are just a pool, without waves, not a single wave arises; the whole being silent, still; inside, at the center, silence – and on the periphery, celebration and laughter. And only silence can laugh, because only silence can understand the cosmic joke.

I tell you, the silence that exists with sadness cannot be true. Something has gone wrong. You have missed the path; you are off the track. Only celebration can give proof that the real silence has happened.

What is the difference between a real silence and a false silence? A false silence is always forced. Through effort it is achieved. It is not spontaneous, it has not happened to you. You have made it happen.

You are sitting silently and there is much inner turmoil. You suppress it and then you cannot laugh. You will become sad because laughter will be dangerous – if you laugh you will lose silence, because in laughter you cannot suppress. Laughter is against suppression. If you want to suppress, you should not laugh; if you laugh, everything will come out. The real will come out in laughter, and the unreal will be lost.

This is the key – the inner part of it is silence, and the outer part of the key is celebration, laughter. Be festive and silent. Create more and more possibility around you – don't force the inner to be silent, just create more and more possibility around you so that the inner silence can flower in it.

Meditation doesn't lead you to silence. Meditation only creates the situation in which the silence happens. And this should be the criterion – that whenever silence happens, laughter will come into your life. A vital celebration will happen all around.

When silence is too much, it becomes laughter. It becomes so overflooded that it starts overflowing in all directions. He laughed. It must have been a mad laughter, and in that laughter there was no Mahakashyap. Silence was laughing. Silence had come to a blossoming.

Your enlightenment is perfect only when silence has come to be a celebration. Hence my insistence that after you meditate, you must celebrate. After you have been silent, you must enjoy it, you must have a thanksgiving. A deep gratitude must be shown towards the whole just for the opportunity that you are, that you can meditate, that you can be silent, that you can laugh. [5]

Rising in Love: A Partnership in Meditation

There are a few very fundamental things to be understood.

First, a man and a woman are on the one hand halves of the other, and on the other hand, opposite polarities.

Their being opposites attracts them to each other. The farther away they are, the deeper will be the attraction; the more different from each other they are, the more will be the charm and beauty and attraction. But there lies the whole problem.

When they come close, they want to come closer, they want to merge into each other, they want to become one, a harmonious whole – but their whole attraction depends on opposition, and the harmony will depend on dissolving the opposition.

Unless a love affair is very conscious, it is going to create great anguish, great trouble. All lovers are in trouble. The trouble is not personal; it is in the very nature of things. They would not have been attracted to each other – they call it falling in love – they cannot give any reason why they have such a tremendous pull towards each other. They are not even conscious of the underlying causes;

hence a strange thing happens: the happiest lovers are those who never meet.

Once they meet, the same opposition that created the attraction becomes a conflict. On each small point, their attitudes are different, their approaches are different. Although they speak the same language, they cannot understand each other.

The way a man looks at the world is different from a woman. For example, a man is interested in faraway things – in the future of humanity, in the faraway stars, whether there are living beings on other planets or not.

A woman simply giggles at the whole nonsense. She is only interested in a very small, closed circle – in the neighbors, in the family, in who is cheating his wife, whose wife has fallen in love with the chauffeur. Her interest is very local and very human. She is not worried about reincarnation; neither is she concerned about life after death. Her concern is more pragmatic. She is concerned with the present, here and now.

Man is never here and now. He is always somewhere else. He has strange preoccupations – reincarnation, life after death.

If both partners are conscious of the fact that it is a meeting of opposi-

tions, that there is no need to make it a conflict, then it is a great opportunity to understand the totally opposite point of view and absorb it. Then the life of a man and woman together can become a beautiful harmony. Otherwise, it is a continuous fight.

There are holidays. One cannot continue to fight twenty-four hours a day, one needs a little rest too – a rest to get ready for a new fight.

But it is one of the strangest phenomena that for thousands of years men and women have been living together, yet they are strangers. They go on giving birth to children, but still they remain strangers. The feminine approach and the masculine approach are so opposed to each other that unless a conscious effort is made, unless it becomes your meditation, there is no hope of having a peaceful life.

It is one of my deep concerns: how to make love and meditation so involved in each other that each love affair automatically becomes a partnership in meditation – and each meditation makes you so conscious that you need not fall in love, you can *rise* in love. You can find a friend consciously, deliberately.

You feel a deep harmony with me, moments of peace, love and silence, and naturally the question has arisen in you that if this is pos-

sible with me, why is it not possible with the man you love?

The difference has to be understood.

You love me, but you don't love me in the same way you love your husband, your wife. Your love towards me is not biological; with me your love is a totally different phenomenon – it is of the spirit, not of the body.

And secondly, you are connected with me because of your search for truth. My relationship with you is that of meditation. Meditation is the only bridge between me and you. Your love will deepen as your meditation deepens, and vice-versa: as your meditation blossoms, your love will also blossom. But it is on a totally different level.

With your husband, you are not connected in meditation. You never sit silently for one hour together just to feel each other's consciousness. Either you are fighting or you are making love, but in both cases, you are related with the body, the physical part, the biology, the hormones. You are not related with the innermost core of the other. Your souls remain separate. In the temples and in the churches and in the courts, only your bodies are married. Your souls are miles apart.

If you want a harmonious relationship with your man, you will have to learn to be more meditative. Love alone is not enough.

Love alone is blind; meditation gives it eyes. Meditation gives it understanding. And once your love is both love and meditation, you become fellow travelers. Then it is no longer an ordinary relationship between husband and wife. Then it becomes a friendliness on the path towards discovering the mysteries of life.

Man alone, woman alone, will find the journey very tedious and very long, as they have found it in the past: seeing this continuous conflict, all the religions decided that those who wanted to seek should renounce the other – the monks should be celibate, the nuns should be celibate. But in five thousand years of history, how many monks and how many nuns have become realized souls? You cannot even give me enough names to count on ten fingers. And millions of monks and nuns of all religions – Buddhist, Hindu, Christian, Mohammedan – what has happened?

The path is not so long. The goal is not that far away. But even if you want to go to your neighbor's house, you will need both your legs. Just jumping on one leg, how far can you go?

I am introducing a totally new vision, that men and women together in deep friendship, in a loving, meditative relationship, as organic wholes, can reach the goal any moment they want. Because the goal is not outside you; it is the center of the cyclone, it is the innermost part of your being. But you can find it only when you are whole, and you cannot be whole without the other. Man and woman are two parts of one whole.

So rather than wasting time in fighting, try to understand each other. Try to put yourself in the place of the other; try to see as a man sees, try to see as a woman sees. And four eyes are always better than two eyes – you have a full view; all four directions are available to you.

But one thing has to be remembered: that without meditation, love is destined to fail; there is no possibility of its being a success. You can pretend and you can deceive others, but you cannot deceive yourself. You know deep down that all the promises love has given to you have remained unfulfilled.

Only with meditation does love start taking on new colors, new music, new songs, new dances – because meditation gives you the insight to understand the polar opposite, and in that very understanding the conflict disappears.

All the conflict in the world is because of misunderstanding. You say something, your wife understands something else. Your wife says something, you understand something else.

I have seen couples who have lived together for thirty or forty years; still, they seem to be as immature as they were on their first day together. Still the same complaint: "She doesn't understand what I am saying." Forty years being together and you have not been able to figure out some way that your wife can understand exactly what you are saying, and so you can understand exactly what she is saying.

I think there is no possibility for it to happen except through meditation, because meditation gives you the qualities of silence, awareness, a patient listening, a capacity to put yourself in the other's position.

It is possible with me: I am not concerned with the trivia of your life. You are here basically to listen and understand. You are here to grow spiritually. Naturally there is no question of conflict, and the harmony arises without any effort.

You can love me with totality, because with me your relationship is of meditation. With any other man or with any other woman, if you want to live in harmony you will have to bring the same atmosphere and the same climate that you have brought here.

Things are not impossible, but we have not tried the right medicine. I would like to remind you that the word 'medicine' comes from the same root as 'meditation'. Medicine cures your body; meditation cures your soul. Medicine heals the material part of you; meditation heals the spiritual part of you.

People are living together and their spirits are full of wounds; hence, small things hurt them so much. People are living without any understanding. Hence, whatsoever they do is going to end in disaster.

If you love a man, meditation will be the best present that you can give to him. If you love a woman, then the Kohinoor, the world's largest diamond, is nothing; meditation will be a far more precious gift – and it will make your life sheer joy.

We are potentially capable of sheer joy, but we don't know how to manage it. Alone, we are at the most sad. Together, it becomes really hell.

Even a man like Jean-Paul Sartre, a man of great intelligence, has to say that the other is hell, that to be alone is better, you cannot make it with the other. He became so pessimistic that he said it is impossible to make it with the other, the other is hell. Ordinarily, he is right. With meditation the other becomes your heaven. But Jean-Paul Sartre had no idea of meditation.

That is the misery of Western man. Western man is missing the flowering of life because he knows nothing about meditation, and Eastern man is missing because he knows nothing of love.

And to me, just as man and woman are halves of one whole, so are love and meditation. Meditation is man; love is woman. In the meeting of meditation and love is the meeting of man and woman. And in that meeting, we create the transcendental human being – which is neither man nor woman.

Unless we create the transcendental man on the earth, there is not much hope. But I feel my people are capable of doing the apparently impossible. [1]

Shiva said: Feel the fine qualities of creativity permeating your breast and assuming delicate configurations.

Just concentrate on the breasts, become one, forget the whole body. Move your total consciousness to the breasts and there will be many phenomena happening to you. If you can do this, concentrate totally near the breasts, the whole body will lose weight, and a very sweet, deep sweetness will envelop you. It will pulsate around you, within you, above,

Circle of Love

below, everywhere – a deep feeling of sweetness.

Really, all the techniques that have been developed have been developed more or less by men, so they always give centers which are easier for men to follow. As far as I know, only Shiva has given some techniques which are basically for women.

A man cannot do this technique.

Really if a man tries to concentrate near the breasts he will become very uneasy. Try it. Even within five minutes you will feel perspiration, you will become very uneasy, because male breasts are negative, they will give you negativity. You will feel uneasy, uncomfortable, feel that something is going wrong in the body, unhealthy, ill.

But female breasts are positive. If

women concentrate near the breasts, they will feel very happy, very blissful, a sweetness will pervade all over their being and the body will lose gravity. They will feel light, as if they can fly. And with this concentration many things will change: you will become more motherly. You may not be a mother but you will become more motherly. To everyone your relationship will become motherly – more compassion, more love will happen. But this concentration near the breasts should be done very relaxedly, not tensely. If you are tense about it there will be a division between you and the breasts. Relax and melt into them, and feel that you are no more, only the breasts are there.

If man has to do the same he will have to do it with the sex center, not with the breasts. Hence the importance of the first chakra in all kundalini yogas. He has to concentrate just at the root of the penis – there he has the creativity, there he is positive. And remember this always: never concentrate on anything negative because with the negative everything negative will follow. With the positive, everything positive will follow.

When man and woman meet, these two poles – negative is in the upper part of man, and positive in the lower; negative is in the lower part of woman and positive in the upper – these two poles of positive and negative meet and a circle is created. That circle is blissful, but it is not ordinary. In ordinary sexual acts, the circle is not happening – that is why you feel so attracted to-

wards sex, and so repelled also. You feel so much for it, you need so much, you ask so much, but when it is given, when it is there, you feel frustration – nothing happens. This is possible only when both the bodies are so relaxed and so open to each other without any fear, without any resistance. The let-go is so complete that the electricities can merge and meet and become a circle.

Then there is a very strange phenomenon…tantra has recorded it and you may not have heard of that phenomenon. This is the phenomenon, the very strangest one – when two lovers really meet and become a circle, then a flickering happens. For a moment the lover becomes the beloved and the beloved becomes the lover, and the next moment, again the lover is lover and the beloved is beloved. The male becomes the female for a moment, then the female becomes the male for a moment – because the circle is moving, the energy is moving, it has become one circle. So it will happen that the male will be active for a few minutes and then he will relax and the female will become active. That means now the male energy has passed to

the feminine body and she will act and the male will remain passive. And this will go on. Ordinarily you are man, woman. In deep love, in deep orgasm, it will happen that for moments you will become woman, and the woman will become man. And this will be felt, absolutely felt and recognized, that the passivity changes.

In life there is rhythm; in everything there is rhythm. You take a breath, the breath goes in – then for a few seconds it stops, there is no movement. Then again it moves, out it goes – then again there is a stop, a gap, no movement, then again movement. Movement, no movement, movement. Your heart is beating, one beat, gap, another beat, gap. The beat means activity, the gap means passivity. The beat means male, the non-beat means female.

Life is rhythm. While two persons meet, male and female, it becomes a circle: there will be gaps – for both. You will be a woman and suddenly there will be a gap, you are no more a woman, you have become a man. You will be man and woman and man. And when these gaps are felt, then you can feel that you have achieved a circle. [2]

Shiva said: When in such embrace your senses are shaken as leaves, enter this shaking.

"When in such embrace," in such deep communion with the beloved or the lover, "your senses are shaken as leaves, enter this shaking." We have even become afraid: while making love you do not allow your bodies to move much, because if your bodies are allowed much movement the sex act spreads all over your body. You can control it when it is localized

Shaking in Sex

at the sex center. The mind can remain in control. When it spreads all over your body, you cannot control it. You may start shaking, you may start screaming, and you will not be able to control your body once the body takes over. We suppress movements. Particularly, all over the world, we suppress all movements, all shaking for women. They remain just like dead bodies. You are doing something to them; they are not doing anything to you. They are just passive partners. Why is this happening? Why all over the world do men suppress women in such a way? There is fear – because once a woman's body becomes possessed, it is very difficult for a man to satisfy her because a woman can have chain orgasms; a man cannot. A man can have only one orgasm; a woman can have chain orgasms. There are cases of multiple orgasms reported. Any woman can have at least three orgasms in a chain, but man can have only one. And with man's orgasm, the woman is aroused and is ready for further orgasms. Then it is difficult. Then how to manage it!

Shake! Vibrate! Allow every cell of your body to dance, and this should be for both. The beloved is also dancing, every cell vibrating. Only then can you both meet, and then that meeting is not mental. It is a meeting of your bio-energies.

Shaking is just wonderful because when you shake in your sex act the energy starts flowing all over the body, the energy vibrates all over the body. Every cell of the body is involved then. Every cell becomes alive because every cell is a sex cell.

When you were born, two sex cells met and your being was created, your body was created. Those two sex cells are everywhere in your body. They have multiplied and multiplied and multiplied, but your basic unit remains the sex cell. When you shake all over your body, it is not only a meeting of you with your beloved. Within your body also, each cell is meeting with the opposite cell. This shaking shows it. It will look animal like, but man is an animal and there is nothing wrong in it.

Enter this shaking, and while shaking don't remain aloof. Don't be a spectator, because mind is the spectator. Don't stand aloof! Be the shaking, become the shaking. Forget everything and become the shaking. It is not that your body is shaking: it is *you,* your whole being. You become the shaking itself. Then there are not two bodies, two minds. In the beginning, there are two shaking energies, and in the end just a circle – not two.

What will happen in this circle? One, you will be part of an existential force – not a societal mind, but an existential force. You will be part of the whole cosmos. In that shaking you will be part of the whole cosmos. That moment is of great creation. You are dissolved as solid bodies. You have become liquid – flowing into each other. The mind is lost, the division is lost. You have a oneness.

This is *adwaita:* this is non-duality. And if you cannot feel *this* non-duality, then all the philosophies of non-duality are useless. They are just words. Once you know *this* non-dual existential moment, then only can you understand the *Upanishads.* Then only you can understand the mystics – what they are talking about when they talk of a cosmic oneness, a wholeness. Then you are not separate from the world, not alien to it. Then existence becomes your home. And with that feeling that "Now I am at home in existence," all worries are lost. Then there is no anguish, no struggle, no conflict. This is what Lao Tzu calls *Tao,* what Shankara calls *adwaita.* You can choose your own word for it, but through a deep love embrace, it is easy to feel it. Be alive, shaking, and become the shaking itself. [3]

Shiva said: Even remembering union, without the embrace, the transformation!

Once you know these previous two meditations, even the partner is not needed. You can simply remember the act and enter into it. But first you must have the feeling. If you know the feeling, you can enter into the act without the partner. This is a little difficult, but it happens. And unless it happens, you go on being dependent: a dependency is created. For so many reasons it happens.

Circle of Love Alone

If you have had the feeling, if you have known the moment when *you* were not there but only a vibrating energy – you had become one and there was a circle with the partner – in that moment there was no partner. In that moment only you are, and for the partner you are not: only he or she is. That oneness is centered within you; the partner is no more there. And it is easier for women to have this feeling because they are always making love with closed eyes.

During the technique, it is good if you have your eyes closed. Then only an inner feeling of a circle is there, only an inner feeling of oneness. Then just remember it. Close your eyes; lie down as if you are with your partner. Just remember and start feeling it. Your body will begin to shake and vibrate. Allow it! Forget completely that the other is not there. Move as if the other is present. Only in the beginning is it 'as if'. Once you know, then it is not 'as if'. Then the other is there. Move as if you are actually going into the love act. Do whatsoever you would have done with your partner. Scream, move, shake. Soon the circle will be there, and this circle is miraculous. Soon you will feel that the circle is created, but now this circle is not created with a man and woman. If you are man, then the whole universe has become woman; if you are woman, then the whole universe has become man. Now you are in a deep communion with existence itself, and the door, the other, is no more there. The other is simply a door. While making love to a woman, you are really making love to existence itself. The woman is just a door, the man is just a door. The other is just a door for the whole, but you are in such a hurry you never feel it. If you remain in communion, in deep embrace for hours together, you will forget the other and the other will just become an extension of the whole. Once this technique is known you can use it alone, and when you can use it alone it gives you a new freedom – freedom from the other.

Really, it happens that the whole existence becomes the other – your beloved, your lover – and then this technique can be used continuously, and one can remain in constant communion with existence. And then you can do it in other dimensions also. Walking in the morning, you can do it. Then you are in communion with the air, with the rising sun and the stars and the trees. Staring at the stars in the night, you can do it. Looking at the moon, you can do it. You can be in the sex act with the whole universe once you know how it happens.

But it is good to start with human beings because they are nearest to you – the nearest part of the universe. But they are dispensable. You can take a jump and forget the door completely. "Even remembering union, the transformation." And you *will* be transformed: you will become new.

Tantra says move in it totally. Just forget yourself, your civilization, your religion, your culture, your ideology. Forget everything. Just move in the sex act: move in it totally; don't leave anything out. Become absolutely non-thinking. Then only does the awareness happen that you have become one with someone. And this feeling of oneness can then be detached from the partner and it can be used with the whole universe. You can be in a sex act with a tree, with the moon, with anything. Once you know how to create this circle, it can be created with anything – even without anything.

You can create this circle within yourself because man is both man and woman, and woman is both woman and man. You are both because you were created by two. You were created by man and woman both, so half of you remains the other. You can forget everything completely, and the circle can be created within you. Once the circle is created within you – your man is meeting your woman; the inner woman is meeting the inner man – you are in an embrace within yourself. And only when this circle is created is real celibacy attained. Otherwise all celibacies are just perversions, and then they create their own problems. When this circle is created inside, you are freed. [4]

PART FOUR

Obstacles to Meditation

The Two Difficulties

There are only two difficulties on the path of meditation: one is the ego. You are continuously prepared by the society, by the family, by the school, by the church, by everybody around you, to be egoistic. Even modern psychology is based on strengthening the ego.

The ego

The whole idea of modern psychology, modern education, is that unless a person has a very strong ego he will not be able to struggle in life where there is so much competition that, if you are a humble man, anybody will push you aside; you will always remain backward. You need a very steely, strong ego to fight in this competitive world; then only can you become a success. In any field – it may be business, it may be politics, it may be any profession – you need a very assertive personality, and our whole society is geared to produce the assertive personality in the child. From the very beginning we start telling him, "Come first in your class"; when the child does come first in the class, everybody praises him. What are you doing? You are feeding his ego from the very beginning. You are giving him a certain ambition: "You can become the president of the country, you can become the prime minister of the country." He starts the journey with these ideas, and his ego goes on becoming bigger and bigger as he succeeds.

In every way the ego is the greatest disease that can happen to man. If you succeed, your ego becomes big – that is a danger, because then you will have to remove a big rock which is blocking the path. Or if the ego is small, you have not been successful, you have proved to be a failure, then your ego will become a wound. Then it hurts, then it creates an inferiority complex – then too it creates a problem. You are always afraid to enter into anything, even meditation, because you know you are a failure, that you are going to fail – that has become your mind. Everywhere you have failed, and meditation is such a great thing…you cannot succeed.

If you enter into meditation with this idea – that failure is bound to be, that it is your destiny, that it is your fate – then of course you cannot succeed. So if the ego is big it prevents you. And if the ego

216

is very small it becomes a wound which also prevents you. In each case the ego is one of the problems. [1]

In the mother's womb each child is profoundly blissful. Of course he is unaware of it, not knowing anything about it. He is so one with his bliss that there is no knower left behind. Blissfulness is his being, and there is no distinction between the knower and the known. So of course the child is not aware that he is blissful. You become aware only when you have lost something.

It is so. It is very difficult to know something without losing it, because when you have not lost it you are so totally one with it. There is no distance: the observer and the observed are one; the known and the knower are one.

Every child is in a profoundly blissful state. Psychologists also agree with this. They say that the whole search of religion is nothing but a way to again find the womb of the mother. They use it as a criticism of religion, but to me it is not criticism at all. It is simply true. Yes, the search for religion is again a search for the womb. The search for religion is again a search to make this whole existence a womb.

The child is absolutely in tune with the mother. The child is never out of tune with the mother. The child does not know that he is separate from the mother. If the mother is healthy the child is healthy; if the mother is ill the child is ill. If the mother is sad the child is sad; if the mother is happy the child is happy. If the mother is dancing the child is dancing; if the mother is sitting silently the child is silent. The child has no boundaries of his own yet. This is the purest bliss, but it has to be lost.

The child is born, and suddenly he is thrown off-center. Suddenly he is uprooted from the earth, from the mother. He loses his moorings and he does not know who he is. There was no need to know it when he was with the mother. There was no need to know – he was all, and there was no need to know, there was no distinction. There was no 'you', so there was no question of 'I'. The reality was undivided. It was *adwaita* – pure *adwaita*, pure non-duality.

But once the child is born, the umbilical cord is cut and he starts breathing on his own; suddenly his whole being becomes a quest to know who he is. It is natural. Now he starts becoming aware of his boundaries – his body, his needs. Sometimes he is happy, sometimes unhappy; sometimes he is fulfilled, sometimes not fulfilled; sometimes he is hungry and crying and there is no sign of mother anywhere; sometimes he is on the mother's breast, again enjoying oneness with the mother. But now there are many moods and many climates, and he will start, by and by, to feel the separation. A divorce has happened; the marriage is broken.

He was absolutely married to the mother; now he will always be separate. And he has to find out who he is. For the whole life one goes on trying to find out who one is. This is the most fundamental question.

First the child becomes aware of 'mine', then of 'me', then of 'you', then of 'I'. This is how it proceeds. This is precisely the procedure, exactly in this order. First he becomes aware of 'mine'. Watch it, because this is your construction, the structure of your ego. First the child becomes aware of 'mine' – this toy is mine, this mother is mine. He starts possessing. The possessor enters first; possessiveness is very basic. Hence all the religions say: become non-possessive, because with possession hell starts.

Watch small children: very jealous, possessive, each child trying to snatch everything from everybody else and trying to protect his own toys. And you will see children who are very violent, almost indifferent to others' needs. If a child is playing with his toy and another child comes you can see an Adolf Hitler, a Genghis Khan, a Nadirshah. He will cling to his toy; he is ready to hit, he is ready to fight. It is a question of territory, a question of domination.

Possessiveness enters first; that is the basic poison. And the child starts saying, "This is mine."

Once the 'mine' enters then you are a competitor with everybody. Once the 'mine' enters, your life will now be a life of competition, struggle, conflict, violence, aggression.

The next step after 'mine' is 'me'. When you have something to claim as yours, suddenly through that claim arises the idea that now you are the center of your possessions. The possessions become your territory, and through those possessions arises a new idea: 'me'.

Once you are settled with 'me', you can see clearly that you have a boundary, and those who are outside the boundary are 'you'. The other becomes clear; now things start falling apart.

The universe is one, it is a unity. Nothing is divided. Everything is connected with everything else; it is a tremendous connectedness.

You are connected with the earth, you are connected with the trees, you are connected with the stars; stars are connected with you, stars are connected with the trees, with the rivers, with the mountains. Everything is interconnected. Nothing is separate; nothing can be separate. Separation is not possible.

Each moment you are breathing – you breathe in, you breathe out – continuously there is a bridge with existence. You eat, existence enters into you; you defecate, it becomes manure – the apple on the tree will become part of your body tomorrow, and some part of your body will go and become manure, will become food for the tree…a continuous give-and-take. Not for a single moment does it stop. When it stops, you are dead.

What is death? – separation is death. To be in unity is to be alive, to be out of unity is to be dead. So the more you think, "I am separate," the less sensitive you will be, more dead, dragging, dull. The more you feel you are connected, the more this whole existence is part of you and you are part of this whole existence. Once you understand that we are members of each other, then suddenly the vision changes. Then these trees are not alien; they are continuously preparing food for you. When you breathe in, you take oxygen in, when you breathe out, you give carbon diox-ide; the trees breathe in carbon dioxide and breathe out oxygen – there is a continuous communion. We are in tune. The reality is a unity, and with the idea of 'me', 'you', we are falling out of reality. And once a wrong conception settles inside, your whole vision becomes upside down….

'Me', then 'you', and then as a reflection arises 'I'. 'I' is the subtlest, the most crystallized form of the possessiveness. Once you have uttered 'I', you have committed sacrilege. Once you have said 'I', you are broken completely from existence – not really broken, otherwise you would die; but in your ideas you are completely broken from reality. Now you will be in a continuous fight with reality. You will be fighting your own roots. You will be fighting with yourself.

That's why Buddha says: "Be a driftwood." You can be a driftwood only if you have dropped the idea of 'I' – otherwise you cannot be a driftwood; struggle will persist. That's why it becomes so difficult when you come to meditate. If I say to just sit silently, you cannot do that – such a simple thing. One would think it is the most simple thing; there should be no need to teach it. One should simply sit and be. But you cannot sit because the 'I' cannot allow you a moment of relaxation. Once a moment of relaxation is allowed, you will be able to see reality. Once reality is known, the 'I' will have to be dropped. Then it cannot persist. So the 'I' never even allows you a holiday. Even if you go to the hills, to the summer resorts, the 'I' never allows you a holiday even there. You take your radio, you take your TV set; you take all your problems and you remain occupied. You had gone there to relax, but you continue your whole pattern in the same way. You don't relax.

The 'I' cannot relax. It exists through tensions. It will create new tensions, it will create new worries; it will constantly manufacture new problems, it won't allow you any rest. Even a minute's rest and the whole house of the 'I' starts toppling down – because the reality is so beautiful and the 'I' is so ugly.

One continues to fight his way unnecessarily. You are fighting for things which are going to happen of their own accord. You are unnecessarily fighting. You are desiring things which are going to be yours if you don't desire. In fact, by desiring you will lose them.

That's why Buddha says: "Float with the stream. Let it take you to the ocean."

'Mine', 'me', 'you', 'I' – this is the trap. And this trap creates misery, neurosis, madness.

Now the problem is: the child has to go through it, because he does not know who he is and he needs some sort of identity – maybe a false identity, but it is better than no identity. He needs some identity. He needs to know exactly who he is, so a false center is created. The 'I' is not your real center. It is a false center – utilitarian, make-believe, just manufactured by you. It has nothing to do with your real center.

Your real center is the center of all. Your real self is the self of all. At the center, the whole existence is one – just as at the source of light, the sun, all rays are one. The farther away they go, the farther away they are from each other.

Your real center is not only your center, it is the center of the whole. But we have created small centers of our own, homemade, manufactured by ourselves. There is a need …because the child is born without any boundary, with no idea of who he is. It is a survival necessity. How will he survive? He has to be given a name; he has to be given an idea of who he is. Of course this idea comes from the outside: somebody says you are beautiful, somebody says you are intelligent, somebody says you are so vital. You gather the things that people say.

Out of all that people say about you, you gather a certain image. You never look into yourself, at who you are. This image is going to be false – because nobody else can know who you are, and nobody else can say who you are. Your inner reality is not available to anybody else except you. Your inner reality is impenetrable to anybody else except you. Only *you* can be there.

The day you realize that your identity is false, put together, that you have collected opinions from people…sometime just think; just sit silently and think who you are. Many ideas will arise. Just go on watching from where they come and you will be able to find the source. Some things come from your mother – much, about eighty to ninety percent. Something comes from your father, something comes from your schoolteachers, something comes from your friends, something from the society. Just watch: you will be able to divide from where it comes. Nothing comes from you, not even one percent comes from you. What type of identity is this, in which you have not contributed at all? And you are the only one who could have contributed, in fact, the whole hundred percent.

The day you understand this, religion becomes important. The day you realize this you start seeking for some technique, some method to enter into your being; how to know exactly, really, existentially, who you are. No more collections of images from the outside, no more asking others to mirror your reality – but to face it directly, immediately; to enter into your nature, to feel it there. What is the need to ask anybody? And whom are you asking? They are as ignorant about themselves as you are about yourself. They don't know themselves; how can they know you?

Just see how things are functioning, how things go on functioning, how things go on happening: one falsity leads to another falsity. You are almost swindled, duped. You are conned, and those who have swindled you may not have done it knowingly. They may have been swindled by others. Your father, your mother, your teachers, have been duped by others – their fathers, their mothers, their teachers. And they have duped you in turn. Are you going to do the same to your children too?

In a better world, where people are more intelligent, more aware, they will teach the child that the idea of identity is false: "It is needed, we are giving it to you, but it is only for the time being, before you yourself discover who you are."

It is not going to be your reality. And the sooner you find out who you are, the better. The sooner you can drop this idea, the better – because from that very moment you will really be born, and you will be really real, authentic. You will become an individual.

The ideas that we gather from others give us a personality, and the knowledge that we come to know from within gives us individuality. Personality is false, individuality is real. Personality is borrowed; reality, individuality, your authenticity, can never be borrowed. Nobody can say who you are.

At least one thing can never be done by anybody else – that is, to give you the answer to who you are. No, you have to go, you have to dig deep into your own being. Layers and layers of identity, false identity, have to be broken. There is fear when one enters into oneself, because chaos comes in. Somehow you have managed with your false identity. You have settled with it. You know your name is this or that; you have certain credentials, certificates, degrees, universities, colleges, prestige, money, heritage. You have certain ways to define yourself. You have a certain definition – howsoever workable, but it works. Going in means dropping this workable definition...there will be chaos.

Before you can come to your center, you will have to pass through a very chaotic state. That's why there is fear. Nobody wants to go in. People go on teaching: "Know thyself"; we listen, but we never listen. We never bother about it. There is a very certain idea in the mind that chaos will be let loose and you will be lost in it, you will be engulfed in it. Because of the fear of that chaos, we go on clinging to anything from the outside. But this is wasting your life. [2]

The chattering mind

The second hindrance on the path of meditation is your constantly chattering mind. You cannot sit even for a single minute, the mind goes on chattering: relevant, irrelevant, meaningful, meaningless thoughts go on. It is a constant traffic and it is always rush-hour. [3]

You see a flower and you verbalize it; you see a man crossing the street and you verbalize it. The mind can translate every existential thing into a word, everything is being transformed. These words create a barrier, these words become an imprisonment. This constant flow toward the transformation of things into words, of existence into words, is the barrier. It is an obstacle to a meditative mind.

So the first requirement toward a meditative growth is to be aware of your constant verbalizing, and to be able to stop it. Just *see* things; do not verbalize. Be aware of their presence, but do not change them into words.

Let things be without language; let persons be without language; let situations be without language. It is not impossible, this is natural and possible. It is the situation as it now exists that is artificial, it is a created situation, but we have become so habituated to it, it has become so mechanical, that we are not even aware of the transformation, of the translation of experience into words.

The sunrise is there. You are never aware of the gap between seeing it and verbalizing. You see the sun, you feel it, and immediately you verbalize it. The gap between seeing and verbalizing is lost; it is never felt. In that interval, in that gap, one must become aware. One must be aware of the fact that the sunrise is not a word. It is a fact, a presence, a situation. The mind automatically changes experiences into words. These words are accumulated and then come between

existence (the existential) and consciousness.

Meditation means living without words, living non-linguistically. Then these piled up memories, these linguistic memories, become obstacles towards meditative growth. Meditation means living without words, living in a situation non-linguistically. Sometimes it happens spontaneously. When you are in love with someone it happens. If you are really in love, then presence is felt – not language. Whenever two lovers are intimate with one another they become silent. It is not that there is nothing to express; on the contrary, there is an overwhelming amount to be expressed. But words are never there; they cannot be. They come only when love has gone.

If two lovers are never silent, if they are always talking, it is an indication that love has died. Now they are filling the gap with words. When love is alive, words are not there, because the very existence of love is so overwhelming, so penetrating, that the barrier of language and words is crossed. And ordinarily, it is only crossed in love.

Meditation is the culmination of love: love not for a single person, but love for the total existence. To me, meditation is a living relationship with the total existence that

surrounds you. If you can be in love with any situation, then you are in meditation....

Society gives you language, it cannot exist without language; it needs language. But existence does not need it. I am not saying that you should exist without language. You will have to use it, but the mechanism of verbalization must be a mechanism that you can turn on and off. When you are existing as a social being, the mechanism of language is needed; without it you cannot exist in the society. But when you are alone with existence, the mechanism must be turned off; you must be able to turn it off. If you can't turn it off the mechanism has gone mad. If you can't turn it off – if it goes on and on, and you are incapable of turning it off, then the mechanism has taken hold of you. You have become a slave to it. Mind must be an instrument, not the master. But it has become the master.

When mind is the master, a non-meditative state exists. When you are the master, your consciousness is the master, a meditative state exists. So meditation means mastering the mechanism, becoming a master to the mechanism.

Mind, and the linguistic functioning of the mind, is not the ultimate. You are beyond it and existence is beyond it. Consciousness is beyond linguistics; existence is beyond linguistics. When consciousness and existence are one, they are in communion. This state is called meditation. The communion between consciousness and existence is meditation.

Language must be dropped. I don't mean that you must push it aside, that you must suppress it or eliminate it. What I mean is that something which is needed in society has become a twenty-four-hour-a-day habit for you and is not needed as such.

When you walk, you need to move your legs but they must not move when you are sitting. If your legs go on moving while you are sitting then you are mad, then the legs have gone insane. You must be able to turn them off. In the same way, when you are not talking with anyone, language must not be there. It is a talking instrument, a technique to communicate; when you are communicating something, language should be used; but when you are not communicating with anybody it should not be there.

If you are able to do this – and it is possible if you understand it – then you can grow into meditation. I say "you can grow" because life processes are never dead additions, they are always a growing process.

So meditation is a growing process, not a technique. A technique is always dead; it can be added to you, but a process is always living. It grows, it expands.

Language is needed, it is necessary, but you must not always remain in it. There must be moments when you are existential and there is no verbalizing. When you just exist, it is not that you are just vegetating – consciousness is there, and it is more acute, more alive, because language dulls consciousness. Language is bound to be repetitive but existence is never repetitive. So language creates boredom. The more important language is to you, the more linguistically-oriented the mind is – the more bored you will be. Language is a repetition, existence is not.

When you see a rose, it is not a repetition. It is a new rose, altogether new. It has never been and it will never be again. For the first time and the last time, it is there.

But when we say this is a rose, the word 'rose' is a repetition: it has always been there; it will always be there. You have killed the new with an old word.

Existence is always young, and language is always old. Through language you escape existence, through language you escape life, because language is dead. The more

involved you are with language, the more you are being deadened by it. A pundit is completely dead because he is language, words and nothing else. Sartre has written his autobiography. He calls it: *Words*. Meditation means living, living totally, and you can live totally only when you are silent. By being silent I do not mean unconscious. You can be silent and unconscious but that would not be a living silence – again, you would have missed. [4]

So what to do? The question is relevant. Watch – don't try to stop. There is no need to do any action against the mind. In the first place, who will do it? It will be mind fighting mind itself. You will divide your mind into two: one that is trying to boss over, the top-dog, trying to kill the other part of itself – which is absurd, it is a foolish game. It can drive you crazy. Don't try to stop the mind or the thinking – just watch it, allow it. Allow it total freedom. Let it run as fast as it wants. You don't try in any way to control it. You just be a witness. It is beautiful!

Mind is one of the most beautiful mechanisms. Science has not yet been able to create anything parallel to mind. Mind still remains the masterpiece – so complicated, so tremendously powerful, with so many potentialities. Watch it! Enjoy it!

And don't watch like an enemy, because if you look at the mind like an enemy, you cannot watch. You are already prejudiced; you are already against. You have already decided that something is wrong with the mind – you have already concluded. And whenever you look at somebody as an enemy you never look deep. You never look into the eyes; you avoid.

Watching the mind means: look at it with deep love, with deep respect, reverence – it is God's gift to you! Nothing is wrong in mind itself. Nothing is wrong in thinking itself. It is a beautiful process as other processes are. Clouds moving in the sky are beautiful – why not thoughts moving in the inner sky? Flowers coming to the trees are beautiful – why not thoughts flowering in your being? The river running to the ocean is beautiful – why not this stream of thoughts running somewhere to an unknown destiny? Is it not beautiful?

Look with deep reverence. Don't be a fighter, be a lover. Watch the subtle nuances of the mind; the sudden turns, the beautiful turns; the sudden jumps and leaps; the games that mind goes on playing; the dreams that it weaves – the imagination, the memory; the thousand and one pro-

jections that it creates. *Watch!* Standing there, aloof, distant, not involved, by and by you will start feeling....

As your watchfulness becomes deeper, your awareness becomes deeper, gaps start arising, intervals. One thought goes, another has not come; there is a gap. One cloud has passed, another is coming; there is a gap.

In those gaps, for the first time you will have glimpses of no-mind, you will have the taste of no-mind. Call it the taste of Zen, or Tao, or Yoga. In those small intervals, suddenly the sky is clear and the sun is shining. Suddenly the world is full of mystery because all barriers are dropped. The screen on your eyes is no longer there. You see clearly, you see penetratingly; the whole existence becomes transparent.

In the beginning, these will be just rare moments, few and far in between. But they will give you glimpses of what *samadhi* is. Small pools of silence – they will come and they will disappear. But now you know that you are on the right track – you start watching again.

When a thought passes, you watch it; when an interval passes, you watch it. Clouds are beautiful; sunshine also is beautiful. Now you are not a chooser. Now you don't have a fixed mind: you don't say, "I

would like only the intervals." That is stupid – because once you become attached to wanting only the intervals, you have decided again against thinking. And then those intervals will disappear. They happen only when you are very distant, aloof. They *happen*, they cannot be brought. They happen, you cannot force them to happen. They are spontaneous happenings.

Go on watching. Let thoughts come and go – wherever they want to go – nothing is wrong! Don't try to manipulate and don't try to direct; let thoughts move in total freedom. And then bigger intervals will be coming. You will be blessed with small satoris, mini-satoris. Sometimes minutes will pass and no thought will be there; there will be no traffic – a total silence, undisturbed.

When the bigger gaps come, you will not only have clarity to see into the world – with the bigger gaps you will have a new clarity arising; you will be able to see into the inner world. With the first gaps you will see into the world: trees will be more green than they look right now. You will be surrounded by an infinite music – the music of the spheres. You will be suddenly in the presence of God – ineffable, mysterious, touching you although you cannot grasp it; within your reach and yet beyond. With the bigger gaps, the same will happen inside. God will not only be outside, you will be suddenly surprised – he is inside also. He is not only in the seen; he is in the seer also – within and without. But don't get attached to that either.

Attachment is the food for the mind to continue. Non-attached witnessing is the way to stop it without any effort to stop it. And when you start enjoying those blissful moments, your capacity to retain them for longer periods arises.

Finally, eventually, one day, you become master. Then when you want to think, you think; if thought is needed, you use it; if thought is not needed, you allow it to rest. Not that mind is simply no longer there – mind *is* there, but you can use it or not use it. Now it is your decision. Just like legs: if you want to run you use them; if you don't want to run you simply rest – legs are there. In the same way, mind is always there.

No-mind is not against mind; no-mind is beyond mind. No-mind does not come by killing and destroying the mind; no-mind comes when you have understood the mind so totally that thinking is no longer needed. Your understanding has replaced it. [5]

False Methods

Meditation is not concentration

Meditations can be wrong. For example, any meditation that leads you deep into concentration is wrong. You will become more and more closed rather than becoming open. If you narrow down your consciousness, concentrate on something, and you exclude the whole of existence and become one-pointed, it will create more and more tension in you. Hence the word 'attention'. It means 'at-tension'. Concentration, the very sound of the word, gives you a feeling of tenseness.

Concentration has its uses but it is not meditation. In scientific work – in scientific research, in the science lab – you need concentration. You have to concentrate on one problem and exclude everything else – so much so that you almost become unmindful of the remaining world.

Only the problem that you are concentrating upon is your world. That's why scientists become absent-minded. People who concentrate too much always become absent-minded because they don't know how to remain open to the whole world.

I was reading an anecdote.

"I have brought a frog," said a scientist, a professor of zoology, beaming at his class, "fresh from the pond, in order that we might study its outer appearance and later dissect it."

He carefully unwrapped the package he carried and inside was a neatly prepared ham sandwich. The good professor looked at it with astonishment.

"Odd!" he said, "I distinctly remember having eaten my lunch."

That goes on happening to scientists. They become one-pointed and their whole mind becomes narrow. Of course, a narrow mind has its use: it becomes more penetrating, it becomes like a sharp needle; it hits exactly the right point, but it misses the great life that surrounds it.

A buddha is not a man of concentration; he is a man of awareness. He has not been trying to narrow down his consciousness; on the contrary, he has been trying to drop all barriers so that he becomes totally available to existence. Watch ...existence is simultaneous. I am speaking here and the traffic noise is simultaneous. The train, the birds, the wind blowing through the trees – in this moment the whole of existence converges. You listening to me, I speaking to you, and millions of things going on – it is tremendously rich.

Concentration makes you one-pointed at a very great cost: ninety-nine percent of life is discarded. If you are solving a mathematical problem, you cannot listen to the birds – they will be a distraction. Children playing around, dogs barking in the street – they will be a distraction. Because of concentration, people have tried to escape from life – to go to the Himalayas, to go to a cave, to remain isolated, so that they can concentrate on God. But God is not an object, God is this wholeness of existence, this moment; God is the totality. That's why science will never be able to know God. The very method of science is concentration and because of that method, science can never know God.

So what to do? Repeating a mantra, doing transcendental meditation, is not going to help. Transcendental meditation has become very important in America because of the objective approach, because of the scientific mind – it is the only meditation on which scientific work can be done. It is exactly concentration and not meditation, so it is comprehensible for the scientific mind. In the universities, in the science laboratories, in psychological research work, much is being done about TM, because it is not meditation. It is concentration, a method of concentration. It falls under the same category as scientific concentration; there is a link between the two. But it has nothing to do with meditation.

Meditation is so vast, so tremendously infinite, that no scientific research is possible. Only if a man *becomes* compassion will it show whether he has achieved or not. Alpha waves won't be of much help because they are still of the mind and meditation is not of the mind, it is something beyond.

So, let me tell you a few basic things. One, meditation is not concentration but relaxation – one simply relaxes into oneself. The more you relax, the more you feel yourself open, vulnerable, the less you are rigid. You are more flexible, and suddenly existence starts penetrating you. You are no longer like a rock, you have openings.

Relaxation means allowing yourself to fall into a state where you are not doing anything, because if you are doing something, tension will continue. It is a state of non-doing: you simply relax and you enjoy the feeling of relaxation. Relax into yourself, just close your eyes, and listen to all that is happening all around. No need to feel anything as a distraction. The moment you feel it is a distraction, you are denying God.

This moment God has come to you as a bird – don't deny. He has knocked at your door as a bird. The next moment he has come as a dog barking, or as a child crying and weeping, or as a madman laughing. Don't deny; don't reject – accept, because if you deny you will become tense. All denials create tension – accept. If you want to relax, acceptance is the way. Accept whatsoever is happening all around; let it become an organic whole. It is – you may know it or you may not know it – everything is interrelated. These birds, these trees, this sky, this sun, this earth, you, me, all are related. It is an organic unity.

If the sun disappears, the trees will disappear; if the trees disappear, the birds will disappear; if the birds and trees disappear, you cannot be here, you will disappear. It is an ecology. Everything is deeply related with each other.

So don't deny anything, because the moment you deny, you are denying something in you. If you deny these singing birds then something in you is denied.

If you relax, you accept; acceptance of existence is the only way to relax. If small things disturb you then it is your attitude that is disturbing you. Sit silently; listen to all that is happening all around, and relax. Accept, relax, and suddenly you will feel immense energy arising in you.

And when I say watch, don't *try* to watch; otherwise you will become tense again, and you will start concentrating. Simply relax, remain relaxed, loose, and look...because what else can you do? You are there, nothing to be done, everything accepted, nothing to be denied, rejected. No struggle, no fight, no conflict. You simply watch. Remember, simply watch. 6

Meditation is not introspection

Introspection is thinking about yourself. Self-remembering is not thinking at all: it is becoming aware of yourself. The difference is subtle, but very great.

Western psychology insists on introspection, and Eastern psychology insists on self-remembering. When you introspect, what do you do? For example, you are angry: you start thinking about anger, how it is caused. You start analyzing why it is caused. You start judging whether it is good or bad. You start rationalizing that you had been angry because the situation was such. You brood about anger, you analyze anger, but the focus of attention is on the anger, not on the self. Your whole consciousness is focused on the anger: you are watching, analyzing, associating, thinking about it, trying to figure out how to avoid, how to get rid of it, how not to do it again. This is a thinking process. You will judge it "bad" because it is destructive. You will take a vow that "I will never commit the same mistake again." You will try to control this anger through will. That's why Western psychology has become analytical: analysis, dissection.

Eastern psychology says, "Be aware. Don't try to analyze anger, there is no need. Just look at it, but look with awareness. Don't start thinking." In fact if you start thinking then thinking will become a barrier to looking at the anger. Then thinking will garb it. Then thinking will be like a cloud surrounding it; the clarity will be lost. Don't think at all. Be in a state of no thought, and *look*.

When there is not even a ripple of thinking between you and the anger, the anger is faced, encountered. You don't dissect it. You don't bother to go to its source, because the source is in the past. You don't judge it, because the moment you judge it, thinking starts. You don't take any vow that "I will not do it," because that vow leads you into the future. In awareness you remain with the feeling of anger, exactly herenow. You are not interested in changing it, you are not interested in thinking about it – you are interested to look at it directly, face to face, immediate. Then it is self-remembering.

And this is the beauty of it: that if you can look at anger it disappears. It not only disappears in that moment – the very disappearance of it by your deep look gives you the key – there is no need to use will, there is no need to make any decision for the future, and there is no need to go to the original source from which it comes. It is unnecessary. You have the key now: look at anger, and anger disappears. And this look is available forever. Whenever anger is there you can look; then this looking grows deeper.

There are three stages of looking. First, when the anger has already happened and gone; as if you look at a tail disappearing – an elephant has gone; only the tail is there. When the anger was there, you were so deeply involved in it you could not really be aware. When the anger has almost disappeared, ninety-nine percent gone – only one percent, the last part of it, is still going, disappearing into the far horizon – then you become aware. This is the first state of awareness – good, but not enough. The second state is when the elephant is there – not the tail – when the situation is ripe. You are really angry to the peak, boiling, burning – then you become aware.

Then there is still a third stage: the anger has not come, is still coming – not the tail but the head. It is just entering your area of consciousness and you become aware, then the elephant never materializes. You killed the animal before it was born. That is birth control. The phenomenon has not happened; then it leaves no trace. [7]

Tricks of the Mind

Don't be fooled by experiences

All experiences are just tricks of the mind, all experiences are just escapes. Meditation is not an experience, it is a realization. Meditation is not an experience; rather, it is a stopping of all experience.

Experience is something outside you. The experiencer is your being. And this is the distinction between true spirituality and false: if you are after experiences, the spirituality is false; if you are after the experiencer, then it is true. And then you are not concerned about kundalini, not concerned about chakras, not concerned about all these things. They will happen, but you are not concerned, you are not interested, and you will not move on these by-paths. You will go on moving towards the inner center where nothing remains except you in your total aloneness. Only the consciousness remains, without content.

Content is the experience; whatsoever you experience is the content. I experience misery; then the misery is the content of my consciousness. Then I experience pleasure; the pleasure is the content. I experience boredom; then boredom is the content. You can experience silence; then silence is the content. You can experience bliss; then bliss is the content. So you go on changing the content – you can go on changing ad infinitum – but this is not the real thing. The real is the one to whom these experiences happen – to whom boredom happens, to whom bliss happens.

The spiritual search is not *what* happens, but to *whom* it happens. Then there is no possibility for the ego to arise. [8]

Mind can enter again

In meditation sometimes you feel a sort of emptiness that is not really emptiness. I call it just "a sort of emptiness." When you are meditating, for certain moments, for a few seconds, you will feel as if the thought process has stopped. In the beginning these gaps will come. But because you are feeling as if the thought process has stopped, this is again a thought process, a very subtle thought process.

What are you doing? You are saying inside, "The thought process has stopped." But what is this? This is a secondary thought process which has started. And you say, "This is emptiness." You say, "Now something is going to happen." What is this? Again a new thought process has started.

Whenever this happens again, don't become a victim of it. When you feel a certain silence is descending, don't start verbalizing it, because you are destroying it. Wait – not for something – simply wait. Don't do anything. Don't say, "This is emptiness." The moment you have said that, you have destroyed it. Just look at it, penetrate into it, encounter it – but wait, don't verbalize it. What is the hurry? Through verbalization the mind has again entered from a different route, and you are deceived. Be alert about this trick of the mind.

In the beginning it is bound to happen, so whenever this happens, just wait. Don't fall in the trap. Don't say anything, remain silent. Then you will enter into emptiness, and then it will not be temporary, because once you have known the real emptiness you cannot lose it. The real cannot be lost; that is its quality. Once you have known the inner treasure, once you have come in contact with your deepest core, then

you can move in activity, then you can do whatsoever you like, then you can live an ordinary worldly life but the emptiness will remain with you. You cannot forget it. It will go inside. The music of it will be heard. Whatsoever you are doing, the doing will be only on the periphery; inside you will remain empty. [9]

Mind can deceive you

There are patterns the seeker gets entangled with.

The first thing is: most seekers get lost in an illusory feeling that they have arrived. It is like the kind of dream in which you feel you are awake. You are still dreaming – your feeling of being awake is part of the dream. The same kind of thing happens to the seeker.

The mind is capable of creating the illusion that "now there is nowhere to go, you have arrived." The mind is a deceiver, and the function of the master for one in this condition is to make him alert that this is not the reality but only a dream, that he has not arrived.

This can happen at many points, again and again. And one can get very irritated and annoyed with the master for the simple reason that whenever you feel you have got it,

he simply takes it away and puts you back into your ignorant state.

For example, it was happening to a German disciple continually – he would get the feeling that he had become enlightened. And the force of the illusion was so much that he could not keep it to himself, he would tell others.

He was *so* certain. This happened three times, and because of his certainty he came to India to get my blessings. Naturally, it shows his certainty that he came for my blessings.

Each time I had to tell him, "You are just being deceived by your own mind. Nothing has happened to you, you are simply the old man – the new man has not arrived. And all that you are doing – writing letters to the U.N., to other governments – are just ways of the ego. You are in the grip of the ego."

It is very easy to live in a beautiful dream. It is hard to see your dreams shattered by reality.

In the ancient scriptures of the East it is called the power of *maya*. Mind has the hypnotic power to create any illusion. If you are after a certain thing, desperately, it is one of the functions of the mind to create the illusion to stop your desperateness. It happens every day to everybody in their dreams, but people don't learn things.

If at night you go to bed hungry, that night you are going to have a dream about eating delicious food. The mind is trying to help you so that your sleep is not disturbed; otherwise you are hungry and you are bound to be awakened by your hunger. The mind gives you a dream that you are eating delicious food of your choice, which satisfies your mind. The hunger remains but sleep is not disturbed. The hunger is covered by the illusion of the dream; it protects your sleep.

You feel in sleep that your bladder is full. If the mind does not create the dream that you have gone to the toilet, come back and gone to sleep again, then your sleep will be disturbed – and sleep is a great necessity for the body. The mind is taking care that you are not disturbed again and again; you can have a long sleep, rest, so in the morning you are rejuvenated.

This is the ordinary function of the mind; on a higher plane the same thing happens. One is an ordinary sleep and an ordinary awakening that mind prevents. On the path, it is an extraordinary sleep and an extraordinary awakening, but the mind is programmed – it is just a mechanical thing. It simply does its work without bothering, because it has no way of checking whether it is ordinary sleep or spiritual sleep, ordinary awakening or spiritual awakening.

To the mind it is all the same. Its function is to keep your sleep intact and create a barrier for anything that disturbs your sleep. If you are hungry it gives you food; if you are desperately in search of truth, it gives you truth, it gives you enlightenment. You ask for anything, and it is ready to give it to you. It can create the illusion of the real thing – that is its intrinsic power. [10]

PART FIVE

Questions to the Master

Only a Witness Can Really Dance

You continuously tell us to "be aware," to "be a witness." But can a witnessing consciousness really sing, dance and taste life? Is a witness a mere spectator of life and never a participant?

Mind is bound to raise this question sooner or later, because mind is very much afraid of *you* becoming a witness. Why is the mind so much afraid of you becoming a witness? – because becoming a witness is the death of the mind. Mind is a doer – it wants to do things – and witnessing is a state of non-doing. The mind is afraid that, "If you become a witness, I will not be needed any more." And in a way the mind is right.

Once the witness arises in you the mind has to disappear, just as when you bring light into your room and the darkness *has* to disappear; it is inevitable. Mind can exist only if you remain fast asleep because mind is a state of dreaming, and dreams can exist only in sleep.

By becoming a witness you are no more asleep; you are awake. You become awareness – so crystal-clear, so young and fresh, so vital and potent. You become a flame, intense, as if burning from both ends. In that state of intensity, light, of consciousness, mind dies, mind commits suicide.

Hence the mind is afraid, and mind will create many problems for you. It will raise many, many questions. It will make you hesitate to take the jump into the unknown; it will try to pull you back. It will try to convince you: "With me is safety, security; with me you are living under a shelter, well guarded. I take every care of you. With me you are efficient, skillful. The moment you leave me you will have to leave all your knowledge, and you will have to leave all your securities, safeties.

You will have to drop your armor and you will be going into the unknown. You are unnecessarily taking a risk for no reason at all." It will try to bring beautiful rationalizations. This is one of the rationalizations which almost always happens to every meditator.

It is not you who is asking the question; it is the mind, your enemy, who is putting the question through you. It is mind who is saying "Bhagwan, you continuously tell us to 'be aware,' to 'be a witness.' But can a witnessing consciousness really sing, dance and taste life?"

Yes! In fact, *only* a witnessing consciousness can really sing, dance and taste life. It will appear like a paradox – it is! – but all that is true is always paradoxical. Remember: if truth is not paradoxical then it is not truth at all, then it is something else.

Paradox is a basic, intrinsic quality of truth. Let it sink into your heart forever: truth as such is paradoxical. Although all paradoxes are not truths, all truths are paradoxes. The truth has to be a paradox because it has to be both poles, the negative and the positive, and yet a transcendence. It has to be life and death, and *plus*. By 'plus' I mean the transcendence of both – both, and both not. That is the ultimate paradox.

When you are in the mind, how can you sing? The mind creates misery; out of misery there can be no song. When you are in the mind, how can you dance? Yes, you can go through certain empty gestures called dance, but it is not a real dance.

Only a Meera knows a real dance, or a Krishna, or a Chaitanya; these are the people who know real dance. Others know only the technique of dancing, but there is nothing overflowing; their energies are stagnant. People who are living in the mind are living in the ego, and the ego cannot dance. It can make a performance but not a dance.

The real dance happens only when you have become a witness. Then you are so blissful that the very bliss starts overflowing you; that is the dance. The very bliss starts singing, a song arises on its own accord. And only when you are a witness can you taste life.

I can understand your question. You are worried that by becoming a witness you will become merely a spectator of life. No, to be a spectator is one thing, and to be a witness is a totally different thing, qualitatively different.

A spectator is indifferent; he is dull, he is in a kind of sleep. He does not participate in life. He is afraid, he is a coward. He stands by the side of the road and simply goes on seeing others living. That's what you are doing all your life: somebody else acts in a movie and you see it. You are a spectator! People are glued to their chairs for hours together before their TVs – spectators. Somebody else is singing, you are listening. Somebody else is dancing, you are just a spectator. Somebody else is loving and you are just seeing, you are not a participant. Professionals are doing what you should have done on your own.

A witness is not a spectator.

Then what is a witness? A witness is one who participates yet remains alert. A witness is in the state of *wei-wu-wei*. That is Lao Tzu's word; it means action through inaction. A witness is not one who has escaped from life. He lives in life, lives far more totally, far more passionately, but yet remains a watcher deep down, goes on remembering, "I am a consciousness."

Try it. Walking on the road, remember that you are a consciousness. Walking continues, and a new thing is added – a new richness is added, a new beauty. Something interior is added to the outward act. You become a flame of consciousness, and then the walking has a totally different joy to it: you are on the earth and yet your feet are not touching the earth at all.

That's what Buddha has said: Pass

through a river but don't let the water touch your feet.

That's the meaning of the Eastern symbol of the lotus. You must have seen Buddha's statues, pictures, sitting on a lotus; that is a metaphor. A lotus is a flower that lives in the water and yet the water cannot touch it. The lotus does not escape to the Himalayan caves; he *lives* in the water and yet remains far, far away. Being in the marketplace but not allowing the marketplace to enter into your being, living in the world and yet not of the world: that is what is meant by 'witnessing consciousness'.

That's what I mean by saying to you again and again: Be aware! I am not against action, but your action has to be enlightened by awareness. Those who are against action, they are bound to be repressive, and all kinds of repressions make you pathological, not whole, not healthy.

The monks living in the monasteries – Catholic or Hindu, the monks of the Jains and the Buddhists – who have escaped from life are not true sannyasins. They have simply repressed their desires and they have moved away from the world, the world of action. Where can you be a witness if you move away from the world of action? The world of action is the best opportunity to be aware. It gives you a challenge, it remains constantly a challenge. Either you can fall asleep and become a doer – then you are a worldly man, a dreamer, a victim of illusions; or you can become a witness and yet go on living in the world. Then your action has a different quality to it: it is *really* action. Those who are not aware, their actions are not real actions but *reactions*. They only react.

Somebody insults you and you react. Insult the Buddha – he does not react, he *acts*. Reaction is dependent on the other: he pushes a button and you are only a victim, a slave; you function like a machine.

The *real* person who knows what awareness is never reacts; he acts out of his own awareness. The action does not come from the other's act; nobody can push his button. If he feels spontaneously that this is right to do, he does it; if he feels nothing is needed he keeps quiet. He is not repressive; he is always open, expressive. His expression is multi-dimensional: in song, in poetry, in dance, in love, in prayer, in compassion, he flows.

If you don't become aware, then there are only two possibilities: either you will be repressive or indulgent. In both ways you remain in bondage.

A nun was raped just outside the monastery. When she was finally found, she was carried inside and the nearby physician was called.

He came, raised his hands and said, "This is work for a plastic surgeon!"

A plastic surgeon was called. When he saw the poor nun he exclaimed. "Oh, my God! What a mess! Where should I start?"

The Mother Superior replied, "Well, that is easy. First get that smile off her face!" ¹

The Goose Has Never Been In!

Sometimes, when dark sides of my mind come up, it really scares me. It is very difficult for me to accept that it is just the polar opposite of the bright ones. I feel dirty and guilty and not worth sitting with You in Your immaculate presence. I want to face all facets of my mind and accept them because I hear You often say that acceptance is the condition to transcend the mind. Can You please talk about acceptance?

The basic thing to be understood is that you are not the mind – neither the bright one nor the dark one. If you get identified with the beautiful part, then it is impossible to disidentify yourself from the ugly part; they are two sides of the same coin. You can have it whole, or you can throw it whole, but you cannot divide it.

And the whole anxiety of man is, he wants to choose that which looks beautiful, bright. He wants to choose all the silver linings, leaving the dark cloud behind. But he does not know silver linings cannot exist without the dark cloud. The dark cloud is the background, absolutely necessary for the silver linings to show.

Choosing is anxiety. Choosing is creating trouble for yourself.

Being choiceless means: the mind is there and it has a dark side and it has a bright side – so what? What has it to do with you? Why should you be worried about it?

The moment you are not choosing, all worry disappears. A great acceptance arises, that this is how the mind has to be, this is the nature of the mind. And it is not your problem, because you are not the mind. If you were the mind, there would have been no problem at all. Then who would choose and who would think of transcending? And who would try to accept and understand acceptance?

You are separate, totally separate. You are a witness and nothing else, an observer who gets identified with anything that he finds pleasant – and forgets that the unpleasant is coming just behind it as a shadow.

You are not troubled by the pleasant side – you rejoice in it. The trouble comes when the polar opposite asserts; then you are torn apart. But you started the whole trouble. Falling from being just a witness, you became identified.

The biblical story of the fall is just a fiction. But this is the real fall: the fall from being a witness into getting identified with something and losing your witnessing.

Just try once in a while: let the mind be whatever it is. Remember, you are not it. And you are going to have a great surprise. As you are less identified, the mind starts becoming less powerful because its power comes from your identification; it sucks your blood. But when you start standing aloof and away, the mind starts shrinking.

The day you are completely unidentified with the mind, even for a single moment, there is the revelation: mind simply dies, it is no longer there. Where it was so full, where it was so continuously – day in, day out; waking, sleeping, it was there – suddenly it is not there.

You look all around and it is emptiness, it is nothingness. And with the mind disappears the self.

Then there is only a certain quality of awareness with no 'I' in it. At the most you can call it something similar to 'am-ness', but not 'I-ness'. To be even more exact, it is 'is-ness', because even in 'am-ness' some shadow of the 'I' is still there. The moment you know its is-ness, it has become universal. With the disappearance of the mind disappears the self. And so many things disappear which were so important to you, so troublesome to you. You were trying to solve them and they were becoming more and more complicated; everything was a problem, an anxiety, and there seemed to be no way out.

I will remind you of the story *The Goose is Out*. It is concerned with the mind and your is-ness.

The master says to the disciple to meditate on a koan. A small goose is put into a bottle, fed and nourished. The goose goes on becoming bigger and bigger and bigger, and fills the whole bottle. Now it is too big; it cannot come out of the bottle's mouth, the mouth is too small. And the koan is that you have to bring the goose out without destroying the bottle, without killing the goose.

Now it is mind-boggling.

What can you do? The goose is too big; you cannot take it out unless you break the bottle, but that is not allowed. Or, you can bring it out by killing it; then you don't care whether it comes out alive or dead. That is not allowed either.

Day in, day out, the disciple meditates, finds no way, thinks this way and that way – but in fact there is no way. Tired, utterly exhausted, a sudden revelation – suddenly he understands that the master cannot be interested in the bottle and the goose; they must represent something else. The bottle is the mind, you are the goose...but with witnessing it is possible. Without being *in* the mind, you can become identified with it so much that you start feeling you *are* in it!

He runs to the master, to say that the goose is out. And the master says, "You have understood it. Now keep it out. It has never been in."

If you go on struggling with the goose and the bottle there is no way for you to solve it. It is the realization that "It must represent something else; otherwise the master cannot give it to me. And what can it be?" – because the whole function between the master and the disciple, the whole business is about the mind and awareness.

Awareness is the goose which is not in the bottle of the mind. But you are believing that it *is* in it, and asking everyone how to get it out. And there are idiots who will help you with techniques to get out of it. I call them idiots because they have not understood the thing at all.

The goose *is* out, has never been in;

238

so the question of bringing it out does not arise.

Mind is just a procession of thoughts passing in front of you on the screen of the brain. You are an observer. But you start getting identified with beautiful things – those are bribes. And once you get caught in the beautiful things you are also caught in the ugly things, because mind cannot exist without duality. Awareness cannot exist with duality, and mind cannot exist without duality.

Awareness is non-dual, and mind is dual. So just watch.

I don't teach you any solutions. I teach you *the* solution.

Just get back a little and watch. Create a distance between you and your mind. Whether it is good, beautiful, delicious, something that you would like to enjoy closely, or it is ugly – you remain as far away as possible. Look at it just the way you look at a film. But people get identified even with films.

I have seen, when I was young – I have not seen any movie for a long time – but I have seen people weeping, tears falling. It is good that it is dark in a movie house; it saves them from feeling embarrassed – and nothing is happening! I used to ask my father, "Did you see? The fellow by your side was crying!"

He said, "The whole hall was crying. The scene was such…"

"But," I said, "there is only a screen and nothing else. Nobody is killed, there is no tragedy happening – just a projection of a film. Just pictures moving on the screen; and people laugh, and people weep, and for three hours they are almost lost. They become part of the movie, they become identified with some character."

My father said to me, "If you are raising questions about people's reactions, then you cannot enjoy the film."

I said, "I can enjoy the film, but I don't want to cry, I don't see any enjoyment in it. I can see it as a film, but I don't want to become a part of it. These people are all becoming part of it."

You get identified with anything. People get identified with other persons and then they create misery for themselves. They get identified with things, then they get miserable if that thing is missing.

Identification is the root cause of your misery. And every identification is identification with the mind. Just step aside, let the mind pass.

And soon you will be able to see that there is no problem at all – the goose is out.

You don't have to break the bottle, you don't have to kill the goose either. [2]

The Watcher on the Hill

I seem to be neither totally in the world, nor the watcher on the hill. How to be someplace? I feel like I am in between everything I do.

Then that is exactly the place you should be.

You go on creating problems. Wherever you are, be there. There is no need to be a watcher on the hills. There should be no 'should'. Once 'should' enters life you are already poisoned. There should be no goal. There should be no right or wrong. This is the only sin: to think in terms of division, values, condemnation, appreciation.

Wherever you are...nothing is wrong in between the watcher on the hills and a man in the world. That's *exactly* where you should be. And I say: wherever you are, if you can accept it, immediately then and there you have become the watcher on the hills. Even in hell, if you accept it, hell disappears, because hell can remain only through your re-

jection. Hell disappears and heaven appears. Whatsoever you accept becomes heavenly, and whatsoever you reject becomes hell.

It is said that a saint cannot be thrown into hell because he knows the alchemy to transform it. You have heard that sinners go to hell and saints to heaven – but you have heard the wrong thing. The case is just the other way around: wherever sinners go, they create hell and wherever saints go, they create heaven. Saints are not sent to heaven. There is nobody to send and manage all this – there is nobody. But wherever they go, this is the way they are: they create their heaven. They carry their heaven with them, within them. And sinners? – you can send them to heaven: they will create hell. They cannot do otherwise.

So what is the definition of a saint or a sinner? My definition is: a saint is one who has come to know the alchemical secret of transforming everything into heaven. And a sinner is one who does not know the secret of transforming things into beautiful existences. Rather, on the contrary, he goes on making things ugly.

Whatsoever you are will be reflected around you. So don't try to be anything else. And don't try to be some other place. That is the disease called man: always to become somebody, to be some other place, always rejecting that which is, and always hankering for that which is not. This is the disease called man.

Be alert! Do you see it?! It is a simple fact to be seen. I am not theorizing about it; I am not a theoretician. I am simply indicating a bare, naked fact – that if you can live in this moment wherever you are and forget about the future, goals, the idea of becoming something else, immediately, the whole world around you is transformed; you have become a transforming force.

Acceptance...a deep, total acceptance is what religion is all about.

A wants to become B; B wants to become C. Then the fever of becoming is created.

You are not a becoming; you are a being. You are already that which you can be, which you can ever be – you are already that. Nothing more can be done about you; you are a finished product.

This is the meaning I give to the story that God created the world: when the perfect creates, the creation is perfect. When God creates, how can you improve upon it? Just think of the whole absurdity; the whole idea is absurd.

You. are trying to improve upon God; you cannot improve. You can be miserable, that's all. And you can suffer unnecessarily. And you will suffer diseases which are just in your imagination and nowhere else. God creating means: out of perfection comes perfection.

You are perfect! Nothing else is needed. Look right now, this very moment, within yourself. Have a direct insight. What is needed? Everything is simply perfect and beautiful. Not even a cloud can I see. Just look within yourself – not even a cloud in your inner space. Everything is full of light.

But the mind will say, sooner or later, to be something else, to be somewhere else, to become. The mind doesn't allow you to be. The mind is becoming, and your soul is being. That's why Buddhas go on saying: "Unless you drop all desiring you will not attain!"

Desiring means becoming. Desiring means to be something else. Desiring means not to accept the case as you are, not to be in a total 'yes' mood – no matter what the situation.

To say "yes" to life is to be religious; to say "no" to life is to be irreligious. And whenever you desire something you are saying "no." You are saying that something better is possible.

The trees are happy and the birds are happy and the clouds are happy – because they have no becoming. They are simply whatsoever they are.

The rosebush is not trying to become a lotus. No, the rosebush is absolutely happy to be a rosebush. You cannot persuade the rosebush. Howsoever you advertise the lotus, you will not be able to corrupt the mind of the rosebush to become a lotus. The rosebush will simply laugh – because a rosebush is a rosebush is a rosebush. It is simply settled and centered in its being. That's why the whole nature is without any fever: calm and quiet and tranquil. And settled!

Only the human mind is in a chaos, because everybody is hankering to be somebody else. This is what you have been doing for a thousand and one lives. And if you don't awaken now, when are you thinking to awaken? You are already ripe for awakening.

Just start from this very moment to live and enjoy and delight. Drop desiring! Whatsoever you are, enjoy it.

Delight in your being. And then suddenly time disappears, because time exists only with desiring. Future exists because you desire.

Then you will be like birds; listen to them. Then you will be like trees; look – the freshness, the greenery, the flowers.

Please be where you are. I am not here to create a new desire in you; I am simply here to make you aware of the whole absurdity of desiring. Desiring is *sansar.*

Understanding the futility of desire is to become enlightened. One who has found out that he is already that which he always wanted to be is a buddha. And you are all buddhas, howsoever fast asleep and snoring. That makes no difference.

Let me be your alarm. Open your eyes. You have slept long enough. It is time to awaken. The morning is knocking at the door. [3]

Where Did You Leave Your Bicycle?

During the meditations, my mind still goes five hundred miles per hour. I never experience silence, and whatever witnessing happens is very short, like flashes. Am I wasting my time?

Your mind is mighty slow. Five hundred miles per hour, only?! And do you think this is speed? Mighty slow you are. Mind goes so fast it knows no speed. It is faster than light. Light travels 186,000 miles in one second; mind is faster than that. But nothing to be worried about – that is the beauty of the mind, that is a great quality! Rather than taking it negatively, rather than fighting with it, befriend the mind.

You say: "During the meditations, my mind still goes five hundred miles per hour" – let it go! Let it go faster. You be a watcher. You watch the mind going around so fast, with such speed. Enjoy this! Enjoy this play of the mind.

In Sanskrit we have a special term for it; we call it *chidvilas* – the play of consciousness. Enjoy it! – this play of mind rushing towards the stars, moving so fast from here and there, jumping all over existence. What is wrong in it? Let it be a beautiful dance. Accept it.

My feeling is that what you are doing is trying to stop it – you cannot do that. Nobody can stop the mind! Yes, mind stops one day, but nobody can stop it. Mind stops, but that is not out of your effort. Mind stops out of your understanding.

You just *watch* and try to see what is happening, why this mind is rushing. It is not rushing without any reason. Try to see *why* this mind is rushing, where it is rushing – you must be ambitious. If it thinks about money, then try to understand. Mind is not the question. You start dreaming about money, that you have won a lottery or this and that, and then you even start planning how to spend it, what to purchase and what not. Or, the mind thinks you have become a president, a prime minister, and then you start thinking what to do now, how to run the country, or the world. Just *watch* the mind! – what mind is going towards.

There must be a deep seed in you. You cannot stop the mind unless that seed disappears. The mind is simply following the order of your innermost seed. Somebody is thinking about sex; then somewhere there is repressed sexuality. Watch where mind is rushing. Look deep into yourself, find where the seeds are.

I have heard: The parson was very much worried. "Listen," he said to his verger, "somebody has stolen my bicycle."

"Where have you been on it, Rector?" inquired that worthy.

"Only around the parish on my calls."

The verger suggested that the best plan would be for the rector to direct his Sunday sermon to the ten commandments. "When you get to 'Thou shalt not steal,' you and I will watch the faces – we will soon see."

Sunday came, the rector started in fine flow about the commandments, then lost his thread, changed his subject, and trailed off lamely.

"Sir," said the verger, "I thought you were going to…"

"I know, Giles, I know. But you see, when I got to 'Thou shalt not commit adultery,' I suddenly remembered where I had left my bicycle."

Just see where you have left your bicycle. The mind is rushing for certain reasons.

The mind needs understanding, awareness. Don't try to stop it. If you try to stop it, in the first place you cannot succeed; in the second place, if you *can* succeed – one can succeed if one makes persevering effort for years – if you *can* succeed, you will become dull. No satori will happen out of it.

In the first place, you cannot succeed; and it is good that you cannot succeed. If you *could* succeed, if you managed to succeed, that would be very unfortunate – you would become dull, you would lose intelligence. With that speed there is intelligence, with that speed there is continuous sharpening of the sword of thinking, logic, intellect. Please don't try to stop it. I am not in favor of dullards, and I am not here to help anybody to become stupid.

In the name of religion, many people have become stupid, they have almost become idiots – just trying to stop the mind without any under-

standing about why it is going with such speed…why in the first place? The mind cannot go without any reason. Without going into the reasons, in the layers, deep layers of the unconscious, they just try to stop. They *can* stop, but they will have to pay a price, and the price will be that their intelligence will be lost.

You can go around India, you can find thousands of sannyasins, mahatmas; look into their eyes – yes, they are good people, nice, but stupid. If you look in their eyes there is no intelligence, you will not see any lightning. They are uncreative people; they have not created anything. They just sit there. They are vegetating, they are not alive people. They have not helped the world in *any* way. They have not even produced a painting or a poem or a song, because even to produce a poem you need intelligence, you need certain qualities of the mind.

I would not suggest that you stop the mind, rather, that you understand it. With understanding a miracle happens. The miracle is that with understanding, by and by, when you understand the causes and those causes are looked into deeply, through looking deeply into those causes, those causes disappear, mind slows down. But intelligence is not lost, because mind is not forced.

What are you doing if you don't remove the causes by understanding? You are driving a car, for example, and you go on pressing the accelerator and at the same time you try to press the brake. You will destroy the whole mechanism of the car. And there is every possibility you will have some accident. This cannot be done together. If you are pushing the brake, then leave the accelerator alone; don't push it any more. If you are pushing the accelerator, then don't push the brake. *Don't* do both the things together, otherwise you will destroy the whole mechanism; you are doing two contradictory things.

You carry ambition – and you try to stop the mind? Ambition creates the speed, so you are accelerating the speed – and putting a brake on the mind. You will destroy the whole subtle mechanism of the mind, and mind is a very delicate phenomenon, the most delicate in the whole of existence. So don't be foolish about it.

There is no need to stop it.

You say: "I never experience silence, and whatever witnessing happens is very short, like flashes." Feel happy! Even that is something of tremendous value. Those flashes, they are not ordinary flashes. Don't just take them for granted! There are millions of people for whom even those small glimpses have not happened. They will live and die and they will never know what witnessing is – even for a single moment. You are happy, you are fortunate.

But you are not feeling grateful. If you don't feel grateful, those flashes will disappear; feel grateful, they will grow. With gratitude, everything grows. Feel happy that you are blessed – they will grow. With that positivity, things will grow.

"And whatever witnessing happens is very short."

Let it be very short! If it can happen for a single split moment, it is happening; you will have the taste of it. And with the taste, by and by, you will create more and more situations in which it happens more and more.

"Am I wasting my time?"

You cannot waste time, because you don't possess time. You can waste something that you possess. Time you don't possess. Time will be wasted anyway whether you meditate or not – time will be wasted. Time is rushing by. Whatsoever you do, do anything or don't do anything, time is going. You cannot save time so how can you waste time? You can waste only something which you can save. You don't possess time. Forget about it! And the best use you can have of time is to have these small glimpses – because finally you will come to see only those moments have been saved which were moments of witnessing, and all else has gone down the drain. The money that you earned, the prestige that you earned, the respectability that you earned, is all gone down the drain. Only those few moments that you had some flashes of witnessing, only those moments are saved. Only those moments will go with you when you leave this life – only those moments can go, because those moments belong to eternity, they don't belong to time.

Feel happy it is happening. It always happens slowly, slowly. One drop by one drop, a great ocean can become full. It happens in drops; in drops the ocean is coming. You just receive it with gratitude, with celebration, with thankfulness.

And don't try to stop the mind. Let the mind have its speed – you watch. 4

Just a 180° Turn

Two Polacks were driving along in the front seat of their car. As they approached a corner, the one who was driving said to his friend, "Will you look out of the window and see if the indicator, the turn signal, is working?" He promptly leaned out of the window and looked at the indicator light and shouted back at his friend, "Yes it is – no it's not, yes it is – no it's not, yes it is – no it's not." Bhagwan, if anybody were to ask me whether I was witnessing or not, my answer would have to be the same: Yes I am, no I'm not; yes I am, no I'm not. Is it like that all the way home?

It is not, because as far as your witnessing is concerned, it may be coming and going, and your answer may be perfectly the same as the Polack who said that the indicator is working, "Yes – no – yes again…"

That is the function of the indicator; to be, not to be; to be, not to be. But don't laugh at the poor Polack. As far as *his* awareness is concerned, he is fully aware. Whenever it is working he says "yes"; whenever it is not working he says "no." His awareness of the indicator is continuous. The indicator goes on changing, but the Polack remains fully aware of when it is working, when it is not working, when it is on, when it is off. His awareness is a continuity.

If you can give the same answer about your witnessing: "Yes I am witnessing, no I am not witnessing, yes I am witnessing, no I am not witnessing," then you have to remember that there is something more behind these witnessing moments which is witnessing all this process. Who is witnessing that sometimes you are witnessing and sometimes you are not witnessing? Something is constant.

Your witnessing has become just an indicator; don't be bothered by it. Your emphasis should be on the eternal, the constant, the continuum – and it is there. And it is in everyone, we have just forgotten it.

But even in times when we have forgotten it, it is there in its absolute perfection. It is like a mirror which is able to mirror everything, is still mirroring everything, but you are standing with your back towards the mirror. The poor mirror is mirroring your back.

Turn, it will mirror your face.

Open your heart, it will mirror your heart.

Put everything on the table, don't hide even a single card and it will reflect your whole reality.

But if you go on standing with your back to the mirror looking all around the world asking people, "Who am I?" then it is up to you. Because there are idiots who will come and teach you that "This is the way. Do this and you will know who you are."

No method is needed, just a 180-degree turn – and that is not a method.

And the mirror is your very being.

You may not have looked at the joke in this light. If you tell the joke to anybody he is going to laugh because the Polack is so stupid, because that is the function of the indicator – to be on, off, on, off. But you have brought me a joke – I cannot simply laugh at it because I see something more in it which perhaps nobody will see.

The Polack is constant, alert. He does not miss a single point, a single moment.

And when you say "witnessing, yes" and then it disappears and you say "no" – again it appears, you say "yes"…it simply shows that there is something behind all these moments of witnessing and not witnessing. The *true* witness, which is reflecting the changing process of what you *think* is your witness, is behind. It is not the true witness, it is only the indicator.

Forget the indicator.

Remember the constant mirroring that goes on twenty-four hours within you, silently watching everything. Slowly, slowly clean it – there is so much dust on it, centuries of dust. Remove the dust.

And one day, when the mirror is completely clean, those moments of witnessing and not-witnessing will disappear; you will be simply a witness.

And unless you find that eternity of witnessing, all other kinds of witnessing are part of mind. They have no value. [5]

All Paths Merge on the Mountain

Is awareness a higher value than love?

The highest peak is the culmination of all values: truth, love, awareness, authenticity, totality. At the highest peak they are indivisible. They are separate only in the dark valleys of our unconsciousness. They are separate only when they are polluted, mixed with other things. The moment they become pure they become one; the more pure, the closer they come to each other.

For example, each value exists on many planes; each value is a ladder of many rungs. Love is lust – the lowest rung, which touches hell; and love is also prayer – the highest rung, which touches paradise. And between these two there are many planes easily discernible.

In lust, love is only one percent: ninety-nine percent are other things: jealousies, ego trips, possessiveness, anger, sexuality. It is more physical, more chemical; it has nothing deeper than that. It is very superficial, not even skin deep.

As you go higher, things become deeper; they start having new dimensions. That which was only physiological starts having a psychological dimension to it. That which was nothing but biology starts becoming psychology. We share biology with all the animals; we don't share psychology with all the animals.

When love goes still higher – or deeper, which is the same – then it starts having something of the spiritual in it. It becomes metaphysical. Only Buddhas, Krishnas, Christs, know that quality of love.

Love is spread all the way and so are other values. When love is one hundred percent pure you cannot make any distinction between love and awareness; then they are no more two. You cannot make any distinction even between love and God; they are no more two. Hence Jesus' statement that God is love. He makes them synonymous. There is great insight in it.

On the periphery everything appears separate from everything else; on the periphery existence is many. As you come closer to the center, the manyness starts melting, dissolving, and oneness starts arising. At the center, everything is one.

Hence your question is right only if you don't understand the highest quality of love and awareness. It is absolutely irrelevant if you have any glimpse of Everest, of the highest peak.

You ask: "Is awareness a higher value than love?"

There is nothing higher and nothing lower; in fact, there are not two values at all. There are two paths from the valley leading to the peak. One path is of awareness, meditation: the path of Zen. The other is the path of love, the path of the devotees, the *bhaktas*, the Sufis. These two paths are separate when you start the journey; you have to choose. Whichever you choose is going to lead to the same peak. And as you come closer to the peak you will be surprised: the travelers on the other path are coming closer to you. Slowly slowly, the paths start merging into each other. By the time you have reached the ultimate, they are one.

The person who follows the path of awareness finds love as a consequence of his awareness, as a by-product, as a shadow. And the person who follows the path of love finds awareness as a consequence, as a by-product, as a shadow of love. They are two sides of the same coin.

And remember: if your awareness lacks love then it is still impure; it has not yet known one hundred percent purity. It is not yet *really* awareness; it must be mixed with unawareness. It is not pure light; there must be pockets of darkness inside you still working, functioning, influencing you, dominating you. If your love is without awareness, then it is not love yet. It must be something lower, something closer to lust than to prayer.

So let it be a criterion: if you follow the path of awareness, let love be the criterion. When your awareness suddenly blooms into love, know perfectly well that awareness has happened, *samadhi* has been achieved. If you follow the path of love, then let awareness function as a criterion, as a touchstone. When suddenly, from nowhere, at the very center of your love, a flame of awareness starts arising, know perfectly well…. Rejoice! You have come home. [6]

Celebrating Consciousness

After working with the cathartic techniques for a few years, I feel that a deep inner harmony, balance and centering is happening to me. But you said that before entering into the final stage of samadhi, one passes through a great chaos. How do I know if I am finished with the chaotic stage?

First, for hundreds of lives you have lived in a chaos. It is nothing new. It is very old. Secondly, the dynamic methods of meditation which have catharsis as their foundation allow all chaos within you to be thrown out. That is the beauty of these techniques. You cannot sit silently, but you can do the dynamic or the chaotic meditations very easily. Once the chaos is thrown out, a silence starts happening to you. Then you can sit silently. If rightly done, continuously done, then the cathartic techniques of meditation will simply dissolve all your chaos into the outside world. You will not need to pass through a mad stage. That's the beauty of these techniques. The madness is being thrown out already. It is in-built in the technique.

But if you sit silently as Patanjali suggests…Patanjali had no cathartic methods; it seems they were not needed in his time. People were naturally very silent, peaceful, primitive. The mind was not yet functioning too much. People slept well, lived like animals. They were not very much thinking, logical, rational, they were more centered in the heart, as primitive people are even now. And life was such that it allowed many catharses automatically.

For example, a woodcutter: he need not have any catharsis because just by cutting wood, all his murderous instincts are thrown out. Cutting wood is like murdering a tree. A stone breaker need not do cathartic meditation. He is doing it the whole day. But for modern man things have changed. Now you live

//////

in such comfort that there is no possibility of any catharsis in your life, except that you can drive in a mad way.

That's why in the West more people die every year through car accidents than by anything else. That is the greatest disease. Neither cancer nor tuberculosis nor any other disease takes such a toll of lives as car driving. In one year of the second world war, millions of people died; more people die every year around the earth just because of mad automobile drivers.

You may have observed if you are a driver, that whenever you are angry you go fast. You go on pushing the accelerator, you simply forget about the brake. When you are very hateful, irritated, the car becomes a medium of expression. Otherwise you live in such comfort, doing less and less with the body, living more and more in the mind.

Those who know about the deeper centers of the brain say that people who work with their hands have less anxiety, less tension; they sleep well because hands are connected with the deepest mind, the deepest center of the brain – your right hand with the left brain, your left hand with the right brain. When you work with the hands, energy is flowing from the head into the hands and being released. People

who are working with their hands don't need catharsis. But people who work with their heads need much catharsis because they accumulate much energy, and there is no way in their body, no opening for it to go out. It goes on and on inside the mind; the mind goes mad.

In our culture and society – in the office, in the factory, in the market – people who work with heads are known as heads: head clerk, or head superintendent, and people who work with hands are known as hands. It is condemnatory. The very word 'hands' has become condemnatory.

When Patanjali was working on these sutras, the world was totally different. People were 'hands'. There was no need for catharsis specifically; life was itself a catharsis. Then they could sit silently very easily, but you cannot sit. Hence, I have been inventing cathartic methods. Only after them can you sit silently, not before.

"After working with the cathartic techniques for a few years, I feel that a deep inner harmony, balance, and centering is happening to me."

Now don't create trouble; let it happen. Now the mind is poking in its nose. The mind says, "How can it happen? First I must pass through chaos." This idea can create chaos. This has been my observation: peo-

ple hanker for silence, and when it starts happening, they can't believe it. It is too good to be true, and particularly people who have always condemned themselves cannot believe that it is happening to them: "Impossible! It may have happened to a Buddha or a Jesus, but to me? No, it is not possible." They come to me; they are so disturbed by silence, that it is happening: "Is it true, or am I imagining it?" Why bother? Even if it is imagination, it is better than imagining anger, it is better than imagining sex, lust.

And I tell you, nobody can imagine silence. Imagination needs some form; silence has no form. Imagination means thinking in images, and silence has no image. You cannot imagine it. There is no possibility. You cannot imagine enlightenment, you cannot imagine satori, samadhi, silence, no. Imagination needs some base, some form, and silence is formless, indefinable. Nobody has ever painted a picture of it; nobody can paint one. Nobody has carved an image of it; nobody could do it.

You cannot imagine silence. The mind is playing tricks. The mind will say, "It must be imagination. How can it be possible for you, such a stupid man as you, and silence happening to you? – must be you are imagining," or, "This guy

Osho has hypnotized you. You must be deceived somehow."

Don't create such problems. Life has enough problems. When silence is happening, enjoy it, celebrate it. It means the chaotic forces have been thrown out. The mind is playing its last game. It plays to the very end; to the very, very end it goes on playing. At the last moment, when enlightenment is just about to happen, then too the mind plays the last game, because it is the last battle.

Don't worry about it, whether it is real or unreal, or whether chaos will come after it or not, because by thinking in this way you have already brought the chaos. It is your idea which can create chaos, and when it is created, the mind will say, "Now listen, I told you so."

Mind is very self-fulfilling. First it gives you a seed, and when it sprouts the mind says, "Look, I was telling you beforehand that you are deceived." The chaos has come, and it has been brought by the idea. So why bother about whether the chaos is still to come in the future or not, or whether it has passed or not? Right this moment, you are silent – why not celebrate it? And I tell you, if you celebrate, it grows.

In this world of consciousness, nothing is so helpful as celebration. Celebration is like watering a plant.

Worry is just the opposite of celebration, it is just like cutting the roots. Feel happy! Dance with your silence. This moment is there – enough. Why ask for more? Tomorrow will take care of itself. This moment is too much; why not live it, celebrate it, share it, enjoy it? Let it become a song, a dance, a poetry; let it be creative. Let your silence be creative; do something with it.

Millions of things are possible because nothing is more creative than silence: no need to become a very great painter, world famous, a Picasso; no need to become a Henry Moore; no need to become a great poet. Those ambitions of being great are of the mind, not of the silence.

In your own way, howsoever small, paint. In your own way, howsoever small, make a haiku. In your own way, howsoever small, sing a song, dance a little, celebrate, and you will find the next moment brings more silence. Once you know that the more you celebrate, the more is given to you; the more you share, the more you become capable of receiving it, each moment it goes on growing, growing.

The next moment is always born out of this moment, so why worry about it? If this moment is silent, how can the next moment be chaos? From where will it come? It

is going to be born out of this moment. If I am happy this moment, how can I be unhappy in the next moment?

If you want the next moment to be unhappy, you will have to become unhappy in this moment, because out of unhappiness, unhappiness is born; out of happiness, happiness is born. Whatsoever you want to reap in the next moment, you will have to sow right now. Once the worry is allowed and you start thinking that chaos will come, it will come; you have already brought it. Now you will have to reap it; it has already come. No need to wait for the next moment; it is already there.

Remember this, and this is really something strange: when you are sad you never think that it may be imaginary. Never have I come across a man who is sad and who says to me that maybe it is just imaginary. Sadness is perfectly real. But happiness? – immediately something goes wrong and you start thinking, "Maybe it is imaginary." Whenever you are tense, you never think it is imaginary. If you can think that your tension and anguish are imaginary, they will disappear. And if you think your silence and happiness are imaginary, they will disappear.

Whatsoever is taken as real, becomes real. Whatsoever is taken as unreal, becomes unreal. You are the creator of your whole world around you; remember this. It is so rare to achieve a moment of happiness, bliss – don't waste it in thinking. But if you don't do anything, the possibility of worry is there. If you don't do anything – if you don't dance, if you don't sing, if you don't share – the possibility is there. The very energy that could have been creative will create the worry. It will start creating new tensions inside.

Energy has to be creative. If you don't use it for happiness, the same energy will be used for unhappiness. And for unhappiness you have such deep-rooted habits that the energy flow is very loose and natural. For happiness it is an uphill task.

So the first few days you will have to be constantly aware. Whenever there is a happy moment, let it grip you, possess you. Enjoy it so totally; how could the next moment be different? From where would it be different? From where would it come?

Your time is created within you. Your time is not my time. There exist as many parallel times as there are minds. There is no one time. If there were one time, then there would be difficulty. Then amidst the whole miserable humankind, nobody could become a buddha because we belong to the same time. No, it is not the same. My time comes from me – it is my creativity. If this moment is beautiful, the next moment is born more beautiful – this is my time. If this moment is sad for you, then a sadder moment is born out of you – that is your time. Millions of parallel lines of time exist. And there are a few people who exist without time – those who have attained to no-mind. They have no time because they don't think about the past; it is gone, so only fools think about it. When something is gone, it is gone.

There is a Buddhist mantra: *Gate gate, para gate – swaha;* "Gone, gone, absolutely gone; let it go to the fire." The past is gone, the future has not yet come. Why worry about it? When it comes, we will see. You will be there to encounter it, so why worry about it?

The gone is gone, the not-come has not come yet. Only this moment is left, pure, intense with energy. Live it! If it is silence, be grateful. If it is blissful, thank God, trust it. And if you can trust, it will grow. If you distrust, you have already poisoned it. [7]

Tune In to Uncertainty

The more I watch myself, the more I experience the falseness of my ego. I have started to feel like a stranger to myself, no longer knowing what is false. This leaves me with an uncomfortable feeling of having no guidelines, as I sensed I had before.

This happens; this is bound to happen. And remember that one should be happy that it has happened; it is a good indication. When one starts on the inner journey everything seems to be clear, rooted, because the ego is in control and the ego has all the guidelines. The ego has all the maps, the ego is the master.

When you move a little further into the journey, the ego starts evaporating, seems to be more and more false, seems to be more and more a deception, a hallucination. When one starts awakening out of the dream, then guidelines are lost. Now the old master is no more the master, and the new master has not yet arisen. There is a confusion, a chaos. This is a good indication.

Half the journey is over, but there will be an uncomfortable feeling, an uneasiness, because you feel lost, a stranger to yourself, not knowing who you are. Before, you knew who you were: your name, your form, your address, your bank balance – everything was certain, this was you. You had an identification with the ego. Now the ego is evaporating, the old house is falling and you don't know who you are, where you are. Everything is murky, cloudy, and the old certainty is lost.

This is good because the old certainty was a false certainty. It was not a certainty, in fact. Deep behind it there was uncertainty. That's why, when the ego evaporates, you feel uncertain. Now the deeper layers of your being are revealed to you – you feel a stranger. You were always a stranger, only the ego deceived you into feeling that you knew who you were. The dream was too much, it looked too real.

In the morning when you are coming out of a dream, suddenly you don't know who or where you are. Have you felt this feeling sometimes in the morning? – when suddenly you are awakened out of a dream, and for some moments you don't know where you are, who you are and what is happening? The same happens when one comes out of the dream of the ego. Discomfort, uneasiness, uprootedness will be felt, but one should be happy about it. If you become miserable about it, you will fall back to the old state of affairs where things were certain, where everything was mapped, charted, where you knew, where guidelines were clear.

Drop uneasiness. Even if it is there, don't be too impressed by it. Let it be there, watch, and that too will go. Soon uneasiness will disappear. It is just there because of the old habit of certainty. You don't know how to live in an uncertain universe. You don't know how to live in insecurity. The uneasiness is there because of the old security. It is just because of the old habit, a hangover. It will go. One just has to wait, watch, relax, and feel happy that something has happened. And I tell you, it is a good indication.

Many have turned back from that point just to feel comfortable again, at ease, at home. They have missed. They were just coming nearer the goal, and they turned back. Don't do that; go ahead. Uncertainty is good, nothing is wrong with it. You have only to be tuned, that's all.

You are tuned with the certain universe of the ego, the secure universe of the ego. Howsoever false on the surface, everything seems to be perfectly as it should be. You need a little tuning with the uncertain existence.

Existence is uncertain, insecure, dangerous. It is a flux – things moving, changing. It is a strange world; get acquainted with it. Have a little courage and don't look backwards, look forward; soon the uncertainty itself will become beautiful, the insecurity itself will become beautiful.

In fact, only insecurity is beautiful, because insecurity is life. Security is ugly, it is a part of death – that's why it is secure. To live without guidelines is the only way to live. When you live with guidelines, you live a false life. Ideals, guidelines, disciplines – you force something on your life, you mold your life, you don't allow it to be, you try to make something out of it. Guidelines are violent and all ideals are ugly. Through them you will miss

yourself. You will never attain to your being.

Becoming is not being. All becoming, and all effort to become something, will force something on you. It is a violent effort. You may become a saint, but in your saintliness there will be ugliness. I tell you, and I emphasize it: to live life without any guidelines is the only saintliness possible. Even then, you may become a sinner; but in being a sinner, there will be a holiness, a saintliness.

Life is holy; you need not force anything upon it, you need not mold it, you need not give it a pattern, a discipline and an order. Life has its own order, it has its own discipline. You simply move with it, you float with it, you don't try to push the river. The river is flowing – you become one with it and the river takes you to the ocean. This is the life of a sannyasin: a life of happening, not of doing. Then your being reaches, by and by, above the clouds, beyond the clouds and conflicts. Suddenly you are free. In the disorder of life you find a new order. But the quality of the order is totally different now. It is nothing imposed by you, it is intimate to life itself.

Trees also have an order, as do rivers, mountains, but those are not orders imposed by moralists, puritans, priests. They don't go to somebody to find the guidelines. Order is intrinsic; it is in life itself. Once the ego is not there to manipulate, to push and pull here and there – "Do this and that" – when you are completely freed from the ego, a discipline comes to you, an inner discipline. It is unmotivated. It is not seeking something, it simply happens: as when you breathe, as when you feel hungry and you eat, as when you feel sleepy and you go to bed. It is an inner order, an intrinsic order. That will come when you become tuned with insecurity, when you become tuned with your strangeness, when you become tuned with your unknown being.

In Zen they have a saying, one of the most beautiful: when a person lives in the world, mountains are mountains, rivers are rivers. When a person moves into meditation, now mountains are no more mountains, rivers are no more rivers. Everything is a confusion and a chaos. But when a man has attained to satori, to samadhi, again rivers are rivers and mountains are mountains.

There are three stages: in the first, you are certain with the ego, in the third you are absolutely certain with the non-ego, and just in between the two, the chaos; when the certainty of the ego disappears and the certainty of life has not yet come. This is a very, very potential moment, very pregnant. If you become afraid and turn back, you will miss the possibility.

Ahead is the real certainty. That real certainty is not against uncertainty. Ahead is the real security, but that security is not against insecurity. That security is so vast that it contains insecurity within itself. It is so vast that it is not afraid of insecurity. It absorbs insecurity into itself, it contains all contradictions. So somebody can call it insecurity and somebody can call it security. In fact it is neither, or both. If you feel that you have become a stranger to yourself, celebrate it, feel grateful. Rare is this moment; enjoy it. The more you enjoy, the more you will find that the certainty is coming nearer to you, coming faster and faster towards you. If you can celebrate your strangeness, your uprootedness, your homelessness, suddenly you are at home – the third stage has come. [8]

Count the Moments of Awareness

You tell us to be aware of everything – which means to be a witness to everything, every act. When I decide to be aware in work, I forget about awareness, and when I become aware that I was not aware, I feel guilty; I feel that I have made a mistake. Could You please explain?

It is one of the basic problems for anybody who is trying to be aware while at work – because work demands that you should forget yourself completely. You should be involved in it so deeply ... as if you are absent. Unless such total involvement is there, the work remains superficial.

All that is great, created by man – in painting, in poetry, in architecture, in sculpture, in any dimension of life – needs you to be totally involved. And if you are trying to be aware at the same time, your work will never be first rate, because you will not be in it.

So awareness while you are working needs a tremendous training and discipline, and one has to start from very simple actions, for example, walking. You can walk, and you can be aware that you are walking – each step can be full of awareness. Eating ... just the way they drink tea in Zen monasteries – they call it the 'tea ceremony', because sipping the tea, one has to remain alert and aware.

These are small actions but to begin with they are perfectly good. One should not start with something like painting, dancing – those are very deep and complex phenomena. Start with small actions of daily routine life. As you become more and more accustomed to awareness, as awareness becomes just like breathing – you don't have to make any effort for it, it has become spontaneous – then in any act, any work, you can be aware.

But remember the condition: it has to be effortless; it has to come out of spontaneity. Then painting or composing music, or dancing, or even fighting an enemy with a sword, you can remain absolutely aware. But that awareness is not the awareness you are trying for. It is not the beginning; it is the culmination of a long discipline. Sometimes it can happen without discipline too.

But this can happen only rarely – in extreme conditions. In everyday life you should follow the simple course. First become aware about actions which do not need your involvement. You can walk and you can go on thinking; you can eat and you can go on thinking. Replace thinking by awareness. Go on eating, and remain alert that you are eating. Walk, replace thinking by awareness. Go on walking; perhaps your walking will be a little slower and more graceful. But awareness is possible with these small acts. And as you become more and more articulate, use more complicated activities.

A day comes that there is no activity in the world in which you cannot remain alert at the same time, doing the act with totality.

You are saying, "When I decide to be aware in work, I forget about awareness." It has not to be your decision, it has to be your long discipline. And awareness has to come spontaneously; you are not to call it, you are not to force it.

"And when I become aware that I was not aware, I feel guilty." That is absolute stupidity. When you become aware that you were not aware, feel happy that at least now you are aware. For the concept of guilt, there is no place in my teachings.

Guilt is one of the cancers of the soul. And all the religions have used guilt to destroy your dignity, your pride, and to make you just slaves. There is no need to feel guilty, it is natural. Awareness is such a great thing that even if you can be aware for a few seconds, rejoice. Don't pay attention to those moments when you forgot. Pay attention to that state when you suddenly remember, "I was not aware." Feel fortunate that at least, after a few hours, awareness has returned.

Don't make it a repentance, a guilt, a sadness – because by being guilty and sad, you are not going to be helped. You will feel, deep down, a failure. And once a feeling of failure settles in you, awareness will become even more difficult.

Change your whole focus. It is great that you became aware that you had forgotten to be aware. Now don't forget for as long as possible. Again, you will forget; again, you will remember – but each time, the gap of forgetfulness will become smaller and smaller. If you can avoid guilt, which is basically Christian, your gaps of unawareness will become shorter, and one day they will simply disappear. Awareness will become just like breathing or heartbeat, or the blood circulating in you – day in, day out. So be watchful that you don't feel guilty. There is nothing to feel guilty about. It is immensely significant that the trees don't listen to Catholic priests. Otherwise, they would make the roses feel guilty: "Why do you have thorns?" And the rose, dancing in the wind, in the rain, in the sun, would suddenly become sad. The dance would disappear; the joy would disappear; the fragrance would disappear. Now the thorn would become his only reality, a wound – "Why do you have thorns?"

But because there are no rosebushes so foolish as to listen to any priest of any religion, roses go on dancing, and with the roses, thorns also go on dancing.

The whole existence is guiltless. And the moment a man becomes guiltless, he becomes part of the universal flow of life. That is enlightenment, a guiltless consciousness, rejoicing in everything that life makes available: the light is beautiful; so is darkness.

When you cannot find anything to be guilty about, to me you have become a religious man. To the so-called religions, unless you are guilty you are not religious; the more guilty you are, the more religious you are.

People are torturing themselves as punishment, as penance. People are fasting; people are beating their chests with their fists till blood oozes from their chests. These people, to me, are psychopaths; they are not religious. Their so-called religions have taught them that if you commit anything wrong, it is better to punish yourself than to be punished by God on Judgment Day – because that punishment is to be thrown into the abysmal darkness of hell for eternity. There is no escape, no exit – once you enter hell, you have entered.

The whole humanity has been made guilty in some measure or other. It has taken away the shine from your eyes; it has taken away the beauty from your face; it has taken away the grace of your being. It has reduced you to a criminal – unnecessarily.

Remember: man is frail and weak, and to err is human. And the people who invented the proverb, "To err is human," have also invented the proverb, "To forgive is divine." I don't agree with the second part.

I say, "To err is human and to forgive is also human." And to forgive oneself is one of the greatest virtues, because if you cannot forgive yourself, you cannot forgive anybody else in the world – it is impossible. You are so full of wounds, of guilt, how can you forgive anybody? Your so-called saints go on saying that you will be thrown into hell. The reality is, they are living in hell! They cannot allow even God to forgive you!

One great Sufi poet, Omar Khayyam, has written in his *Rubaiyat,* his world-famous collection of poetry: "I am going to drink, to dance, to love. I am going to commit every kind of sin because I trust God is compassionate – he will forgive. My sins are very small; his forgiveness is immense."

When the priests came to know about his book – because in those days books were written by hand, there were no printing presses.... The priests discovered that he was writing such sacrilegious things, that he was saying, "Don't be worried, go on doing anything you want because God is nothing but pure compassion and love. How much sin can you commit in seventy years of life? – in comparison to his forgiveness, it is nothing."

He was a famous mathematician too, renowned in his country. The priests approached him and said, "What kind of things are you writing? You will destroy people's religiousness! Create fear in people, tell people that God is very just: if you have committed a sin, you will be punished. There will be no compassion."

Omar Khayyam's book was burned in his day. Whenever a copy was found, it was burned by the priests, because this man was teaching such a dangerous idea.

If it spreads among human beings and everybody starts rejoicing in life, what will happen to the priests? What will happen to the saints? What will happen to their mythologies of hell and heaven and God? All will disappear into thin air.

At least with me, Omar Khayyam is one of the enlightened Sufi mystics, and what he is saying has immense truth in it. He does not mean that you should commit sin. What he means simply is that you should not feel guilty. Whatever you do – if it is not right, don't do it again. If you feel it hurts somebody, don't do it again. But there is no need to feel guilty, there is no need to be repentant, there is no need to do penance and torture yourself.

I want to change your focus completely. Rather than counting how many times you forgot to remember to be aware, count those few beautiful moments when you were crystal clear and aware. Those few moments are enough to save you, are enough to cure you, to heal you. And if you pay attention to them, they will go on growing and spreading in your consciousness. Slowly, slowly the whole darkness of unawareness will disappear.

In the beginning you will also find many times that perhaps it is not possible to be working and to be aware together. But I say unto you that it is not only possible, it is very easily possible. Just begin in the right way. Just don't start from XYZ; start from ABC.

In life, we go on missing many things because of wrong starts. Everything should be started from the very beginning. Our minds are impatient; we want to do everything quickly. We want to reach the highest point without passing through every rung of the ladder.

But that means an absolute failure. And once you fail in something like awareness – it is not a small failure – perhaps you will not try it again, ever. The failure hurts.

So anything that is as valuable as awareness – because it can open all the doors of the mysteries of existence, it can bring you to the very temple of God – you should start very carefully and from the very beginning and move very slowly.

Just a little patience and the goal is not far away. [9]

Make Things as Simple as Possible

How can I tell the difference between one part of the mind watching another part of the mind, and the watcher. Can the watcher watch itself? One time, I thought I had got it, and then that same day I heard you say in discourse, "If you think you've got the watcher, you've missed." Since then, I've tried watching feelings in the body, thoughts and emotions. Mostly, I'm just caught in them, but, once in a while, rarely, I feel tremendously relaxed, and nothing stays – it just keeps moving. Is there anything to do?

One has to start watching the body walking, sitting, going to bed, eating. One should start from the most solid because it is easier. And then one should move to subtler experiences. One should start watching thoughts. And when one becomes an expert in watching thoughts, then one should start watching feelings. After you feel that you can watch your feelings, then you should start watching your moods, which are even more subtle than your feelings, and more vague.

The miracle of watching is that as you are watching the body, your watcher is becoming stronger; as you are watching the thoughts, your watcher is becoming stronger; as you are watching the feelings, the watcher is becoming even more strong. When you are watching your moods, the watcher is so strong that it can remain itself – watching itself, just as a candle in the dark night not only lights everything around it, it also lights itself.

To find the watcher in its purity is the greatest achievement in spirituality, because the watcher in you is your very soul, the watcher in you is your immortality. But never for a single moment think, "I have got it," because that is the moment when you miss.

Watching is an eternal process; you always go on becoming deeper and deeper, but you never come to the end where you can say "I have got it." In fact, the deeper you go, the more you become aware that you have entered into a process which is eternal – without any beginning and without any end.

But people are watching only others; they never bother to watch themselves. Everybody is watching – that is the most superficial watching – what the other person is doing, what the other person is wearing, how he looks. Everybody is watching; watching is not something new to be introduced in your life. It has only to be deepened, taken away from others and arrowed towards your own inner feelings, thoughts, moods – and finally, the watcher itself.

A Jew is sitting in a train opposite a priest.

"Tell me, your worship, why do you wear your collar back to front?"

"Because I am a father," answers the priest.

"I am also a father, and I don't wear my collar like that," says the Jew.

"Ah," says the priest, "but I am a father to thousands."

"Then maybe," replies the Jew, "it is your trousers you should wear back to front."

People are very watchful about everybody else.

Two Polacks went out for a walk when suddenly it began to rain. "Quick," said one man, "open your umbrella."

"It won't help," said his friend, "my umbrella is full of holes."

"Then why did you bring it in the first place?"

"I did not think it would rain."

You can laugh very easily about ridiculous acts of people, but have you ever laughed about yourself? Have you ever caught yourself doing something ridiculous? No, you keep yourself completely unwatched; your whole watching is about others, and that is not of any help.

Use this energy of watchfulness for a transformation of your being. It can bring you so much bliss and so much benediction that you cannot even dream about it. A simple process, but once you start using it on yourself, it becomes a meditation. One can make meditations out of anything.

Anything that leads you to yourself is meditation. And it is immensely significant to find your own meditation, because in the very finding you will find great joy. And because it is your own finding – not some ritual imposed upon you – you will love to go deeper into it. The deeper you go into it, the happier you will feel – peaceful, more silent, more together, more dignified, more graceful.

You all know watching, so there is no question of learning it, it is just a question of changing the objects of watching. Bring them closer.

Watch your body, and you will be surprised. I can move my hand without watching, and I can move my hand with watching. You will not see the difference, but I can feel the difference. When I move it with watchfulness, there is a grace and beauty in it, a peacefulness, and a silence. You can walk watching each step, it will give you all the benefit that walking can give you as an exercise, plus it will give you the benefit of a great simple meditation.

The temple in Bodhgaya where Gautam Buddha became enlightened has been made in memory of two things – one is a Bodhi tree under which he used to sit. Just by the side of the tree there are small stones for a slow walk. He was meditating, sitting, and when he would feel that sitting had been too much – a little exercise was needed for the body – he would walk on those stones. That was his walking meditation.

When I was in Bodhgaya, having a meditation camp there, I went to the temple. I saw Buddhist lamas from Tibet, from Japan, from China. They were all paying their respect to the tree, and I saw not a single one paying his respect to those stones on which Buddha had walked miles and miles. I told them, "This is not right. You should not forget those stones. They have been touched by Gautam Buddha's feet millions of times. But I know why you are not paying any attention to them, because you have forgotten completely that Buddha was emphasizing that you should watch every act of your body: walking, sitting, lying down."

You should not let a single moment go by unconsciously. Watchfulness will sharpen your consciousness. This is the essential religion – all else is simply talk. But you ask me, "Is there something more?" No, if you can do only watchfulness, nothing else is needed.

My effort here is to make religion as simple as possible. All the religions have done just the opposite: they have made things very complex – so complex that people have never tried them. For example, in the Buddhist scriptures there are thirty-three thousand principles to be followed by a Buddhist monk; even to remember them is impossible. Just the very number thirty-three thousand is enough to freak you out: "I am finished! My whole life will be disturbed and destroyed." I teach you: just find a single principle that suits you, that feels in tune with you – and that is enough. [10]

Witnessing Is Like Sowing Seeds

How does watching lead to no-mind? I am more and more able to watch my body, my thoughts and feelings and this feels beautiful. But moments of no thoughts are few and far between. When I hear you saying "Meditation is witnessing," I feel I understand. But when you talk about 'no-mind', it doesn't sound easy at all. Would you please comment?

Meditation covers a very long pilgrimage. When I say "Meditation is witnessing," it is the beginning of meditation. And when I say "Meditation is no-mind," it is the completion of the pilgrimage. Witnessing is the beginning, and no-mind is the fulfillment. Witnessing is the method to reach to no-mind.

Naturally you will feel witnessing easier. It is close to you. But witnessing is only like seeds and then is the long waiting period – not only waiting, but trusting that this seed is going to sprout, that it is going to become a bush, that one day the spring will come and the bush will have flowers. No-mind is the last stage of flowering.

Sowing the seeds is of course very easy. It is within your hands. But bringing the flowers is beyond you.

You can prepare the whole ground, but the flowers will come on their own accord. You cannot manage to force them to come. The spring is beyond your reach. But if your preparation is perfect, spring comes. That is absolutely guaranteed.

The way you are moving is perfectly good. Witnessing is the path and you are starting to feel a thoughtless moment once in a while. These are glimpses of no-mind, but just for a moment.

Remember one fundamental law: that which can exist just for a moment, can also become eternal, because you are given always one moment – not two moments together. And if you can transform one moment into a thoughtless state, you are learning the secret. Then there is no hindrance why

264

you cannot change. The second moment will also come alone with the same potential and the same capacity.

If you know the secret, you have the master key which can open every moment into a glimpse of no-mind. No-mind is the final stage, when mind disappears forever, and the thoughtless gap becomes your intrinsic reality. If these few glimpses are coming, they show you are on the right path and you are using the right method.

But don't be impatient. Existence needs immense patience. The ultimate mysteries are opened only to those who have immense patience.

Once a man is in a state of no-mind, nothing can distract him from his being. There is no power bigger than the power of no-mind. No harm can be done to such a person. No attachment, no greed, no jealousy, no anger, nothing can arise in him. No-mind is absolutely a pure sky without any clouds.

You say, "How does watching lead to no-mind?" There is an intrinsic law: thoughts don't have their own life. They are parasites. They live on your identification with them. When you say, "I am angry," you are pouring life energy into anger, because you are getting identified with anger.

But when you say, "I am watching anger flashing on the screen of the mind within me," you are not giving any life, any juice, any energy to anger any more. You will be able to see that because you are not identified. The anger is absolutely impotent, has no impact on you, does not change you, does not affect you. It is absolutely hollow and dead. It will pass on and it will leave the sky clean and the screen of the mind empty.

Slowly, slowly, you start getting out of your thoughts. That's the whole process of witnessing and watching. In other words, George Gurdjieff used to call it 'non-identification'. You are no more identifying with your thoughts. You are simply standing aloof and away – indifferent, as if they may be anybody's thought. You have broken your connections with them. Only then can you watch them.

Watching needs a certain distance. If you are identified, there is no distance, they are too close. It is as if you are putting the mirrors too close to your eyes – you cannot see your face. A certain distance is needed, only then can you see your face in the mirror.

If thoughts are too close to you, you cannot watch, you become impressed and colored by your thoughts. Anger makes you angry, greed makes you greedy, lust makes you lustful, because there is no distance at all. They are so close that you are bound to think that you and your thoughts are one.

Watching destroys this oneness and creates a separation. The more you watch, the bigger is the distance; the bigger the distance, the less energy your thoughts are getting from you and they don't have any other source.

Soon they start dying, disappearing. In these disappearing moments you will have the first glimpses of no-mind – as you are experiencing. You say, "I am more and more able to watch my body, my thoughts and feelings. And this feels beautiful." This is only just the beginning. Even the beginning is immensely beautiful. Just to be on the right path, even without taking a single step, will give you immense joy for no reason at all.

And once you start moving on the right path, your blissfulness, your beautiful experiences are going to become more and more deep, more and more wide with new nuances, with new flowers, with new fragrances.

You say, "But moments of no-thoughts are few and far between." It is a great achievement, because people don't know even a single gap. Their thoughts are always in a rush hour. Thoughts upon thoughts,

265

bumper to bumper. The line continues – whether you are awake or asleep. What you call your dreams are nothing but thoughts in the form of pictures, because the unconscious mind does not know alphabetical languages.

What you are feeling is a great indication that you are on the right path. It is always a question for the seeker whether he is moving in the right direction or not. There is no security, no insurance, no guarantee. All the dimensions are open; how are you going to choose the right one?

These are the ways and the criterion of how one has to choose. If you move on any path, any methodology, and it brings joy to you, more sensitivity, more watchfulness and gives a feeling of immense well-being, this is the only criterion that you are going on the right path. If you become more miserable, more angry, more egoist, more greedy, more lustful, those are the indications you are moving on a wrong path.

On the right path your blissfulness is going to grow more and more every day. And your experiences of beautiful feelings will become tremendously psychedelic, more colorful, colors that you have never seen in the world, fragrances that you have never experienced in the world. Then you can walk on the path without any fear that you can go wrong.

These inner experiences will keep you always on the right path. Just remember that they are growing. That means you are moving. Now you have only a few moments of thoughtlessness. It is not a simple attainment, it is a great achievement because people in their whole life know not even a single moment when there is no thought. These gaps will grow. As you will become more and more centered, more and more watchful, these gaps will start growing bigger and the day is not far if you go on moving without looking back, without going astray. If you keep going straight, the day is not far away, when you will feel for the first time that the gaps have become so big that hours pass and not even a single thought arises. Now you are having bigger experiences of no-mind.

The ultimate achievement is when you are surrounded with no-mind for twenty-four hours. That does not mean that you cannot use your mind. That is a fallacy propounded by those who know nothing about no-mind.

No-mind does not mean that you cannot use the mind. It simply means that the mind cannot use you. No-mind does not mean that the mind is destroyed. No-mind simply means that the mind is put aside. You can bring it into action any moment you need to communicate with the world, then it will be your servant. Right now, it is your master. Even when you are sitting alone, it goes on: yakkety-yak, yakkety-yak, and you cannot do anything. You are so utterly helpless.

No-mind simply means that the mind has been put in its right place. As a servant, it is a great instrument. As a master, it is very unfortunate. It is dangerous. It will destroy your whole life.

Mind is only a medium when you want to communicate with others. But when you are alone, there is no need of the mind. So whenever you want to use it, you can use it. And remember one thing more: when the mind remains silent for hours, it becomes fresh, young, more creative, more sensitive, rejuvenated through rest.

Ordinary people's minds start somewhere around three or four years of age and then they go on continuing for seventy years, eighty years without any holiday. Naturally they can not be very creative. They are utterly tired, and tired with rubbish. Millions of people in the world live without any creativity. And creativity is one of the greatest blissful experiences.

But their minds are so tired. They are not in a state of overflowing energy.

The man of no-mind keeps the mind in rest, full of energy, immensely sensitive, ready to jump into action the moment it is ordered. It is not a coincidence that the people who have experienced no-mind …their words start having a magic of their own. When they use their mind, it has a charisma, it has a magnetic force. It has tremendous spontaneity and the freshness of the dew-drops in the early morning before the sun rises. And the mind is nature's greatest evolved medium of expression and creativity.

So the man of meditation, or in other words, the man of no-mind, changes even his prose into poetry. Without any effort – his words become so full of authority that they don't need any arguments, they become their own arguments. The force that they carry becomes a self-evident truth. There is no need for any other support from logic or from scriptures. The words of a man of no-mind have an intrinsic certainty about them. And if you are ready to receive and listen, you

will feel it in your heart: the self-evident truth.

You say, "When I hear you say 'meditation is witnessing,' I feel I understand. But when you talk about no-mind, it doesn't sound easy at all." How can it sound easy? It is your future possibility. Meditation you have started, it may be in the beginning stages, but you have a certain experience of it that makes you understand me. But if you can understand meditation, don't be worried at all. Meditation surely leads to no-mind, just as every river moves towards the ocean without any maps, without any guides.

Every river without exception finally reaches to the ocean. Every meditation, without exception finally reaches to the state of no-mind.

But naturally when the Ganges is in the Himalayas wandering in the mountains and in the valleys, it has no idea what the ocean is, cannot conceive the existence of ocean, but it is moving towards the ocean because water has the intrinsic capacity of always finding the lowest place, and the oceans are the lowest place. So the rivers are born on the peaks of the Himalayas and start

moving immediately towards lower spaces and finally they are bound to find the ocean.

Just the reverse is the process of meditation – it moves upwards to higher peaks. And the ultimate peak is no-mind. No-mind is a simple word, but it exactly means enlightenment, liberation, freedom from all bondage, the experience of deathlessness and immortality.

Those are big words and I don't want you to be frightened. So I use a simple word: no-mind. You know the mind. You can conceive a state when this mind will be non-functioning.

Once this mind is non-functioning, you become part of the mind of the cosmos, the universal mind. When you are part of the universal mind your individual mind functions as a beautiful servant. It has recognized the master. And it brings news from the universal mind to those who are still chained by the individual mind. When I am speaking to you, it is in fact the universe using me. My words are not my words. They belong to the universal truth. That is their power, that is their charisma, that is their magic. 11

Witnessing Is Enough

I have always heard You say, "Stop doing. Watch." Several times lately I've heard You say that the mind should be the servant instead of our master. It feels that there is nothing to do except watch. But the question still arises: is there anything to do with this unruly servant but to watch?

There is nothing else to do with this unruly servant, but just to watch. Apparently it appears too simple a solution for too complex a problem. But this is part of the mysteries of existence. The problem may be too complex, the solution can be very simple.

Watching, witnessing, being aware seem to be small words to solve the whole complexity of mind. Millions of years of heritage, tradition, conditioning, prejudice, how will they disappear just by watching? But they disappear.

As Gautam Buddha used to say, if the lights of the house are on, thieves don't come close to that house – knowing that the master is awake because the light is shown from the windows, from the doors, you can see that the light is on. It is not the time to enter into the house. When the lights are off, thieves are attracted to the house. Darkness becomes an invitation. As Gautam Buddha used to say, the same is the situation about your thoughts, imaginations, dreams, anxieties, your whole mind.

If the witness is there, the witness is almost like the light. These thieves start dispersing. And if these thieves find there is no witness, they start calling their brothers, and cousins and everybody saying, "Come on." It is as simple a phenomenon as the light. The moment you bring the light in, the darkness disappears. You don't ask, "Is just light enough for darkness to disappear?" Or, "When we have brought the light, will we have to do something more for the darkness to disappear?"

No, just the presence of the light is the absence of the darkness and the absence of the light is the presence of darkness. The presence of the witness is the absence of the mind and the absence of the witness is the presence of the mind.

So the moment you start watching, slowly, slowly as your watcher becomes stronger, your mind will become weaker. The moment it realizes that the watcher has come to maturity, the mind immediately submits as a beautiful servant. It is a mechanism. If the master has arrived, then the machine can be used. If the master is not there or is fast asleep, then the machine goes on working things, whatsoever it can do on its own. There is nobody to give orders, there is nobody to say: "No, stop. That thing has not to be done." Then the mind is slowly convinced that it itself is the master and for thousands of years, it has remained your master.

So when you try to be a witness, it fights, because it is a question of survival of the mind. It has completely forgotten that it is only a servant. You have been so long absent – it does not recognize you. Hence the struggle between the witness and the thoughts. But final victory is going to be yours, because nature and existence both want you to be the master and the mind to be the servant. Then things are in harmony. Then the mind cannot go wrong. Then everything is existentially relaxed, silent, flowing towards its destiny.

You don't have to do anything else but to watch.

Paddy bought a parrot at an auction. He asked the auctioneer: "I have spent a great deal of money for this parrot – are you sure he can talk?" The auctioneer replied, "Of course I am sure; he was bidding against you."

Such is the unawareness of the mind and such are the stupidities of the mind. I have heard that the Irish atheists – seeing that the theists have started a dial-a-prayer service – also started one although they are atheists. The competitive mind... they have also started a dial-a-prayer service. When you phone them up, nobody answers.

Two tramps were sitting by a camp fire one night. One of them was very depressed. "You know Jim," he mused, "the life of a tramp is not as great as it is made out to be. Nights on park benches, or in a cold barn. Traveling on foot and always dodging the police. Being kicked from one town to another. Wondering where your next meal is coming from; being sneered at by your fellow man...." His voice trailed off and he sighed heavily.

"Well," said the other tramp, "if that is how you feel about it, why don't you go and find yourself a job?" "What!" said the first tramp in amazement, "and admit that I'm a failure?"

Mind has become accustomed to being a master. It will take a little time to bring it to its senses. Witnessing is enough. It is a very silent process, but the consequences are tremendously great. There is no other method which can be better than witnessing as far as dispersing the darkness of the mind is concerned. In fact, there are one hundred twelve methods of meditation. I have gone through all those methods – not intellectually. It took me years to go through each method and to find out its very essence.

And after going through one hundred twelve methods, I was amazed that the essence is witnessing; the methods' non-essentials are different, but the center of each is witnessing.

Hence I can say to you, there is only one meditation in the whole world and that is the art of witnessing. It will do everything – the whole transformation of your being – and it will open the doors of *Satyam, Shivam, Sundram:* the truth, the godliness and the beauty of it all. [12]

INTRODUCTION
NOTES TO THE READER

1. Philosophia Ultima, Session 2.
2. Hsin Hsin Ming, Session 3.
3. Philosophia Ultima, Session 1.
4. Unio Mystica, Vol. I, Session 4.
5. The Guest, Session 6.
6. The Dhammapada, Vol. I, Session 2.

ABOUT MEDITATION

1. The Orange Book, p. 94.
2. The Rajneesh Bible, Vol. IV, Session 2.
3. The Rajneesh Upanishad, Session 3.
4. Light on the Path: Talks in the Himalayas.
5. The Search, Session 7.
6. The Book, Series I, pp. 87–88.
7. Beyond Enlightenment, Session 9.
8. The Psychology of the Esoteric, Session 2.
9. The Golden Future, Session 1.
10. Beyond Enlightenment, Session 28.
11. The Search, Session 7.
12. Guida Spirituale, Session 15.
13. The Book, Series I, p. 230.
14. The Secret of Secrets, Vol. II, Session 3.
15. Guida Spirituale, Session 12.
16. The Book, Series I, p. 28, 30.
17. Ibid., p. 30.
18. Ibid., p. 31.
19. The Book of the Books, Vol. II, Session 8.
20. Guida Spirituale, Session 2.

THE SCIENCE OF MEDITATION

1. The Book of the Secrets, Vol. III, Session 15.
2. Tantra: The Supreme Understanding, Session 8.
3. The Book of the Secrets, Vol. IV, Session 2.
4. The Book of the Secrets, Vol. III, Session 9.
5. The Book of the Secrets, Vol. IV, Session 9.
6. The Book of the Secrets, Vol. I, Session 1.
7. The Book of Wisdom, Vol. I, Session 1.
8. The Book of the Secrets, Vol. V, Session 11.
9. The Book of the Secrets, Vol. V, Session 7.

THE SCIENCE OF MEDITATION

10. The Secret of Secrets, Vol. II, Session 1.
11. Ibid.
12. Yoga: The Alpha and the Omega, Vol. VI, Session 7.
13. Meditation: The Art of Ecstasy, Session 4.
14. The Great Zen Master: Ta Hui, Session 20.
15. Ibid., Session 14.
16. Ancient Music in the Pines, Session 7.
17. A Cup of Tea, Letter 72.
18. The Book of Wisdom, Vol. I, Session 9.
19. Yoga: The Science of the Soul, Vol. III, Session 10.
20. YAA-HOO! The Mystic Rose, Session 8.
21. The Hidden Splendor, Session 10.
22. The Book of Wisdom, Vol. II, Session 7.
23. Sermons in Stones, Session 4.
24. What Is, Is, What Ain't, Ain't, Session 10.
25. Light on the Path: Talks in the Himalayas.

THE MEDITATIONS

Two Powerful Methods for Awakening
1. My Way: The Way of the White Clouds, Session 4.
2. Instructions currently in use at Osho Commune International, Poona, India.
3. Meditation: The Art of Ecstasy.
4. The Orange Book, pp. 29-30.
5. Ibid., pp. 132-136.

Dancing as a Meditation
1. The Orange Book, pp. 49-52.
2. Ibid., pp 143-145.

The Meditative Therapies
1. YAA-HOO! The Mystic Rose, Session 30.
2. Instructions currently in use at Osho Commune International, Poona, India.
3. Live Zen, Session 17.
4. The Supreme Doctrine, Session 1.

Anything Can Be a Meditation
1. The Orange Book, p. 64.
2. Ibid., pp. 23-26.
3. A Sudden Clash of Thunder, Session 9.

THE MEDITATIONS

4. The Orange Book, p. 16.
5. The Secret of Secrets, Vol. II, Session 4.
6. The Orange Book, pp. 65-69.

Breath – a Bridge to Meditation
1. The Book of the Secrets, Vol. I, Session 3.
2. The New Dawn, Session 16.
3. Instructions currently in use at Osho Commune International, Poona, India.
4. The Book of the Secrets, Vol. I, Session 3.
5. Ibid., Session 5.
6. Ibid.
7. Yoga: The Science of the Soul, Volume II, Session 95.

Opening the Heart
1. The Book, Series I, p. 634.
2. The Book of the Secrets, Vol. I, Session 12.
3. The Orange Book, pp. 195-196.
4. The Book of the Secrets, Vol. V, Session 7.
5. The Book of the Secrets, Vol. I, Session 11.
6. The Book of Wisdom, Vol. I, Session 1.
7. Ibid., Session 5.

Inner Centering
1. Unio Mystica, Vol. I, Session 2.
2. The Book of Wisdom, Vol. II, Session 2.
3. The Book of the Secrets, Vol. III, Session 1.
4. Ibid., Session 5.
5. Ibid., Session 3.
6. The Book of the Secrets, Vol. IV, Session 13.

Looking Within
1. The Book of the Secrets, Vol. II, Session 5.
2. Ibid.
3. Ibid.
4. The Secret of Secrets, Vol. I, Session 7.

Meditations on Light
1. The Book of the Secrets, Vol. IV, Session 1.
2. The Secret of Secrets, Vol. II, Session 13.
3. The Book of the Secrets, Vol. IV, Session 1.
4. Ibid., Session 15.
5. The Book of the Secrets, Vol. III, Session 15.

THE MEDITATIONS

Meditations on Darkness
1. The Shadow of the Bamboo, Session 11.
2. The Book of the Secrets, Vol. IV, Session 3.
3. Ibid.

Moving Energy Upwards
1. You Ain't Seen Nothin' Yet, Session 7.
2. The Book of the Secrets, Vol. III, Session 15.
3. Ibid.

Listening to the Soundless Sound
1. The Secret of Secrets, Vol. I, Session 13.
2. The Orange Book, pp. 153-154
3. Ibid.
4. The Book of the Secrets, Vol. II, Session 11.
5. Yoga: The Science of the Soul, Vol. III, Session 6.
6. The Orange Book, pp. 201-202.
7. The Book of the Secrets, Vol. II, Session 11.
8. Ibid., Session 9.
9. Ibid., Session 11.

Finding the Space Within
1. The Book of the Secrets, Vol. IV, Session 8.
2. Ibid., Session 1.
3. Ibid., Session 13.
4. The Orange Book p. 62-63.
5. Yoga: The Science of the Soul, Vol. III, Session 7.
6. Tantra: The Supreme Understanding, Session 4.

Entering into Death
1. The Revolution, Session 9.
2. The Book of the Secrets, Vol. IV, Session 5.
3. Vedanta – Seven Steps to Samadhi, Session 15.

Watching with the Third Eye
1. The Orange Book, pp. 199-200.
2. Ibid., pp. 26-37
3. The Book of the Secrets, Vol. I, Session 5.
4. The Book of the Secrets, Vol. IV, Session 15.
5. The Secret of Secrets, Vol. I, Session 11.

THE MEDITATIONS

Just Sitting
1. The Book of the Books, Vol. I, Session 9.
2. Ibid.
3. The Orange Book, pp. 114-115.
4. Instructions currently in use at Osho Commune International, Poona, India.
5. Roots and Wings, Session 10.

Rising in Love: A Partnership in Meditation
1. Beyond Enlightenment, Session 16.
2. The Book of the Secrets, Vol. V, Session 3.
3. The Book of the Secrets, Vol. III, Session 1.
4. Ibid.

OBSTACLES TO MEDITATION

1. Light on the Path: Talks in the Himalayas.
2. The Discipline of Transcendence, Vol. IV, Session 3.
3. Light on the Path: Talks in the Himalayas.
4. The Psychology of the Esoteric, Session 2.
5. A Sudden Clash of Thunder, Session 2.
6. Ancient Music In the Pines, Session 3.
7. Yoga: The Alpha and the Omega, Vol. VI, Session 6.
8. The Book of the Secrets, Vol. IV, Session 8.
9. Ibid.
10. Light on the Path: Talks in the Himalayas.
11. The Rebel, Session 17.

QUESTIONS TO THE MASTER

1. The Book of the Books, Vol. IV, Session 10.
2. Beyond Psychology, Session 18.
3. The True Sage, Session 5.
4. The Tantra Vision, Vol. I, Session 8.
5. The Rajneesh Upanishad, Session 10.
6. Ah, This!, Session 8.
7. Yoga: The Science of the Soul, Vol.III, Session 4.
8. Yoga: The Alpha and the Omega, Vol. IV, Session 10.
9. The Hidden Splendor, Session 11.
10. The Golden Future, Session 19.
11. Satyam-Shivam-Sundram, Session 7.
12. Ibid., Session 22.

About Osho

Most of us live out our lives in the world of time, in memories of the past and anticipation of the future. Only rarely do we touch the timeless dimension of the present – in moments of sudden beauty, or sudden danger, in meeting with a lover or with the surprise of the unexpected. Very few people step out of the world of time and mind, its ambitions and competitiveness, and begin to live in the world of the timeless. And of those who do, only a few have attempted to share their experience. Lao Tzu, Gautam Buddha, Bodhidharma…or more recently, George Gurdjieff, Ramana Maharshi, J. Krishnamurti…. They are thought by their contemporaries to be eccentrics or madmen; after their death they are called "philosophers". And in time they become legends – not flesh-and-blood human beings, but perhaps mythological representations of our collective wish to grow beyond the smallness and trivia, the meaninglessness of our everyday lives.

Osho is one who has discovered the door to living his life in the timeless dimension of the present – he has called himself a "true existentialist" – and he has devoted his life to provoking others to seek this same door, to step out of the world of past and future and discover for themselves the world of eternity.

From his earliest childhood in India, it was clear that Osho was not going to follow the conventions of the world around him. He spent the first seven years of his life with his maternal grandparents, who allowed him a freedom to be himself which few children enjoy. He was a solitary child, preferring to spend long hours sitting quietly by a lake, or exploring his surroundings on his own. The death of his maternal grandfather, he says, had a profound effect on his inner life, provoking in him a determination to discover that in life which is deathless. By the time he joined his parents' growing family and entered school, he was firmly grounded in a clarity and sense of himself that gave him the courage to challenge all attempts by his elders to shape his life according to their own ideas of who he should be.

He has never shied away from controversy. For Osho, truth cannot compromise, or it is no longer the truth. And truth is not a belief but an experience. He never asks people to believe what he says, but rather to experiment and see for themselves whether what he is saying is true or not. And at the same time, he is relentless in finding ways and means to expose beliefs for what they are – mere consolations to soothe our anxieties in the face of the unknown, and barriers to encountering a mysterious and unexplored reality. After his enlightenment at the age of twenty-one, Osho completed his academic studies and spent several years teaching philosophy at the University of Jabalpur. Meanwhile, he traveled throughout India giving talks, challenging orthodox religious leaders in public debate, and meeting people from all walks of life. He read extensively, everything he could find to broaden his understanding of the belief systems and psychology or contemporary man. By the late 1960s Osho had begun to develop his unique dynamic meditation techniques. Modern man, he said, was so burdened with the outmoded traditions of the past and the anxieties of modern-day living that he must go through a deep cleansing process before he could hope to discover the thought-less, relaxed state of meditation. He began to hold meditation camps around India, giving talks to the participants and personally conducting sessions of the meditations he had developed.

In the early 1970s, the first Westerners began to hear of Osho, and joined the growing numbers of Indians who had been initiated by him into neo-sannyas. By 1974 a commune had been established

around Osho in Poona, India, and the trickle of visitors from the West was soon to become a flood. Many of the first Westerners who came were therapists who had found themselves facing the limitations of Western therapies and were seeking an approach that could reach and transform the more profound depths of the human psyche. Osho encouraged them to contribute their skills to the commune, and worked closely with them to develop their therapies in the context of meditation.

The problem with therapies developed in the West, he said, is that they confine themselves to treating the mind and its psychology, while the East has long understood that mind itself, or rather, our identification with it, is the problem. The therapies can be useful – like the cathartic stages of the meditations he has developed – in unburdening people of their repressed emotions and fears, and in helping people to see themselves more clearly. But unless we begin to detach ourselves from the mechanism of the mind and its projections, desires and fears, we will climb out of one ditch only to fall into another of our own invention. Therapy, therefore, must go hand in hand with the process of disidentification

and witnessing known as meditation.

By the end of the 1970s the commune in Poona housed the largest therapy and growth center in the world, and thousands of people were coming to participate in therapy groups and meditations, to sit with Osho in his daily morning discourse, and to contribute to the life of the commune or to return to their countries and set up meditation centers there.

Between 1981 and 1985, the communal experiment found itself in the United States, on a 126-square-mile section of high desert in eastern Oregon. Here, Osho was in a period of silence and isolation from the world, except for his daily drives into the surrounding countryside. The primary emphasis of commune life was the work of building the City of Rajneeshpuram, an "oasis in the desert". In a miraculously short time the commune had built housing for 5000 people and had begun to reverse decades of damage to the abused and overgrazed earth, restoring creeks, building lakes and reservoirs, developing a self-sufficient agriculture and planting thousands of trees.

Meditations and therapy programs in Rajneeshpuram were carried on by Rajneesh International

Meditation University. The modern facilities built for the university, and its protected environment, enabled a depth and expansion of its programs which had not been possible before. Longer courses and trainings were developed and attracted a broader range of participants, including many who were already established in the world and wanted to expand their professional skills and understanding of themselves. The annual festivals held in July to celebrate "Master's Day" drew as many as 20,000 people, to sit in Osho's presence and greet him on his daily drives.

But the United States did not take kindly to this new experiment within its borders, and soon a vast array of government agencies, privately-funded lobbying organizations and fundamentalist Christians had joined forces to try to prevent Rajneeshpuram's continued existence. Its residents were subjected to verbal and physical abuse when they traveled outside the city's boundaries, and the city and various corporations within it were constantly engaged in lengthy court battles and appeals. Osho's personal secretary, who had managed affairs during his period of retirement from public life, began to take on the characteristics of her opponents, attacking

them with a murderous zeal and ruling the commune with an iron hand.

Around this time, Osho resumed public speaking. He turned his attention to Christianity, and its fundamental values of obedience and blind faith, its methods of guilt and repression, its manifestations of fanaticism and violence. He talked about freedom and responsibility, and reverence for life. And he sharply challenged the commune's opponents to come and see the experiment for themselves, and to pay more attention to upholding their own Constitution.

Osho's secretary finally left the commune, leaving behind a trail of crimes and misdeeds, some against her enemies outside, but most against the residents of the commune itself. Local, state and federal officials used the opportunity to move against the city and commune structures, filing charges against the corporations and threatening to seize all their assets. Osho was arrested and held without bail and, in an attempt to discredit him and link him with the crimes of his secretary, he was taken across country on a prisoner transport plane, shackled and in chains. The five-hour journey was extended into five days, including a period of two days in which

Osho's whereabouts were kept secret from his attorneys and he was registered into an Oklahoma prison under a false name. A progressive deterioration in his health following this period eventually led doctors to believe that he was poisoned during the two days in Oklahoma, probably with thallium.

On the advice of his attorneys, who feared for his life, Osho allowed himself to be deported from the U.S. on minor immigration violations. He embarked on a world tour, but pressure from the U.S. State Department resulted in twenty-one countries either denying him entry altogether, or deporting him without explanation after a short stay. He returned to India in mid-1986, where he was immediately joined by hundreds of disciples and friends from around the world.

By January, 1987, Osho was back in Poona, giving talks twice a day. Within a few months the Poona commune had begun a full program of activities and was expanding far beyond its previous scope. The standard of modern, air-conditioned facilities had been set in America, and Osho made it clear that the new Poona commune should be a 21st-century oasis, even in developing India. More and more people were coming from the East – from Japan, particularly – and their presence brought a corresponding enrichment of the healing and martial arts programs. The visual and performing arts also flourished, along with the new "Mystery School". This diversification and expansion was reflected in Osho's choice of the name "Multiversity" as the umbrella for all the programs.

And the emphasis on meditation grew even stronger – it was a constantly recurring theme in Osho's discourses, and he developed and introduced several new meditation therapies, including No-Mind, the Mystic Rose, and Born Again.

In the middle of 1987, Osho gradually began to withdraw from public activities. His fragile health often prevented him from giving discourses, and the periods of his absence grew longer. In mid-1988 he introduced a new element into his discourses, guiding his audience into a three-stage meditation at the end of each of his talks. In April of 1989 he delivered his last discourse, answering questions and commenting on Zen sutras. For the following months, whenever his health permitted he would come in the evening to sit with his disciples and friends in a meditation of music and silence, after which he would retire to his room and the assembly would watch one of his videotaped discourses. Osho left his body on January 19, 1990. Just a few weeks before that time, he was asked what would happen to his work when he was gone. He said:

My trust in existence is absolute. If there is any truth in what I am saying, it will survive…. The people who remain interested in my work will be simply carrying the torch, but not imposing anything on anyone….

I will remain a source of inspiration to my people. And that's what most sannyasins will feel. I want them to grow on their own – qualities like love, around which no church can be created, like awareness, which is nobody's monopoly; like celebration, rejoicing, and maintaining fresh, childlike eyes….

I want my people to know themselves, not to be according to someone else. And the way is in.

Before he left his body, Osho dictated the inscription for his Samadhi, the marble and mirrored-glass crypt containing his ashes. It says:

OSHO

Never Born – Never Died
Only Visited this Planet Earth
between
December 11, 1931 – January 19, 1990

AT THE FEET OF THE MASTER

This handsome volume of Osho's words, illustrated with black and white photos of Osho and sannyasins in the Commune, is a compilation from thirty published darshan diaries. Osho speaks directly to individuals, addressing issues concerned with their personal growth. What is a disciple? What is a master? What does it mean to take sannyas? These and innumerable other aspects of the search, as relevant today as ever, are covered.

THE BOOK OF WISDOM

DISCOURSES ON ATISHA'S SEVEN POINTS OF MIND TRAINING
2 VOLUMES COMBINED

"These Seven Points of Mind Training are the fundamental teaching that he [Atisha] gave to Tibet," Osho states. "They are of immense value. They are the whole of religion condensed. They are like seeds; they contain much. The moment you move into them deeply, when you contemplate and meditate and start experimenting with them, you will be surprised – you will be going into the greatest adventure of your life."

COME, COME, YET AGAIN COME

Osho's invitation echoes the words of the Sufi mystic, Jalaluddin Rumi: "Come, come, whoever you are; wanderer, worshiper, lover of learning, it does not matter. Ours is not a caravan of despair. Come, even if you have broken your vow a thousand times. Come, come, yet again come." Seekers from all over the world bring their questions to Osho: "Why do your sannyasins celebrate death?" "What does it mean when a woman says she is afraid of a man?" "Why is it so difficult for me to laugh?" And dozens of others. And Osho, indefatigably loving, just keeps on giving.

THE EMPTY BOAT

TALKS ON THE STORIES OF CHUANG TZU

Osho revitalizes the 3000-year-old Taoist message of self realization through the stories of the Chinese mystic, Chuang Tzu. He speaks about the state of egolessness, "the empty boat"; about spontaneity, dreams and wholeness; about living life choicelessly and meeting death with the same equanimity. Set in a poetic format, this series overflows with the wisdom of one who is an empty boat Himself.

THE HIDDEN HARMONY

According to Osho, if Heraclitus had been born in India rather than Greece, he would have been recognized as not simply a philosopher but as a mystic. Further, He says that if Heraclitus had been accorded his rightful status, the whole course of Western history would have been totally different.

Though only fragments remain of his words, Osho finds in them a poetry that is refreshing in its simplicity and clarity. Through this series of eleven discourses, Osho acts as a via media to this mystic of twenty-five centuries ago.

A MUST FOR MORNING CONTEMPLATION
A MUST FOR CONTEMPLATION BEFORE SLEEP

2 VOLUMES

Excerpts from talks Osho has given to His disciples and other seekers during *darshan*, the intimate evening meetings He conducted for many years. These books are divided into twelve months, of thirty-one days each, and the passages have been designed to be read chronologically rather than randomly.

Osho's suggestion is, on first awakening, to read the passage designated for that morning before one's mind becomes engaged in the day's activities; and similarly, in the evening, to read the assigned passage just before going to sleep. As He explains, the words of a mystic are not theories to accept or reject, they are fingers pointing towards the transcendental.

MY WAY, THE WAY OF THE WHITE CLOUDS

A comprehensive introduction to the world of Osho. In an intimate setting He responds directly to spontaneous questions on happiness and misery, relationship and aloneness, ego and consciousness, energy and sex, love and prayer, logic and madness, meditation and surrender, enlightenment and the master-disciple relationship.

Books by Osho are available from all good bookshops. If you have difficulty obtaining the book you want, please write to either address listed in the back for your nearest bookshop or distributor.

For a complete catalog of Osho's books or to have your name added to our mailing list, just send us your name and address and you will receive information about forthcoming titles.

The Osho Commune International in Poona, India, is the world's largest meditation and growth center. It is the meeting place and spiritual home of hundreds of thousands of people from nearly every country in the world. Guided by the vision of the enlightened master Osho, the Commune might be described as a laboratory, an experiment in creating a "New Man" – who lives in harmony with himself and his environment, and who is free from all ideologies and belief systems which now divide humanity.

The Commune's Osho Multiversity offers hundreds of workshops, groups and trainings, presented by its nine different faculties:

Osho School for Centering
Osho School of Creative Arts
Osho International Academy of Healing Arts
Osho Meditation Academy
Osho School of Mysticism
Osho Institute of Tibetan Pulsing
Osho Center for Transformation
Osho School of Zen Martial Arts
Osho Academy of Zen Sports and Fitness

All these programs are designed to help people to find the knack of meditation: the passive witnessing of thoughts, emotions, and actions, without judgment or identification. Unlike many traditional Eastern disciplines, meditation at Osho Commune is an inseparable part of everyday life – working, relating or just being. The result is that people do not renounce the world but bring to it a spirit of awareness and celebration, in a deep reverence for life.

For information about visiting the Commune or participating in its programs, see our overleaf.

Music to support and guide many of Osho's meditations has been composed with His guidance, and is available on cassette and CD. For information about where to order this music, and for more information about Osho, His meditations, books and tapes, contact:

Osho America
P.O. Box 12517 • Scottsdale, Arizona 85267-2517
1-800-777-7743 • E-mail: osho_america@osho.org

Osho International
24 St. James's Street, London, SWIA IHA

Osho Commune International
17 Koregaon Park, Poona 411 001, India

Also see:
http://www.osho.org